Some other books by A. J. Liebling

The Most of

A. J. Liebling

Selected by

WILLIAM COLE

Simon and Schuster

New York

1963

PUBLISHED BY SIMON AND SCHUSTER, INC.
ROCKEFELLER CENTER, 630 FIFTH AVENUE
NEW YORK 20, N. Y.

FIRST PRINTING

LIBRARY OF CONGRESS CATALOG CARD NUMBER: 63–17729
MANUFACTURED IN THE UNITED STATES OF AMERICA
BY H. WOLFF BOOK MFG. CO., INC., NEW YORK, N. Y.

To James A. Macdonald (Col. John R. Stingo)
at 90

Contents

Foreword

PAINTERS often have retrospective shows, and there is no reason to suspect writers of being less vain. This book contains pieces written over a period of thirty years, and I have let William Cole, who is by way of being a professional anthologist, do the selecting, because I could not myself get the manuscript down below a million words. I think Mr. Cole has done as good a job as anybody could, with such a redundance of great stuff to choose from, but I regret the rest of the million.

We have put first in the book a small number of the pieces that I wrote about (and mostly during) the last World War, because it was a watershed in my working life. I had worked fourteen years when I went to France in 1939 at the age of thirty-five, and since I came back in 1945, there have been eighteen more years. The antebellum pieces are placed *after* the ones about the war, because the thirties are so far away in feeling that the reader, we think, needs a transition from now. The war provides it.

The principal preoccupation of almost everybody in the 1930s was getting by, and the humor, as during a blitz, was rueful and concerned with the imminence of individual disaster. New York, for the first time since the Revolution, remained physically unchanged for those ten years, because nobody had money to build with. This brought a shabby stability that encouraged place-fondness—walks by the half-deserted piers and excursions to decayed bathing resorts, like the one in the sketch "What Do You Expect for Two Dollars?" There was the greatest sudden wave of nostalgia for the past that ever hit the United States north of the Mason and Dixon line, and it became a social convention to act as if you assumed that everybody you met had, like yourself, been in easy circumstances Befo de Crash—even though you hadn't either. This abolished that demon of the twenties and fifties—"status." The 1920s, with their smugness and their underlying sense of guilt, were much more like now. In the materially miserable thirties, few had time to feel guilty and certainly nobody had reason to feel smug.

The pieces written after 1945 need no gloze.

A. J. Liebling

March 5, 1963

Bellum

❧ ❧

Aux Armes: 1939

AT THAT PERIOD—it sounds like talking about stagecoach days—the Clippers still left from a yacht-club setting at Port Washington, Long Island. A friend of mine named Fred Schwed, a romantic soul who had been reared on Richard Harding Davis, although in early manhood he had switched to Scott Fitzgerald, had asked to drive me out to my plane in the early morning. Passengers were supposed to be at the plane with their luggage at eight o'clock.

Schwed picked me up at an hour I never had experienced while sober, at the door of the house where I was living, and headed in what I took to be the direction of Long Island because the sun was rising over it. He drove me over one bridge, which was all right, and then around a wild farming country, in which I distinctly saw a hen and on another occasion what I took to be a cow—in one jump more I figured he would have me among the coyotes and Republicans—and then over another bridge, which was all wrong because it landed us in Westchester County. By then I had only an hour or so to catch the plane, so I began to curse, which I do well. The secret of good cursing lies in cadence, emphasis, and antiphony. The basic themes are always the same. Conscious striving after variety is not to be encouraged, because it takes your mind off your cursing. By the time Schwed got me to the landing, he felt what a proper swine he was for having gotten up early in the morning to take me to the plane, and if the experience had broken him of volunteering to do favors for people, it would have been worth while.

I rushed into the dinky frame ticket and customs office they had there, still drooling obscenity, and saw my mother, who had gotten up early in another part of Long Island and come out to see me off. Sucking back four bloody oaths that I could already feel pressing against the back of my teeth, I switched to a properly filial expression, embraced the dear woman, and got aboard the Clipper feeling like Donald Duck.

When I got tired of talking to the other passengers, I thought about women. I frequently do this for hours without becoming bored; they are much pleasanter than sheep to think of when you are trying to fall asleep. Thinking about women also makes you insensible to mild fright or minor discomforts. Once I was sleeping with another fellow under a pup tent in a rainstorm in Tunisia, and at about two o'clock in the morning he woke me up. I said, "What's up?" and he said, "The tent's just blown away." The rain had turned into a cloudburst, and my blankets were soaked through. I got into the front seat of a jeep and wrapped the wet blankets around me. The top and windshield afforded some help, but the water lashed in from both sides. I thought about women for four and a half hours and never even caught cold.

Aux Armes: 1941

[Second Voyage]

I SPENT THE NIGHT of my arrival in Britain at the Central Hotel in Glasgow. The Central has an indefinite number of rooms, alcoves, and lounges, all meant to drink in, spread along the sides of a corridor on the first floor. At that date it was still easy to get whiskey in any of them early in the evening (by 1942 there was very little of it).

At eleven o'clock service ceased except in a lounge marked "For Use of Residents Only." This was in deference to the eleven-o'clock closing law in public drinking places. If you are living in a hotel, it counts as your home. Everybody from the other rooms moved into this lounge and continued to drink, but at midnight a lame waiter whom any ex-Walter Scott fan could identify instantly as a crusty old servitor, announced that drinks would be sold only to *actual* residents of the hotel. After he had weeded out small tippers and Englishmen whose faces he did not like, he waved the survivors, mostly Scotsmen, Norwegians, Americans, and trulls, into another, more exclusive lounge. He applied the fine comb again at one o'clock and again we moved, to a lounge for bona fide residents of the hotel.

At four in the morning I found myself in what I thought was my eleventh drinking nook of the night, together with a Major in kilts, a Lieutenant in kilts, and a merchant-navy skipper.

The Major spoke a trifle brusquely to the waiter, and the waiter said, "Major, you've had enough. Go to bed now."

The Major sulked for a couple of minutes and then went, for he knew the waiter was the only man in Glasgow who could give him a drink.

The merchant-navy man had been glaring at the Lieutenant disapprovingly, and now he said, "It amuses me to see you wearing a kilt when I have better Highland blood than you." This sounded like a quotation from a Waverley novel, but I could not identify it.

The Lieutenant said, "I have just come from a place called Crrete. Have you heard of it? I am a MacInnes of Skye."

The merchant-navy man said, "I never cared for Skye."

The Lieutenant said, "That is no' imporrtant."

The seafarer said, "I am a MacNeill of Barra."

The Lieutenant said, "You lie. You have not the faceel appearrance of a MacNeill of Barra."

The crusty old servitor got between them and said, "Gentlemen, you've a wee thingie on, both. There'll be no more drink tonight."

I went to bed still trying to figure whether they had framed me with some amateur theatricals. But it had all been on the level. The first fact one must accept about Britain is that all British literature, no matter how improbably it reads, is realistic. You meet its most outrageous models everywhere you turn, because Britain is full of improbable people, behaving in what an American or a Frenchman wrongly suspects is a fictitious manner.

Before coming to Britain I had intended to write about it from an American point of view, but the project reminded me of one Jack Johnson once described: "It would be like a man who only understand Italian trying to teach French to a man who do not understand Italian either." The essential point in writing about Britain is never to try to explain it, and in talking to Britons, never to try to make them explain themselves.

Where They Are: 1941

❧ ❧

IN THE MEN'S BAR of the Ship Hotel at Grimsby, Englishmen speak to other Englishmen after less than five drinks. This is a tribute to Grimsby's genius, which is bacchic and maritime in equal parts. Grimsby sent ships to the fleet of King John and still sends its ships to the wars with Grimsby skippers and Grimsby crews, eked out, it is true, by a supplement of fellows from other parts of England, to whom Grimsby men refer impartially as "they dommed farmers." The farmers drown like the Grimsby men, but they cause them a lot of vexation in the interim. In the Ship bar one may meet fifty-year-old sublieutenants of the Royal Navy (Reserve, naturally) who have tattooed fists and unbutton their uniform jackets to allow room for beer. They are not quite gentlemen, of course, any more than middle-aged Lt. James Cook was a gentleman when he sailed to find a continent. The gentlemen lose the continents. The sublieutenants come ashore from the minesweepers and patrol boats that used to be trawlers. Only the very old boats with maimed or ancient skippers fish now. As for the convivial part of the Grimsby tradition, Sir Fretcheville Hollis, a Parliament man for Grimsby, told Samuel Pepys in 1667 that to win an election there he had to spend £352 for beer. Pepys set this down as a "develish lie," but Pepys was no Grimsby man. Under the combined influence of Grimsby beer and Grimsby informality, even pink-cheeked and well-turned-out young officers off destroyers become relatively effusive. They say "Beastly weathah we ah having" to men to whom they have never been introduced. Since ships bigger than destroyers seldom come to Grimsby, the town is relaxingly free of officers of senior grade.

The highest-ranking officer in the bar as I entered one evening was a Lieutenant Commander named Armstrong, whom I had met at the naval base, where I had been getting material for a story. He was a big man who looked to be about forty but must have been a good deal older than that, because he had once told me that he had been in sail in 1904. He had fought in the other war and then been a captain in the merchant marine and then retired, and now he was in service again. Armstrong was a kind of patrol-boat admiral. He had under his command at least a dozen converted fishing boats, of about two hundred tons each, carrying crews of thirty men.

Most of the patrons of the Ship get their drinks at the bar and then carry them to the long wooden tables. Armstrong was at a table with a pint of the local brew in front of him, and he motioned me to come and sit beside him. I got my beer and joined him.

"One of my fellows had a do with a German plane," he said, by way of beginning. "Plane was attacking some fishing boats, and my fellow went to help. Between all of them they shot the plane down, but they're rowing about who did it. Fishermen say they did; my chaps say they did, naturally. One fishing boat sank. A bomb dropped close to her and she just came apart. My fellow said that the bomb hit the water, and the next thing he thought he heard was a burst of machine-gun fire. 'But it wasn't machine-gun fire,' he said. 'It was her rivets popping out so fast it just sounded like machine-gun fire.' All of her crew were saved. I thought you'd like that description. Same chap once told me he'd seen a trawler bombed, and she went so high he could see the top of a nearby lighthouse under her keel. And two sea gulls over the lighthouse, he said."

I said something about wishing the fellow would write a book.

Armstrong said, "I once had one chap who did. Well, it wasn't a book exactly, but a diary, anyway."

I got up and brought another round of beer.

"You know how it is in our boats," Armstrong said when I had sat down again. "The chap in command gets lonely. When the ship is fishing, most of the space in her hull is used for a fishhold. The men all muck in together, eating and sleeping in the smallest possible space, and the skipper mucks in with everyone else. They don't mind that, because they're on shares, and the more fish they carry the more money they get. But when we take the boat over for the Navy, we convert the fishhold into quarters for the crew. The skipper has a cabin forward, and since he's the only commissioned officer aboard, he can't eat with the rest. He has to take his meals alone, and the others say 'sir' to him. That makes him moody and sometimes inclines him to drink. Spirits are tax-free in the Navy, as you probably know, and that is a temptation. Then he begins to brood about the new chaps in the crew. It would be splendid if we could man our boats a hundred per cent with fishermen, but it's impossible. A fishing boat carries a crew of thirteen, but when she goes to the Navy she needs thirty—gunners and fellows to handle mines and all that. And some of the new men have never been to sea. This chap who wrote the diary didn't drink heavily. The writing was his outlet. I came across it when I was going through his effects, poor chap. He copped it in a fight with some motor torpedo boats. A one-pound shell took half of his head off. I sent the diary, along with the rest of his things, to the widow, but I couldn't help copying a few entries."

Armstrong reached inside his jacket and brought out a typewritten page, which he passed to me. There were the entries:

Dec. 11. Coventry, London. Manchester. Ow I wish I could come up with a Jerry plane. I would show them. Today my steward put my knife spoon and fork in bucket of water to wash then forgot they were there chooked water overboard with them in it. I could of chooked im overboard too.

Dec. 16. I of a fine crew. One chap that worked in sweetshop. One bus conductor. One building workman. Two married men that of never been to sea.

What a bloody sample.

Dec. 21. I told cook to make rice pud. Late in day rice floating on galley floor he put about ½ a stone of rice in boiling water nice pud.

January 6. Today men grappled German mine were bringing it over side but not fast enough. I leaned over side and seized cable to help. Opened my mouth to give order and upper and lower plates fell out.

They are not gone. I know where they are.

"Do you know," Armstrong said, "something about that last entry makes me rather sad. So many Grimsby lads, you know."

"Yes," I said. "We know where they are."

Depression Kids: 1943

I KNEW THAT the quality of American troops would be good, once they had paid their entry fee with a couple of bobbles, because Americans are the best competitors on earth. A basketball game between two high-school teams at home will call forth enough hardness of soul and flexibility of ethic to win a minor war; the will to win in Americans is so strong it is painful, and it is unfettered by any of the polite flummery that goes with cricket. This ruthlessness always in stock is one of our great national resources. It is better than the synthetic fascist kind, because the American kid wears it naturally, like his skin, and not self-consciously, like a Brown Shirt. Through long habit he has gained control over it, so that he turns it on for games, politics, and business and usually turns it off in intimacy. He doesn't have to be angry to compete well.

Eggs: 1943

WE USED TO GO DOWN to this village to get eggs when we were too lazy to make the chow line for breakfast or when we felt hungry at any time of day. We'd take them back to the shack a bunch of us were living in and cook them. Solitary Arabs squat along the roadsides all over North Africa, waiting for military vehicles. When one comes into sight, the Arab pulls an egg out from under his rags and holds it up between thumb and forefinger like a magician at a nightclub. The price of eggs —always high, of course—varies in inverse ratio to the distance from a military post.

Near big towns that are a long way from any post, the Arabs get only five francs (ten cents at the new rate of exchange) for an egg, but in villages close to garrisons eggs are sometimes hard to find at any price. Norgaard and I followed a standard protocol to get them. First we went into the general store and barbershop, which was just a couple of almost empty rooms that were part of a mud house, and shook hands with all the male members of the establishment. Naturally, we never saw any of the females. Then we presented a box of matches to the head of the house, an ex-soldier who spoke French, and he invited us to drink coffee. The Arabs have better coffee and more sugar than the Europeans in North Africa. While we drank the coffee, we sat with the patriarch of the family on a white iron bed of European manufacture. The patriarch had a white beard and was always knitting socks; he stopped only to scratch himself.

Once, as we were drinking coffee, we watched our French-speaking friend shave a customer's head. He started each stroke at the top of the cranium and scraped downward. He used no lather; the customer moistened his own poll with spittle after each stroke of the razor. Once, when the customer made a particularly awful face, all the other Arabs sitting around the room laughed.

During the coffee-drinking stage of the negotiations, we presented the Arabs with a can of fifty English cigarettes. After that they presented us with ten to fifteen eggs. Soldiers who were not such good friends of theirs usually got twenty eggs for fifty cigarettes, but it always costs something to maintain one's social life.

One day I asked the barber why the old man scratched himself, and he said, laughing, "Because of the black spots. We all have them, and they itch." With much hilarity the Arabs showed us the hard, black spots, apparently under their skins, from which they were suffering. I judged the trouble to be a degenerate form of the Black Death, tamed during the centuries by the rugged constitutions of our hosts. Norgaard thought that the spots were just chiggers.

Shibboleth: 1943

"GIVE DA PASSWOY," I once heard a First Division sentinel challenge.
   "Nobody told me nuttin," the challenged soldier replied.
   "What outfitchas outuv?"
   "Foy Signals."
   "Whynchas get on da ball? Da passwoy is 'tatched roof.' "
   "What is it mean?"
   "How do I know? Whaddaya tink I yam, da Quiz Kids?"

"My dear little Louise": 1944

❧ ❧

DURING our breaking-out offensive in Normandy, the division artillery headquarters I was traveling with occupied four command posts in five days. A French family was living in one wing of the first house we used, although most of the roof was gone and a couple of the bedrooms had only three walls, but the farmhouses in which we had our second and third command posts were deserted. The Germans had forced all the inhabitants to leave. In our fourth one, we found civilians again. The Germans, not expecting so quick an advance, had not evacuated people from what they still considered the rear area. In the barnyard of that place, we found a dead Panzer Grenadier of a *Schutzstaffel* division. His paybook said that he had been born in Essen, and on his body there was a typewritten form that he had filled out but obviously had not had time to hand in to his company commander, asking for what we would call an emergency leave to go home. His reason was "Bombing deaths in family—urgent telegram from wife." He had been hit by a fragment of shell, but it had not torn him up much. A detail of our fellows buried him in back of the barn.

The dead cows were more of a problem. Now that we had moved on to Brittany, one of the things that made us happy was that we were out of dead-cattle country. The war moves more swiftly, and it isn't necessary to drop artillery shells on every field and crossroad. Besides, the cattle in Brittany are fewer and more scattered than in Normandy, where every pasture was full of them. You need a bulldozer to bury cows properly, unless you are going to take all day about it, and nobody had men to spare for a large-scale interment detail. They lay in the fields with their four legs pointing stiffly in the air, like wooden cows discarded from a child's Noah's Ark, and their smell hung over the land as the dust hung over the roads. Men are smaller than cattle and they are always buried first; we lived in the stench of innocent death.

At our fourth command post, there were more dead cows than usual, because, the people on the farm told us, eighteen extra cows had arrived with the Germans a couple of weeks before. There had been two sets of Germans in the farm buildings—ten paratroopers who had showed up

driving eight cows, and forty SS men who had appeared driving ten
cows. The paratroopers, one of whom was a Captain, had got there first
and taken up quarters in the farmhouse. The SS men, arriving later,
had billeted themselves in the outbuildings, but only after a noisy argument, in which they had failed to get the paratroopers out of the big
house. The Captain had too much rank for them. The paratroopers had
been fighting a long time and were very down in the mouth, the people
of the house said. A soldier who served as interpreter had told the French
family that the war was over, that Germany was beaten. But the SS fellows, who had come from soft berths in Warsaw and Brno, were still
gonflés en bloc (blown up hard) and talked as if they owned the earth.
That was less than two weeks ago, but even the SS men, to judge by
those taken prisoner, have changed now. The SS soldiers had brought a
refugee family with them to milk the cows, the people on the farm said.
Every day the paratroopers drank the cream from their eight cows and
threw the milk away. Both sets of Germans had departed abruptly, but
the SS had left one man to guard the cows, presumably in case the reports of the Allied attack proved exaggerated. A shell had killed the cow
tender.

I am sure that I will remember our two deserted command posts
longer and more vividly than the two that were inhabited. Perhaps that
is because you think more about people when they aren't there, and because you can be your own Sherlock Holmes and reconstruct them in
accordance with your own hypothesis.

The first deserted farm was a solid rectangle of stone and stucco buildings with walls nearly a foot thick. The farmyard, on which all the
buildings fronted, could be reached only by narrow lanes that pierced
the solid row of buildings at the front and at the back. It would have
been a tough defensive position to crack if there had been any tactical
reason to defend it. The farmhouse was very old and must have belonged to an aged, rich, crippled, bigoted woman or to a crippled man
who had a fat old woman for a housekeeper. There was a crutch in the
farmyard, lying as if it had fallen off a departing wagon, and in two of
the bedrooms there was a pair of old, mended crutches that must have
been discarded for newer ones. In the kitchen, by the great open hearth,
there was a reclining chair with an extension on which to rest your legs,
and in one bedroom there were several old and dirty corsets, whose
whalebones, despite the garments' immense girth, had all sprung because
of the continual effort to encompass a bulging body.

There was a tall Norman clock in every room. Clocks of this sort are
made in little towns, like Périers and Colombières and Marigny, which

nobody outside Normandy ever heard of before this summer. Every crossroad seems to have had its clockmaker as well as its baker and its harness maker. The wooden cases of these timepieces are generally rather austere, but the dials are framed by hammered gilt sculpture; sheaves, golden apples, plows, and peasants in donkey carts are favorite motifs. The pendulums are vast, and they too are encrusted with ornament. A bride, I imagine, although no one has told me so, brings a clock as part of her dowry, and a house where there are many clocks has been ruled in turn by many women. This house was full of hideous modern religious images and of wax fruits and flowers under glass bells. There were no books except devotional ones and those that gave quick ways of making the computations a farmer must make in doing business with wholesalers. There were many of each kind.

The farmsteaders had left the place in a great hurry, and some soldiers, either German or American, had been there afterward and rummaged through the house, littering the floors with things, useless to them, that they had pulled from the cupboards—women's high-collared blouses, skirt hoops, dingy photographs of family outings and one of a man in a cuirassier's uniform, with breastplate and horsetail helmet, and three or four parchment manuscripts. One, dated 1779, was the deed of sale of a farm; another was a marriage contract dated the Year 3 of the First Republic. The contract enumerated the items the bride was to bring in her dowry, which included six pillowcases, one canopy for a bed, and ten handkerchiefs; the whole thing was to come to 1,057 francs. If the husband died before the wife, she was to be allowed to withdraw that much from the estate in consideration of her dowry. If the wife died first, the widower was to keep the pillowcases, handkerchiefs, and all the rest, probably to bestow on his next choice. I wondered, naturally, which of them had survived the other. There were canopies over the beds in all the bedrooms; one must have been the canopy listed in the contract. The house had stone floors that did not shake even when some guns just across the road were being fired, which happened for one entire night we spent there.

The guns were only three thousand yards behind the front line, but they were firing at a target—a railroad station or road junction—eleven miles away. They belonged not to division artillery but to a remote, unfamiliar entity called Corps. The battery commander, a harassed-looking little Captain, called on our artillery General as soon as we moved in and said he hoped the General did not mind guns; there were a lot of generals who couldn't sleep on account of the noise, and he had had to move twice already. He was like a man apologizing to his new neighbors for having noisy children; he was sensitive. Our General said that the guns were music to his ears, and we all smiled mechanically and obediently. The Captain said, "I'm sure glad to hear that, because I feel I have an ideal setup here."

Across the yard from the house, in a small storeroom, lived a donkey so old that he had a gray beard. His hoofs were long and misshapen, like the nails of an old dog who gets no exercise, and he stayed in his gloomy cell, blinking out at the world, without enough energy to walk into the adjoining barn and eat the hay, although he would accept cabbages if they were brought to him.

From the crippled woman's, or man's, house we moved into a region that had been heavily bombed on the first day of the offensive and was completely deserted except for the surviving animals. An officer who had done some reconnoitering had found a hamlet, Chapelle en Litige (Chapel in Litigation), which was intact. Bombs had fallen into all the adjoining fields, and bomb craters had made the roads into it almost impassable, but its half-dozen houses and the dependent barns stood untouched.

One officer, who considers the Air Forces a form of artillery totally lacking in professional direction, said, "If they had dropped hundred-pound bombs instead of five-hundred, they'd have killed just as many cows without spoiling the roads."

The façade of the granite house in which we set up shop was hidden by pear trees *en espalier,* laden with fruit and lush with leaves. An old hen had made a nest in a branch under the hayloft window and was rearing her chicks there; they were hard to find, buried among the pears, and produced a noise that was inexplicable to us until we discovered them. Some of the soldiers with us took up quarters in smaller houses, and once they had found niches for themselves, we all strolled about the village looking over the interiors of the houses. The owners had evacuated them in an orderly fashion, taking most of their belongings with them. There was not much left except furniture.

I found a pile of letters, most of them old, a few recent, lying on a dressing table in one of the houses. In a nearby cupboard was a long row of schoolboys' notebooks filled with exercises in drawing, arithmetic, and composition. All the books bore the inscription, written in a hand that became progressively less slack, *"Cahier d'Albert Hédouin."* A couple of recent business letters were addressed to *Veuve* Hédouin, and I assumed that Albert was the widow's son. There were also in the cupboard a number of the usual breviaries and cheap books of devotion, including a pamphlet of prayers for prisoners of war. Idly, because as a camp follower I had nothing else at the moment to do, I took some of the letters and, sitting down on the threshold of the plain little house I was in, started to read them.

One was dated September 25, 1914. It read:

MY DEAR LITTLE LOUISE:

I utilize a little moment to send you news of me. I am in good health and hope my letter finds you the same. I'd rather be at Chapelle en Litige than where I am, for it isn't nice to sleep outdoors. If this thing ends soon, I won't be sorry. I am with Anatole and Désiré, and they are in good health, too. Probably the buckwheat has been harvested, if the weather is as good there as it is here. I'd like to help thresh it and drink a big bowl of cider instead of being here, but it's useless to think about it. When you wean the little colt, leave him in the barn for two days, then turn him into the fields of broom, where the donkey is. Put some branches on top of the gate, so he won't try to jump over it. When you get this letter, send me some news of what goes on at home. Have you made a barrel of cider for Pannel yet and have the cows turned out well? Excuse me for being brief, my dear little Louise and cherished babies. I write this letter in the open air, sitting on my knapsack, and now I must go.

Your husband, who loves you and kisses you again and again,
LOUIS HÉDOUIN, *336th Infantry.*
P. S. Put the donkey in Fernand's field.

The next letter was dated in November, 1914.

MY DEAR LITTLE LOUISE:

It is with great pleasure I learn that you are in good health. I too am in good health. Dear little Louise, I think you should make at least three barrels of cider, although I know it will give you a lot of trouble. Considering the price of apples and the price of cider, it pays better to make cider than to sell apples. And make a good barrel for us, so that we can have the pleasure of drinking it together when I come home. ["Come home," I thought. "That war had four years to go then."] *My dear little Louise, you tell me that you have planted some wheat. Good. Prices are going up. I hope you have sowed oats, dear one. Dear little Louise, I hope you are well. Also the cows and calves. Butter is selling at a pretty good price, if it can only continue. I was glad to hear you had someone help you thresh the buckwheat. Dear little Louise, I wish I could have been there, but it's useless to think about it. Here one is and here one stays—until when, nobody knows.*

Your husband, who loves and will never cease to love you and the dear little children,

Louis.

Looking up, I saw that four or five cows, probably wanting to be milked, were staring hopefully at me, and I wondered how Louis Hédouin would have felt if he had known that in thirty years not even a woman would be left to care for the cattle in Chapelle en Litige.

There was another letter, also written in 1914, in which he said he had been to Mass and then eaten some ham dear little Louise had sent him; he would rather have attended Mass at home, but it was "useless to think of it."

Dear little Louise [he went on], you say you have had a card from Aimable and he is in good health. So much the better, for you can't imagine how unhealthy it is where he finds himself. I couldn't either, unless I had been there, but don't worry, I'm all right. Dear little Louise, you say that Marie has had a letter from Pierre and he is a prisoner. So much the better. That way he is sure to survive. I know that threshing must be a lot of trouble to you. I am sorry you are alone and have so much work to do. Do you remember, on that evening before I went away, Enée said that this business wouldn't be over before Easter? I am afraid he was right. It is sad when I think of it. Days are indeed long.

Louis.

And on March 15, 1915, he wrote that he was sorry to hear that Louise was suffering but hoped she would soon be delivered—the first indication I had had that he knew she was pregnant.

My dear little Louise [he continued], I had a letter from Papa the same time as yours. He says he has sold the old cow for 345 francs. It's not bad, when you think that she only had four teeth left. What about the black cow you thought was going to calve March 8 and what are you doing with the Jersey? Tell me in your next letter. Dear little Louise, you say you have threshed the oats. Good. There must have been some loss, but you did the best you could. The worst of it is we probably won't be home in time for the haying this season. Excuse me for not having written. We were taking ammunition up to the front lines. Lately things go badly. The regiment has refused to march to an attack. Everybody is sick of this business, and we lose courage and ask for an end of this terrible war.

A sweet kiss from your husband,
Louis.

Then, on March 22, the latest date I found on any of his letters, Hédouin wrote:

MY DEAR LITTLE LOUISE:
I have received with great pleasure your letter of the eighteenth. Your mother writes to me that you have had a nine-pound boy and are doing well, and the boy, too. My dear little Louise, you did well to have a midwife from Remilly, and she didn't charge much, either—eight francs. My dear little Louise, I'd like to be with you, but it's useless to think of it. Distance keeps us apart. I hope God will help you in your troubles. My parents write me that at home people are saying this will end soon. So much the better. Dear little Louise, the boy will be called Albert. Before telling you, I waited to see whether you would have a boy or a girl.
Your husband, who loves you,
Louis.
P. S. What about the black cow?

Nineteen-fifteen. I did a bit of subtraction. Albert would have been twenty-four in 1939—just the right age. I thought of the graded notebooks and the pamphlet of prayers for prisoners of war.

Snipers: 1944

I HAVE WRITTEN before of the dual character of the Normandy front during the period of buildup and containment—nasty going up front, and lovely, fat, tranquil farming country a couple of miles back, undisturbed by enemy aviation or artillery. I have noted, too, the odd guilty feeling it gave us who did not have to remain in the front lines but had the option of going there whenever we pleased. We seldom visited Barneville without also puttering around some spot that we could permit ourselves to consider hazardous. On the afternoon after our first dinner, I remember being in a division's command post—I think it was the 79th's—which was in an apple orchard infested with snipers, who, a colonel informed me, were harmless if you kept moving. Division commanders vied in getting their headquarters as far front as possible. This one, whose name I forget, used to sleep on the ground and make his staff do likewise.

The Colonel who reassured me about the snipers was an Ozark type; he said they couldn't have done much shooting before they got into the army, since they didn't know how to lead a moving target. "If you just keep walking, they almost always shoot behind you," he told me.

I looked around, and it was the most perambulatory headquarters personnel I had ever seen. The G-3 and the assistant G-3 were walking arm in arm, discussing something, and the G-4 and the assistant G-4 were walking arm in arm in the opposite direction, discussing something else. Even the warrant officers had for once got up from behind their tables and were walking.

"We got some old Missouri squirrel-hunters in this outfit, and we are hunting the snipers down pretty good," the Colonel said. "But we could do better if we had dogs."

K Rations: 1944

PARIS, we expected, would be short of food. We found the solution of our supply problem on the road ahead of us: a two-and-a-half-ton truck stacked high with cases of K rations, which were flat waxed-cardboard packages—thirty-six to a case—each containing the ready-to-eat components of a nourishing, harmless, and gastronomically despicable meal, calculated, I always supposed, to discourage overindulgence. (Among troops actively engaged, a K ration beat nothing to eat, but it was a photo finish.) These components were a round tin of alleged pork and egg, ground up together and worked to a consistency like the inside of a sick lobster's claw, and tasting like boardwalk cotton candy without any sugar in it; a few sourballs or other boiled sweets (I remember one particularly horrid variety that was flavored with root beer); four cigarettes; and a pinch of soluble coffee, dehydrated vegetarian bouillon, or lemonade powder. You sometimes had to open six packages to find the one with coffee in it, and smokers had to open five to get the equivalent of a pack of cigarettes. The rest of a K ration so opened was then chucked away, except in Arab countries, where it could be traded for shell eggs, fowl, or little girls.

Arrivée: 1944

❧ ❧

I HAD THOUGHT of the whole war as a road back to Paris, and now that I was on the real one, I momentarily felt let down. The car barely crept; I might as well have been riding home to Manhattan on a Sunday night from a weekend in Norwalk. After we got through Longjumeau, though, we made better time, and then, as we approached the Porte d'Orléans, we began to meet cyclists coming out from the city to greet us. These cyclists (the only ones I recall, anyway) were all women, the most beautiful I have ever seen. It is an established fact that women look better at some times than at others. I once knew a chap, for instance, who claimed that a woman is never so attractive as just after a severe bout of flu, because it makes her more ethereal, and when I was a young reporter, I used to think that women looked their best in a house where a man had just died. All such previous theories of environmental cosmetology blew up, however, when I saw the Parisiennes on their bicycles. To make a woman really beautiful, liberate her. It brings her up pounds on any kind of track. She visibly exudes a generalized good will that makes you want to kiss her.

These women wore long, simple summer dresses that left their bodies very free. (Elastic for girdles had disappeared from Occupied France years earlier.) Their bare legs were more smoothly muscled than Frenchwomen's before the war, because they had been riding those bicycles or walking ever since taxis vanished from the streets of Paris, and their figures were better, because the *pâtissiers* were out of business. It was a tribute to the French frame that none of them looked scrawny or knobby. Their hair was done up high on their heads, without silly little ponytails, and they wore wooden platform shoes, because there was no leather. As they bore down upon the oncoming jeeps, I understood how those old Sag Harbor whalers must have felt when the women of the islands came swimming out to them like a school of beautiful tinker mackerel. None of ours came aboard, though. They couldn't abandon their bicycles. One evening after the war, Roach and I were reminiscing about our arrival in Paris, and he told me that I cried. I have no doubt that I did, but I do not remember when.

In the Place d'Orléans, just within the city limits, we came upon a sight unique in my experience—thousands of people, tens of thousands, all demonstratively happy. In any direction we looked, there was an unending vista of cheering people. It was like an entry into Paradise, and all the sweeter because we didn't deserve it. A man goes through life feeling that he is never getting sufficient credit for what he has done, and few are ever cheered for something they haven't done. Neither Roach nor Morrison nor I had fired a single shot, but there was adulation enough for everybody. Gen. Omar Nelson Bradley, who was not there to receive any of it, could have moved an American division into Paris twenty-four hours sooner, but instead he had sent to Normandy for the Daydaybay, because he wanted a French unit to disengage the capital. It was the most potent lift that French morale received during the war. The people crowded about the troops in the trucks and half-tracks and jeeps, sometimes making it impossible for them to move. At one point our Chevrolet was so weighted down that it came to a dead stop.

There were police lines, but the police were celebrating, too. They couldn't find it in their hearts to step on anybody's feet. Resistance organizations of left, center, and right had united in the final insurrection of Paris, and the display of exuberance was therefore that rare phenomenon in France—a demonstration without a counterdemonstration. An open truck crossed the Place loaded with police, all of them carrying Sten guns. The crowd cheered madly: *"La police à l'honneur!"* The police had been the collective heroes of the uprising; they had raised the tricolor over the Prefecture of Police on August 19 and had held it against all attacks. Nobody called them *flics* or *poulets* or *la flicaille*. In a city where cop-hating is a tradition, such cordiality was without precedent. *"La police à l'honneur!"* It was like a dream.

My Award

꙳ ꙳

FROM THE MOMENT of our appearance in the station, we had been attended by a bevy of F.F.I. lads wearing tricolor brassards and strung with bandoleers and lethal weapons, mostly captured *Wehrmacht* machine pistols. They told us they belonged to the *Service de Presse des Forces Françaises du Quartorzième Arrondissement*. I asked a fellow who seemed to be their commanding officer if he could find us a billet. He replied that a hotel had been set aside for the accommodation of *la presse étrangère*—the Hôtel Néron, near the statue of the Lion de Belfort. It was an appetizingly wicked name; a good orgy would be appropriate on such a night.

Our progress to the Néron was a dashing cortege—a cross between an Arab fantasia and the reception accorded Adah Isaacs Menken by the silver miners of the Big Bonanza. Six or eight F.F.I.s, each carrying at least three firearms, hung on to the sides of our jeep, which was preceded by one captured Volkswagen and followed by another, both loaded to the Plimsoll with effervescent firepower. The Néron, despite its name, turned out to have nothing *louche* about it. Standing on a side street off the Avenue d'Orléans and a couple of hundred yards beyond the Lion, it was neither dilapidated nor elaborate. The Fourteenth Arrondissement is a neighborhood of low-salaried white-collar people, mostly civil servants, and the chief peacetime clientele of the Néron, I thought, must have consisted of old bachelor or widower postal clerks and railway conductors. Now the hotel was a combination of barracks and arsenal, with young men in berets, shirt-sleeves, and pistol belts bounding up the stairs three at a time, for no apparent reason, and then dashing down again. The soldiers of the night were strutting openly at last, and enjoying it.

Two ecstatically beaming elderly women were standing in the office downstairs when we arrived at the Néron—the *patronne* and her maid, delighted to be in the midst of such excitement. The hotel, I noticed on the way to my quarters, had a bathroom, and I was soon gratified to discover that the taps worked, although they both ran cold. In all the other French cities I had been through, the Germans had succeeded in blowing the water systems before leaving. The best I had been able to manage at Bagnoles was a swim in a spinachy pond.

I had an invigorating soak, got dressed, putting on a fresh pair of socks —the only change in attire my musette-bag wardrobe permitted—and sallied out into the dusky streets, home again. It was not quite dark, and the *bistros* on either side of the Avenue d'Orléans and on the Place Denfert-Rochereau were full of men—some with F.F.I. brassards and some without—*discutant le coup,* as after a football match. I went into a bar and had one of those sticky red *apéritifs* that partly refute the notion that the French have sensitive palates. It cost a hundred francs, which was two dollars then. I was getting hungry, and looked for a place to eat, but I saw none that was open; the reports of a food shortage in Paris were evidently well founded, and I began to think grimly about my K rations. Walking along the Avenue Denfert-Rochereau, I searched for the plaque that had marked the gatepost of the American Baptist Center, and, unable to find it, presumed that the Germans had closed my old gymnasium during the Occupation.

By now, it was beginning to be really dark. From the direction of the Luxembourg came the sound of steady firing—small-cannon as well as machine-gun; apparently, the Germans inside hadn't listened to the officers sent out from Leclerc's headquarters. I mention this firing because it seemed part of the summer night, like thunder. There was no menace in the sound, and if it were not for plaques on the walls of houses in various parts of Paris that now commemorate the deaths of Frenchmen on that very night, I would find it difficult to believe there was real combat on the evening of my stroll. I walked on down as far as the Closerie des Lilas and crossed the Boulevard du Montparnasse to have a better look at the place. The French were never as thorough as the English were about blackouts, and I could soon see, through chinks in the curtain of a window near the side door of the café, that there was a blue light— a *veilleuse,* or night lamp—burning within.

I banged on the door and shouted, in French, "It's an old customer! An old customer! An American! An American!" I thought that would interest whoever was inside, and it did, but not immediately. After I had shouted it a dozen times, the door opened a crack and a barman I had never seen looked out. I said to him, "Dominique? Where is Dominique?" I couldn't remember the boss's name. For all I knew, Dominique might have been gone seventeen years, for I hadn't visited the Closerie since 1927. In that case, the current barman might never even have heard of him. But I was in luck. Dominique had not left until 1940, when the Germans came in, and this barman had known him.

"Dominique went back to Barcelona in 1940," he said. At least, I had established myself as a former customer.

I could hear another man behind the fellow at the door, talking to him, and now a new face, which I recognized as that of the *patron,* appeared at the crack. "I used to come here with Russell," I said. *"Le vieux Russell.* With the *chapeau melon.* Is he still in Paris?"

The patron's face split in a grin. *"Ah, sacré Russell!"* he said. "He went to England. Come in." He opened the door.

There were no customers in the Closerie—only the *patron,* his wife, the barman, and a waitress. Once inside, I talked to them of Russell, of the celebration at this very bar of Lindbergh's safe arrival in Paris in 1927, of the perils of D Day and the hardships of the road, and of the outstanding character of General Leclerc. It took. The four of them were preparing to dine at one of the deserted tables, and as the waitress brought in a great terrine of potato soup, the boss asked me if I had eaten. I magnanimously consented to join them, even though his wife warned that there would be nothing to follow but an omelet and a salad; the *patronne,* it was plain, had never sampled a K ration.

The firing around the Luxembourg continued. "Apparently they're still holding out," I said.

"A lot of good it will do them," the *patron* observed, with relish. "A shot of red?" He filled my glass with Bordeaux, and, as he did so, his name came back to me—M. Colin. "Do you remember how Russell used to talk about Bouguereau?" he asked. "How he was all for Bouguereau?"

"Sacré vieux Russell!" I said. Never had an acquaintance served me better. The omelet was as big as an eiderdown.

"The Americans will be back soon," I said. "It will be like old times here at the Closerie."

"But you are the first," M. Colin said, in a voice that had taken on a tone of significance. Up to that point, our talk had been friendly but casual, with nothing about it to suggest that we were reunited on a historic occasion. Now, however, M. Colin said, "Monsieur, at the moment of the *débacle,* when the future looked blackest, I set aside two bottles against the arrival of the first American customer to return here. One is a bottle of *véritable* pernod and the other contains Black and White. Later, such bottles became impossible to find in Paris. They were beyond price. But I have never opened either. Which bottle will you drink?"

I chose the whiskey, because I knew I could drink more of that, and after we had finished the wine and the omelet and the salad, M. Colin put the bottle on the table. It was the only trophy or award I won during the war, and I wouldn't have traded it for the D.S.O. We drank to Russell and Bouguereau and Lafayette and General de Gaulle, and to Angèle, upon whom I had once prevailed to accompany me as far out of the student quarter as the bar of the Closerie, where she immediately became homesick for the Taverne Soufflet, half a mile away.

"She said whiskey smelled of bedbugs," I recalled sentimentally. "But she admired the stimulating effect it had on me. She has been dead for seventeen years." By that time, my new honors were beginning to overwhelm me.

"A chagrin of love never forgets itself," the waitress said. "You must not make bile about it."

When we had imbibed the last of my glory, I took an effusive leave and went out into the dark street. The bars that I had passed earlier were still busy, but I had no inclination to enter. Any further drinking that night would have been a letdown. I made but one brief pause—to roar at the Lion. He wouldn't roar back, and I continued to the Hôtel Néron, which I found as easily as if I had lived there all my life.

That Will Stay with You: 1949

WHEN the telephone rang, Marvin Bloom was holding the baby. Rosalind picked up the receiver and said hello, and then appeared surprised at the voice of the person at the other end. She put a hand over the mouthpiece and said to Marvin, "It's somebody asking for Mr. Bloom." Most of the people who called the Blooms said "Hello, Roz," or "Hello, Marty," according to which Bloom responded. "I would say, from the tone of the voice, a policeman, except that the manner is too polite," she said while Marvin was looking for a place to put the baby. "Perhaps somebody who has your name as a prospect to buy something." Rosalind always liked to try to visualize people from their voices. She took the baby from Marvin, and he grabbed the telephone from her hand, leaning across her lap to answer.

As soon as Marvin had said hello, the voice, which he recognized instantly, roared, "Are you the son of a bitch who was in the Coast Guard?"

"Mr. T-Todhunter, sir!" Marvin cried. He always stuttered a little when he was excited.

"Call me Toughy now, Bloom—I mean Marty," the voice continued. "War's over, you know—has been for a long time. Knew you lived somewhere in the Bronx. Been calling every M. Bloom in the Bronx phone book. This was my sixth try. Say, where were you on June the sixth, five years ago today?"

"I was onna—onna *ferry* ride," Marvin said, trying hard to think of something funny fast. Unsatisfied with his first effort, he said, "I was onna luckshury cruise, with all expenses paid."

Lieutenant Todhunter, Senior Grade, had been the skipper of the Landing Craft, Infantry, Large, on which Marvin had been one of the two pharmacist's mates, and she had capsized an hour after being hit, on D Day, off Omaha Beach.

Roz knew all about Mr. Todhunter. She had heard the story often enough before becoming Mrs. Bloom, and there was a framed, enlarged, tinted photograph of the LCIL crew on the radio cabinet. Roz thought Mr. Todhunter, in the picture, looked handsome but weak-willed, and she had once called him, in an argument with Marvin, "a typical-looking representative of an obviously parasitical social group."

So Marvin was not too hopeful when Todhunter said, "There are a couple of us down in the apartment of a friend of mine. Me and Meecham—you know, the war correspondent who was with us—and a couple of babes. It's his apartment, and you were the only one of the crew I knew lived in New York, and we wanted to know if you would care to have a drink."

"I don't think I could, Mr.—uh, Toughy," he said. "You see, I got caught and had to marry the girl, and this is her night with the Great Humphrey. I gotta stay home with the outshoot—I mean the offshoot."

But Roz had been clutching at his biceps during the second half of his speech. "Why don't you go, honey?" she was whispering.

She wasn't a bad kid at all, Marvin thought. He put his hand over the mouthpiece and said to her, "It's my night in. And they're drinking."

"Well, if you have a hangover, you won't mind staying in tomorrow night," Roz said.

He took away his hand and shouted into the phone, "Sure, sure, Toughy! That'll be great! Where is it?"

It was in apartment 15-E in the Buckminster Élysée Hotel, a couple of blocks east of Central Park, and the last Marvin heard from Roz, as he stood in the hall waiting for the automatic elevator, was "Don't forget to tell me all about it." As he walked down Gun Hill Road to the subway station, he felt astonishment at his good luck, particularly since he and Roz had quarreled at supper. He wondered if his wife had known what was getting him down. It seemed to him now that she must have.

In the subway, going downtown, Marvin remembered how he had felt that morning, when he woke at the sound of the alarm clock in the darkened bedroom of the two-and-a-half-room flat. It would have been light even that early, but Rosalind insisted on keeping the shade down, as she said she had thin eyelids and one gleam of sun tortured her. It had been close, too, with the shade barring any improbable motion of air, and Marvin had imagined for a moment that he was in the crew compartment of the LCIL. The sour-milk smell of the baby had brought him back to reality seconds before he had reached over to turn off the alarm. He had shuffled out to the kitchen to make coffee for himself, thinking involuntarily of the galley on the little ship. Only as he shaved had he begun to feel perfectly sure of his surroundings. June 6 was a bad date to have been in something on. Suppose, he thought, you had been in something on a date that didn't mean anything, like maybe March 23. You would maybe begin to forget the date in a couple of years, and it would just slip by without your noticing it, so you would say, "Why, hell, here it is March twenty-seventh already, and I never even remembered!" But a thing that happened on D Day was like having been married on the Fourth of July.

He had already thought about all that in the subway once that day, going down to work in the soda fountain at Lexington and 23rd in the morning. When he had finished work, he had wanted to go out and tie one on, but he had figured Roz wouldn't like it and it wouldn't do him any good anyway. Drinking alone only made him feel lonelier. Seeing Todhunter again would make it a celebration. Bloom hadn't seen anybody from the ship for four years. There had been only eighteen left anyway. Allardyce Meecham, the war correspondent, had seemed all right, too. He had been aboard for only a few days, and while they lay at Weymouth waiting to go over, he had spent all his time with the LCIL's four officers and the three infantry lieutenants aboard, playing cards and shooting the breeze in the tiny wardroom. But he had written a hell of a story "from his hospital bed in a southern English port" a couple of days later, only Marvin knew Meecham had really been in a hotel in London. The story had made out that everybody aboard was a hero and kept a stiff upper lip—probably to keep from swallowing water, Marvin had thought when he read it. Meecham's paper had sent two free copies to each of the heroic survivors. Meecham was a kind of a tall, awkward man, with red hair, Marvin remembered, and was old enough to have had more sense than to be there anyway. Bloom got off at 86th, took a local down to 59th and Lex, and walked up a couple of blocks to get to the address Todhunter had given him.

Marvin was a short, thin man, with a long nose that rose from base to point, like a snipe's, and heavy black eyebrows. He moved with a jerky, slightly comic alacrity, like a punchinello working for a jittery puppetmaster. Before the war, he had played a couple of seasons in dance bands at small summer hotels. Mostly, however, he had worked behind soda fountains, and this association with drugstores had determined his choice of a rating to buck for in the Coast Guard. For years, he had longed to be addressed as Doc. The rating didn't qualify him for a pharmacist's license in civilian life, so he had gone back to jerking sodas. He wore a light-gray double-breasted tropical-worsted suit with a wide chalk stripe, and the point of a dark-red rayon handkerchief stuck up out of his breast pocket, matching his necktie. Roz insisted on conservative clothes for him. He had about twenty dollars in his pocket and was prepared to offer to chip in for any liquor bought for the party. He was pretty sure, however, that Meecham was going to pay for all of it, and as this embarrassed him, he stopped at a liquor store on a cross street and bought a bottle of Cointreau for the women.

The Buckminster Élysée was like a couple of hundred other hotels on the East Side, with a decorative scheme carrying discretion to the point of insignificance. The hall staff wore Jäger-green uniforms, the fit of which indicated a high labor turnover. Marvin was miffed, because even at that they wouldn't let him walk right into an elevator but asked him who he was calling on and made him wait at the desk while they phoned up to Mr. Meecham and asked if it was all right. When he got to the fifteenth floor, the elevator man opened the door and waved a hand with four broken fingernails down a long passageway, off which opened a dozen identical doors. "Down there," he said. Somebody with a deep, hoarse voice was singing "My father was the keeper of the Eddystone Light" behind one of the doors, so Marvin had no trouble identifying it as the one where his friends were.

The door opened almost as soon as he rang the bell, and Meecham, the former war correspondent, his hair thinner and grayer and his face fatter than the way Marvin had remembered him, stood in the doorway holding out his hand and saying, "Howdy, fella!" He had quite a bean belly. Marvin Bloom shook the hand and went in. It was a two-room apartment, furnished with stuffed bits covered in some hard gray-green material. Toughy Todhunter and Meecham and two women, plus glasses, ice, empty soda-water bottles, and ashtrays, just about filled the room nearest the door. Todhunter was a hell of a big man, six feet three inches tall and thick in neck, trunk, and wrists. His face was red, shiny, and soft, like butcher's meat that has been cut and allowed to stand in the showcase. He was in his early thirties, but he seemed to have become middle-aged since the last time Marvin had seen him.

"Marty!" Todhunter yelled, hitting the little man across both shoulder blades with one hand. "Tell these people how I made the shore patrol at Weymouth carry me down to my ship and put me aboard her. 'I'll go if you insist,' I said, 'but you'll have to carry me.' So the suckers did!"

"I was there when they carried you aboard, sir," Marvin said loyally.

"Toughy to you, Marty!" Todhunter bellowed.

One of the women cut in. "You might introduce your friend, Toughy, before you start treating us to any more of your fascinating reminiscences." Marvin could tell from her tone that she hadn't wanted him to be invited—two broads, two guys, and everything would have worked out quicker than with him there. She was a hard-looking broad, Marvin noticed, with one of those wide, generous mouths that was built up with lipstick around a thin, straight slit in her face. She had high cheekbones and her hair was pulled away from her forehead to make her look intelligent, and she had a pretty good shape, with a girdle, or maybe two, under the kind of low-cut black dress that bunched her breasts and pushed them in your face.

"I'm sorry," Toughy said, as if the girl impressed him. "Miss Considine—Mr. Bloom."

"I brought you ladies something, Miss Considine," Marvin said, "on the grounds I knew beforehand I was bound to like you," and he presented her with the Cointreau.

"How amusing!" Miss Considine cried. "Is this all the rage in the smart set, Mr. Bloom?"

"Don't mind her, Marty," Todhunter said. "She's just too sophisticated to live."

The other woman, a droopy blonde, was more friendly. "Kwahntro oleways remands me of ma first seduction," she said. "Thank yawl fa bringin' it."

"Why bring up ancient history?" Miss Considine said, but the other woman pretended not to hear her.

Meecham introduced the blonde as the Princess Something-or-Other.

"Mary Lou was married to a Polish Prince," Meecham said sadly. "But the Prince betrayed his class by staying in Poland."

"My old man came from Poland, too," Marvin said, but the statement did not seem to improve the atmosphere.

Meecham and the Princess went into the bedroom. Marvin found a straight chair and sat down, and Toughy said, "Tell me now, Marty, how did you ever get hold of that penicillin?"

Marvin said, "How the hell did you know I had that?"

Toughy laughed. "How do you think I figured Hovdisian got rid of that dose without reporting to a doctor on shore?" he asked. "And what about Ringdahl?"

"Well, I didn't want to let them get out of the war," Marvin said. "And besides, Ringdahl was the cook. I had steak every night after I cured him, while the officers was eating canned salmon."

"I think your conversation is disgusting," Miss Considine said. "I hardly saw a good steak here during the war, except in restaurants, while you heroes were simply spending our money on tarts and getting sick."

"Oh, Audrey," Toughy said. "It wasn't all like that. The men just had to have a little fun now and then."

"The *men*," Miss Considine said. "How many times did your little ministering angel there have to minister to you?"

"Don't mind Miss Considine," Toughy said to Bloom. "She has a Wall Street mentality." He poured a bathroom water tumbler about half full of whiskey for Marvin and looked about for some water to add, but Marvin drank the whiskey straight, in two gulps.

"That's right. I have a Wall Street mentality," Miss Considine said. "And who is it buys those beach cottages you build?" Todhunter was an architect in civilian life.

The liquor made Marvin feel master of the situation, and he decided to drown Miss Considine out. "You remember the fight we had with them Limey jerks in Gibraltar, sir?" he said brightly, forgetting to call Todhunter Toughy. "The bottles was flying. Boy, I laid a table down and used it for a shield. Then, every time I got my hand on a bottle, I would crouch up and—bam!—let fly."

"A form of lend-lease, I suppose," said Miss Considine coldly.

"Those were great days—great days," Toughy said. And without warning he began to sing, "The dum-te-dum, and the dee-dee-dee, and HO for a life on the rolling sea!"

"Oh, not that, Toughy," Miss Considine protested, screwing up her face.

"Do you remember Mr. Campbell, sir?" Marvin asked when Todhunter had finished singing. "I wish he was here." Campbell had been Todhunter's second in command. "I'd give him a punch in the nose," Marvin said, feeling the whiskey in his chest. "He was chicken. Do you know, sir, I once picked up a pig in the pub near the railway station and took her home, and when we got there, after we had a good time, I wanted to give her a pack of cigarettes, but she said, 'Oh, no. There's a Yank naval officer comes up here gives me *masses* of cigarettes and *bags* of chocolate. Just look.' So she shows me a bureau drawer full of Lucky Strikes and Hershey bars. 'What ship is he from?' I asked her. So she described where we was laying. 'And what does he look like?' I says. So she described him."

"And it was Campbell?" Todhunter roared.

"It wasn't anybody else," Marvin said, and they both began to laugh. "And that's why the PX was always so short of butts and candy," Marvin said when he had finished laughing. He had had another drink and was feeling happy, but at the same time he was dissatisfied. He had almost forgotten before tonight what a big, silly stiff Todhunter had seemed in the long months between actions. What he had remembered was Todhunter standing up in the conning tower, taking the ship in, in to Omaha, without a deviation of an inch, between the rows of concrete blocks with rusty iron rods set in them, in the one narrow path that the navy scouts had cleared of mines on the night before. He remembered the noise and how Todhunter had seemed the one rock of calm and courage.

Todhunter said, probably beginning another bawdy anecdote, to match Marvin's last, "Do you remember Donovan?"

"Do I remember him?" Marvin said, "I had him all over me—pieces of him on my tin hat, pieces in my eyes—"

"Spare us the details," Miss Considine said. "I'm going to the john." She delivered a warning knock on the bedroom door and opened it enough to get through.

While she was gone, the two men talked excitedly.

"Do you remember when the first one hit us, and went into the forward compartment before all those infantrymen were out of it?" Todhunter asked.

"Christ, do I remember!" Marvin said.

"I always respected you after that day, Bloom, because you went down into that compartment to see what you could do."

"There wasn't anything. A whole hospital wouldn't of done any good. Legs, arms, meat—you can't imagine."

"We went right in anyway, didn't we?" Todhunter said. A huge, sweaty man, getting fat now, with a red, childish face, he looked a little as if he might cry.

"We sure did, Toughy."

"And we landed them dry-ass, the ones that were left."

"I think most of them must of been killed, too, on the beach. And then do you remember when the second one hit us, Toughy, after the soldiers were off, and what happened to the winch crews? It reminded me of when you're a kid and you step on a caterpillar—the stuff comes out—the deck."

"It was the cases of rations the soldiers left on deck—the condensed milk and the asparagus soup and corned beef. The shrapnel tore through the cans."

"And Mr. Scammons, an officer, running around the forward deck without a scratch on him. 'Oh, give me a shot of morphine!' he says. 'Give me anything! I can't stand it!' he says. I should have given him a shot of cyanide."

The two women and Meecham, blinking at the light, had returned to the room.

"Never have I seen nobler sacrifices than on that day," the former war correspondent said. Before the war, he had been a drama critic, but now he wrote a syndicated column and gave lectures on international affairs.

"I'll never forget you, Mr. Meecham," Marvin said. He was getting drunk now. "Scrunched up behind the pilothouse, like another coat of paint. You was scared as hell."

"I felt that every additional wounded man would only be an added embarrassment," Meecham said rather self-consciously.

"You looked embarrassed, all right," Marvin howled.

"I think we've heard about enough of this kind of gunk," Miss Considine said, going over and sitting down on the arm of Todhunter's chair. "Poor Toughy is all upset. After all," she said, addressing herself to Marvin, "*some* people had quite a lot to gain in the war—but not people like Toughy. Let's do something amusing. Let's play a game." She produced a pack of cards, each of which had six numbered names printed on one side and the other side blank. "These are horse-race cards," she said. "Each one puts up a quarter and picks a horse, with a name and number. Then I take this damp towel"—she suited the action to the words—"and draw it across the blank side of the card. The moisture brings out a photograph of the finish of a horse race, and the winner has a number on his blanket. Whoever has bet on the number wins."

"But there are six horses," Meecham pointed out, "and only five of us."

"I know," said Miss Considine. "But I have three horses running for me, because I am the bookmaker, and any one of you wins, I pay him a dollar and a quarter, including his own stake."

"How perfectly *wonderful* of you, darling!" cried the Princess, who seemed to Marvin to be slightly drunker than anybody else.

He could still figure percentages and he knew Miss Considine was making a 25 per cent book, but he didn't want to start an argument in a party Toughy had invited him to. He played a couple of games, hoping that by luck he might win once and quit with the tramp's buck, making her mad, but when the photograph was "developed," it always showed one of the house horses winning. If Miss Considine had been a man, he would have tried to grab the cards away and put them under the tap in the bathroom. He had an idea there were only three winning numbers on them.

But it wasn't any good, and he felt mad, because he hadn't picked up what she said about the special stake that he and people like him had had in the war. Now it was too late. "Well, folks," he said, getting up after losing a dollar even, "I had a wonderful time, but it's a long way up to the Bronx and I gotta be up betimes to go to work in the A.M."

"There must be absolutely *no* unemployment," said Miss Considine sweetly.

"Wait till the Republicans get in," Marvin said, and left feeling he had had the last word.

His exhilaration lasted only as far as the elevator. By the time the man with the broken fingernails let him out in the lobby, he felt displeased with himself. It seemed something inside him remained unexpressed, and he didn't want to go home to Roz until it came out. He was tacking slightly as he walked, but his head was clear, and it was only about half past twelve. He headed over toward Third Avenue, where there were a lot of saloons, and took his pick. He passed a couple up because they were too crowded, another because it was too empty, and a fourth because it had too much chromium and pink plastic showing. There was nothing particular about the one he went into, except that it looked normal.

The bartender, who had flat, smoothed-out cheekbones and a thickened left ear, came over for Marvin's order, and he called for Scotch. He knocked one off and then had to wait a couple of minutes to get the bartender's eye again; it was the kind of place where they don't like to pump booze into the customers. The bartender must have sized him up and decided he could stand a few more if he didn't take them too quick, so he came over in his own good time and gave him a drink. By then, Marvin had begun to like the place, and when the bartender arrived, he asked, "You ever in the ring?" The bartender just nodded and went away to draw beers for a couple of other customers. When he thought Marvin was about ready for a third drink, he came back and poured him a light one. Marvin drank a little, and said, "Mac, did you ever see a deck covered with blood and condensed milk, all mixed together?"

The bartender's face didn't change. It was as if he heard questions like that every hour of the day. "No, Mac," he said. "Did you see that?"

"I did," Marvin said, but before he could say anything more, the bartender had started away again, toward the far end of the bar, where he had left part of a drink of his own that he was having with a man who was reading the *Daily Racing Form*.

When he was only halfway, though, he turned around and came back and stood in front of Marvin, as if he felt he should say something further.

"Well, that'll stay with you, Mac," the bartender said consolingly. "That'll stay with you."

Madame Hamel's Cows

ON JULY 18, 1944—a Tuesday, as I remember it—part of the 29th, or Blue-and-Gray, Division, which was formed originally from Maryland, Virginia, and Pennsylvania National Guard units, fought its way into the city of St. Lô, the seat of the prefecture of the Département de la Manche, in lower Normandy. St. Lô, which had a prewar population of about 12,000, was deserted, except for unevacuated German dead. Correspondents—among them me—who entered shortly after the troops saw little, because they either hugged what they hoped would prove to be the lee of a wall or lay flat on their faces during their sojourn. The Germans, having been thrown out of the city, were reacting like a drunk who has been chucked out of a saloon and then throws a beer bottle through the window.

Rising briefly to cross a street at an intersection, I saw the assistant division commander, Brig. Gen. Norman D. Cota, receive a wound in his cane-carrying arm. He shifted his stick to his other hand and stepped inside a gaping shop front while a medic put a dressing on the damaged member. Cota came out in time to see the correspondents departing as rapidly as possible, and my last memory of that victory is of the laughing General waving his stick and yelling, "Don't leave me now, boys! Don't leave me now!" The wound hurt worse later. When I next saw the General, he said, "I was standing out there to give the boys confidence, but it didn't work out right." A couple of days before the wounding, I had encountered him in the wooded country near St. André de l'Épine, a hamlet on the right flank of the German position. He was stopping soldiers who were drifting back from the firing line.

"Where are you going, boys?" I heard him ask a pair of stragglers, and they pulled up sharp when they noticed the star on the helmet of the spindle-shanked, Roman-nosed old man alone in the road with his walking stick.

"The Lieutenant bugged out, sir, and we thought we might as well, too," one of them said.

"Harses! Harses!" the General said in a non-Harvard New England accent. "I haven't seen any lieutenant coming this way. Get up there before he notices you've been away." Cota was a Regular, born in Massachusetts. He waved the stick and they went back.

After leaving General Cota in St. Lô, some of the correspondents went to see Maj. Gen. Charles Gerhardt, the division commander, a couple of kilometers farther back, to congratulate him on his capture of the city, for which the 29th had been fighting hard for a month. General Gerhardt was a sporting type, an old West Point third baseman who had acquired the habit of pepper talk.

"Sir," one correspondent said, in a highly technical tone, "could you explain to us the strategic significance of St. Lô? Why has First Army made such a point of capturing it?"

"Well, Peanut," the General said, "it's a catchy name. It fitted well in headlines, and the newspapers took to using it every day. After that, it became a morale factor, so we had to capture it."

The General knew better, but his answer stirred up the sediment of *War and Peace-cum*-Siegfried Sassoon that lies at the bottom of every civilian's thinking about the Military Mind. St. Lô was the confluence of arterial roads from the south and east, through which the enemy might have been able to pour reserves to smother a breakthrough farther west. Its capture was like a tourniquet on an elbow, permitting an operation on the forearm. The General couldn't have said that without giving the next move away, but he might at least have said something Delphic and stuffy that the fellows could have put in their dispatches.

Gerhardt's reactions were snappy, as an infielder's have to be, but he didn't always stop to think of their effect. For example, there was the occasion, after the storming of Brest, when the Division buried a couple of thousand of its dead. The Division's Catholic chaplain told me afterward in Paris, in the bar of the Hôtel Scribe, that, marching the men away from the cemetery, the General had the band play "Roll Out the Barrel." He wanted to change their mood. The chaplain considered it an inappropriate choice. Furthermore, he objected to the prayer the General had offered at the funeral formation; the chaplain thought the General should have left that to the professionals. "He said, 'May the good God in Heaven, if there be one . . . ,'" the chaplain reported. "Who is he to voice a doubt of the existence of God?" I said it was just a reflex—the General wanted to be sure all bases were covered before he threw the ball. As a matter of fact, Gerhardt used to say grace before every meal in his mess.

When St. Lô fell, there was for the moment nothing for the correspondents to write about, and this was bad for their dispositions. Deprived of the progress-toward-St. Lô report that had been the essential element of their daily stories, my colleagues, especially the press-association men, began to bicker. All of them had used the St. Lô dateline on their stories of the capture (I had seen nobody carry a typewriter into town, much less stay long enough to write a story), but one man was charged by his colleagues with having used the dateline when he had not actually been in the town at all. The others considered this unethical. The press-association boys constantly competed among themselves on a strict time basis, like milers. The day after the capture, a United Press man wandered through my tent and his, carrying a copy of a cable he had received from his home office. "'Beat nearest competitor one minute forty-five,'" he read aloud proudly. "'Kudos, kudos, kudos.'" Then he looked up and asked, "What does 'kudos' mean?"

"It means they've decided not to give you a raise," I said.

The tents were in the First Army press camp, where there were censors and excellent mobile facilities for the transmission of our stuff by Press Wireless. The camp was at a place called Vouilly, which was near Isigny, an early capture, and about fifteen miles north of St. Lô. Vouilly was a crossroads, an old church, a harness maker's shop, and a grocery-café. Down a wooded private road beyond the crossroads lay a big farm with an immense, moated farmhouse that was known as the Château.

In that country of rich peasants and hard-drinking gentry, the line between large farmhouses and small châteaux is seldom clear; houses, like
families, cross and recross social lines. Mme Hamel, the proprietress of
the Château, made no claim to nobility, but she looked a proper chatelaine—tall and straight, with a high forehead, a long, straight nose,
bright-blue eyes, and white hair. She was sixty-two. The living room of
the Château, equipped with army chairs and tables, was our pressroom.
It was bigger than the city room of the Providence *Journal* and the
Bulletin when I worked there a long time ago. The dining room, as long
and almost as wide, was never used; Mme Hamel, her son and daughter-
in-law, the farm servants, and the neighbors made their headquarters in
the kitchen, which was a fine room in itself, with a wall spigot that ran
hard cider. Our tents were in front of the house, along the edge of one
of the great pastures, which we shared with fifty cows. Every morning
during the fighting for St. Lô, we would have a large, hot breakfast in
the mess tent and then climb into jeeps, two or three correspondents to
a driver, and take off for the battlefield. The mess tent was our ace good-
will builder with the farmers; it was run cafeteria style, and all of us
generally left a lot on our plates. The swill was of a magnificence un-
paralleled in that thrifty countryside, and the farmers carted it away
for their young pigs and the mothers of their still younger pigs.

By five o'clock in the afternoon, we would be back. It was a sensible
way to work, but it created what the quarterly-review fellows call a
dichotomy—we were in the war from nine to five and out of it from
five to nine. The weakness of the *Luftwaffe* at that stage increased the
discrepancy between the front and Vouilly. There was no danger on the
roads, and although we maintained a blackout at night, we felt silly
about it. The best route to the front was a sunken road that led up
through St. André de l'Épine. For days, the progress of the 29th along
it was slow, bloody, and sometimes nearly imperceptible. If you stuck
to the road in the Division's wake and went slowly, in order not to raise
dust, you could not be seen, except at gaps in the high hedges that lined
both sides, and there was not much chance of your being hit. There
was always fire going over the road, clipping leaves from trees and
making you feel important, but you would have needed a stepladder to
climb up to it. The Germans believed in firing their weapons often—as
advocated by the distinguished American military critic, Gen. S. L. A.
Marshall, and numerous Chinese tacticians of the fifteenth century—in
order to keep their spirits up. When we got to the point where vehicular
traffic ended—there was always an MP on the spot to say where it was
—we would dismount and walk as far up front as the mood moved us.

It was on one of these forward excursions that I heard Cota talking to the stragglers. The feature writers would try to cull thrilling incidents from company commanders and walking wounded, and the correspondents from places like Minneapolis would go around trying to find soldiers from Minnesota to ask them what RFD route they lived on. During the last days of the battle, I had been heartened by the number of abandoned German bodies in the road; it showed that the survivors were moving backward a lot faster than they wanted, or they would have carried their dead with them. They were unlikable people and they had no business in that part of France anyway.

The infantrymen and artillery spotters, who had to fan out in the fields on both sides of the road, naturally were more likely to be hit than we were. The wounded who could walk had their hurts dressed at first-aid stations by the roadside and then hiked, or hitched jeep rides, to the rear. When we turned back at the end of each day's outing, we picked up as many of them as we could. They would sit on the hood of the jeep, embarrassed because they had been hit. "Looks like we might have some rain," they would say, or "Wonder how the Yankees are doing." This embarrassment is the mark of a good competitor. He neither complains nor tries heroically to pretend it was jolly good fun; he feels that he personally is responsible for whatever happened to him. His prototype is Gen. Joe Stilwell, who said, after his eviction from Burma, "I claim we got a hell of a beating"—not "I claim the cards were stacked against us" or "I claim we won a hell of a moral victory."

Driving homeward, we would look into the faces of the infantrymen coming up to the line, in single file, well spaced, heavily burdened. They were preoccupied faces, neither aggressive nor self-pitying, from a region that was neither Big City nor Wild West. They had been twenty months in Devon before coming to France, and they had fitted in well with the gentle Devon people. "The finest physical men I ever saw," General Cota had told me in England when he first went to the Division. "But there's no meanness in them. I try everything I can think of to make them mean, but it's no use." The General had come from the 1st Division, which was loaded with Brooklyn boys, and they had convinced him that the best premilitary preparation was two brisk battles daily for a seat in the subway. "Those fellows in the First were little, but they didn't care who they stepped on," he said, explaining his theory.

When I got back from my exciting incursion into St. Lô, I rushed to the kitchen of the Château to inform Mme Hamel of our glorious feat of arms. The family still possessed a private stock of old Calvados, and these tidings were, I thought, of a sort to stimulate hospitality. I was in a great hurry to get there before André Rabache, the Agence Française correspondent, who also knew about the Calvados. I arrived to find the Hamels and a large collection of neighbors seated around the long kitchen table. I could sense that they had been engaged in a serious discussion.

"Madame," I said proudly, for I wanted her to think well of the American Army, "I come from St. Lô. The city is ours! Now we can advance!"

"I felicitate you, monsieur," she said. "I am happy to hear it."

"I also, *mon commandant*," said a neighboring farmer, whose name was Lesavoureux. *"Correspondant,"* which is not a military rank, seldom registered with the Normans, who usually promoted us to *commandant*, or major. "But I ask myself what will happen to the pigs."

"The pigs?" I asked. My mind was still on Cota, directing traffic among the shells.

"Yes, *mon commandant*—the young pigs who depend for their nourishment on the leftovers of the mess," he said.

The only ray of hope I could offer was that the enemy might make a tenacious defense of the environs.

Mme Hamel, who had the manners of a marquise, came to the rescue. "The pigs are already well launched," she said, turning a disdainful eye in M. Lesavoureux's direction. "They have had a good start in life and will make out for themselves perfectly. Perhaps monsieur would like a glass of Calvados? The day must have made you some emotion."

The Normans are not a sheeplike people. Give them a lead and they start in the opposite direction. While M. Lesavoureux wanted the army not to advance, a farmer down the road, whom I visited one night with Hamel *fils,* was irritated by our procrastination. He had part of an armored division in his pasture. "I was extremely pleased to see them arrive," he said, "but they are ruining my hay crop." I had been reliably informed that this farmer owned several barrels of old Calvados, and it was my object to obtain one of them for our mess. To do this, I was prepared to buy one of his pigs, also for the mess. (The correspondents made up a pool for these supplementary purchases and declared the army personnel in.) The farmer's counterplan was to use a small amount of the Calvados to get me drunk, and then sell me the pig, but no barrel. After a long evening, I came away with neither the barrel, which he wouldn't sell, nor the pig, which I wouldn't buy without the barrel. But I had the makings of a frightful hangover free, and M. Hamel said that nobody else had ever got anything for nothing from the host of the armored division.

* * *

I was thinking of all these things as I rode west from Colleville to Isigny with Michel, a White Russian chauffeur in a hired car, eleven years later. We were on the road that runs along the top of the cliffs overlooking Omaha Beach, and at Isigny, where our road would end, we would look for a road that led south to Vouilly, where I hoped to find Mme Hamel as magnificent as before. I wondered, too, about the descendants of the pigs. When we got to Isigny, which is famous for producing the thick cream that comes to the table with strawberries in French restaurants ("Isigny: 2,787 inhabitants; specialties: butter, tripe, cream, mussels; sixty per cent destroyed by bombardment on June 8, 1944."—*Guide Bleu, Normandie*), Michel was favorably impressed by the white stone buildings, in the style of Robert Moses comfort stations, that have replaced the 60 per cent destroyed.

"*Moderne!*" he said. "*Pas comme Boolioo.*"

He had been unfavorably impressed by the fishnet of medieval alleys that entangles the cathedral. Isigny is dominated by the large, modern, double-winged plant of the Reunited Butteries & Creameries, a modern-Norman testimonial to God's bounty. At a quartermaster's dump in Isigny in 1944, I drew the best pair of shoes I have ever owned, free. I was sure that it was no use looking for the quartermaster's dump now, however.

Michel stopped in front of the Reunited Butteries & Creameries and went inside to ask the way to Vouilly. He came out visibly depressed, as always when he had to ask directions. "*N'esista pas, moosioo,*" he said, in what I had learned to recognize as his notion of French. "*Voo-lioo, personne a entendoo.*" He stood with folded arms, his great brown eyes liquid with astonishment at his plight, like those of an abandoned straggler from Denikin's army who has heard the first howls of the advancing Bolsheviki. His eyes told me that I had been a fool to leave the caravan routes between Paris and Deauville or Paris and Cannes in order to lead him after a mirage. Nothing to do now but throw our burnooses over our heads and wait for the St. Bernard dogs.

"*Voolioo*, evidently, does not exist," I said to him, in an excessively reasonable tone. "But *Vouilly, Vouilly, Vouilly* exists!" I made a move as if to go myself to ask directions.

"Ah, *Vooyee!*" Michel said, starting back at a run, and adding, over his shoulder, "*Pooquoi moosioo dit Voolioo?*

Michel had lived in France for twenty-seven years, and it was a point of professional honor that he, the resident, should translate for me, the foreigner. It was a little like traveling through the British Isles with a

Gurkha dragoman who insists on carrying on all intercourse with the natives.

Michel returned from the Reunited this time with the expression of a Scotland Yard inspector who has cracked a big case. *"Ça y est,"* he announced. *"Vooyee—ah!"* And he looked at me indulgently before he headed the Versailles in the right direction.

Vouilly is less than a dozen miles inland, but when you get there the sea is forgotten. Bayeux, with its 10,000 inhabitants, seems an incredibly large city in retrospect, and its cathedral, embodying renovations right up through the fifteenth century, is Saarinen compared to the small, un-ornamented Romanesque church of Vouilly, with its front and rear elevations like equilateral triangles on squares and its tower no higher in proportion than a peaked helmet on a Norman swordsman. The Vouilly church hasn't been changed since the eleventh century. The tower is off to one side of the peaked roof, like a fighter's head tucked in behind his shoulder. It surveys a countryside where the fields are surrounded by ditches and banks of earth, with trees, all ensnarled with vines and bushes, growing out of the tops of the banks—the most ancient of cattle fences. The rain falls most days, the grass grows all through the year, and the cattle turn it into milk. During the fighting in Normandy, the Army Civil Affairs branch tried to evacuate peasants from farms that became battlefields, but they wouldn't go. They said the cows had to be milked. The cattle, in the open all year round but never out of call of the milkmaid, develop a character that is neither wild, like that of range cattle, nor passive, like the milk factories that spend most of their lives in front of a manger. They are, like the Normans, independent, gluttonous, and indomitable. The Germans defended the hedged fields as fortresses, and the cattle remained in them as audience, chewing the rich grass as the shells burst among them and falling on their sides like vast milk cans. In the immediate vicinity of Vouilly, however, there had been no fighting.

Michel asked a woman at the café the way to the Château, and she said to turn left on the first "avenue" past the crossroads. She meant the first avenue of trees, but Michel was amused.

"Elle appelle 'avenoo' oona toota petita roo," he said. *"Paysanne."* For Michel, "avenue" was a term reserved for the Avenue des Champs-Élysées, the Avenue Foch, and thoroughfares of equivalent luminosity.

He consented to turn down the bucolic version of an avenue, though, and after about a mile I saw the Château in front of me, sleeping among the trees. Its tower was higher than that of the church, but not high enough to rise above the oldest trees around it.

We drove between the hedged fields, over the bridge and into the farmyard. Mme Hamel and her son were sitting under an apple tree, shelling peas. They were surrounded by fat, sleepy hens, among whom walked peacefully a fat, sleepy tomcat. When Michel stopped the Versailles, madame looked at us, shading her eyes with one strong hand, and called out to her son, "It's he!" She rose—a trifle heavier but even more impressive than I had remembered her—like a great, noble Percheron mare, white with age, getting up in a field, and walked over to the car as I got out. Her son came with her, and as they reached the car, she said to him, "I knew he would come back someday."

To me she said, "Why didn't you come last year with the others?"

In 1949 and 1954, I knew, airlines had organized two junkets to Omaha Beach for former war correspondents who had been there—and some who hadn't—thus reaping a modest harvest of mentions in news stories. I had not been with either party, and Mme Hamel, in consequence, had felt slighted. She liked all her old guests to come back to her. For five weeks in 1944, the Château had been one of the news centers of the world. Scores of millions of people in America had hung on the stories of the ugly fighting among the dead cattle, and every word had gone out through the mysterious wireless trucks on madame's farm. She had not been insensible to the honor, or to the excitement of feeling herself in the know, and she had not begrudged us the use of her pastures. All the old guests who made the junkets came back to visit, she said. She remembered me particularly, because I had hung around the kitchen so much, cadging refreshments.

Her son is a quiet man, short, wide-shouldered, and long-armed. He walks with a limp that dates from the time when, as a prisoner of war of the *Wehrmacht*, he was made to work at clearing French minefields in Alsace. (It was in 1940. Pétain had capitulated, and the Germans were paying only nominal heed to the Geneva Convention rules on the treatment of war prisoners.) Hamel had stepped on some kind of antipersonnel device, crippling himself so badly that the Germans had sent him home during a much-publicized "restoration to their families" of a number of French prisoners incapable of useful labor. The Vichy regime had touted this as a great concession. By 1944, when I first met him, he had got around to thinking of his accident as a stroke of luck. He could walk again—although with a limp—he could work as well as ever, and he was home, on the right side of the Allied line, while the fate of his former fellow prisoners was dubious. They had already had to undergo four years of heavy Allied air bombardments, and it was still possible that the SS would massacre the survivors when Germany was invaded. (As it turned out, they didn't, but the omission was probably due to a loss of nerve.) Hamel *fils*, therefore, didn't hold the minefield incident too strongly against the Germans. Certain aspects of his captivity had even amused him—particularly the fright of the civilian population during the first great air raids.

Every evening, while the correspondents pounded at their typewriters, he would circulate among them with a cup and a jug of milk warm from the cow, like a hospitable precursor of M. Mendès-France. He was married, but the dowager Mme Hamel remained the chatelaine, and I had only to see the Hamels together to know that nothing had changed since 1944. The pastures stretched green and profitable before us, with not a tent in sight. The cows roamed free over the site of the vanished latrine, a part of the pasture that for some bovine reason they always resented being dispossessed from. They upset the simple installation almost every night, I recalled.

I asked Mme Hamel about the health of some of the cows I remembered: L'Anglaise, so called because she came from the Channel Islands; La Nageuse, who leaped into the moat to cool off; La Nitouche, who pretended a maidenly aversion to the bull. None survived, madame said, but they had left daughters and granddaughters to make assault upon their records of lactation. She kept a book listing the names, biographies, and milk records of her cows—usually about fifty. I remembered madame and her lady in waiting, the milkmaid, leading La Nitouche to the bull, who was the terror of the soldiers even though he was fastened to a stake by a chain and nose ring.

"Do you remember the day the bull broke loose and charged the jeep?" she asked me, as if she had been following my unspoken recollections.

I remembered, of course. He had knocked out one of his eyes, which occasioned rejoicing among the men.

In the pasture on the other side of the road, where the mess tent had stood, the grass had the look of never having been disturbed by man. I could not help asking the question that had been on my mind all the way from Omaha Beach.

"And the pigs, madame?" I asked. "The pigs that were fed on the leavings of the *popote* and that we abandoned when the army was compelled to advance?"

"Most of them died," madame said. "But of indigestion. They had been *too* well fed. Figure to yourself, monsieur. A pig fed on pancakes and syrup—God never intended it. It was providence that the army advanced when it did, because in three more days they would all have perished." I was happy to learn that, in effect, the interests of the First Army and of the pigs of M. Lesavoureux had coincided, although M. Lesavoureux was too shortsighted to recognize it.

The day was hot, and Mme Hamel proposed that we go inside the Château. In the long, cool hall that parallels the front of the house, I felt I had come back to one of my homes. (A mobile man has many. There is, for example, a cabin on a Norwegian tanker that I wake in often, although I haven't slept there for fourteen years.) On one of the great oak doors leading off the hall, a sign reading PRESS ROOM preserved the memory of the *grande époque*. Mme Hamel led me into the room next to it, the dining room—a symbol that the Château was on a peacetime footing. M. Hamel and Michel trailed along, Michel with his beret in his hand, and looking about him with a new appreciation of the Hamels' status. These were more than *paysans;* they were kulaks.

The dining room was full of furniture I could not remember from the war days; there was a long Norman table of old, scarred oak, surrounded by carved chairs, and a buffet and an armoire, equally old. All were in what I judged to be the style of the late sixteenth or early seventeenth century; the *ferronerie* of the buffet and the chest was of a chaste hammered crudity that proclaimed the age of all the work.

"I made them myself, all but the armoire," said M. Hamel soberly. "The armoire is real, of the sixteenth century, and I copied it."

"And the hardware? The handles, locks, hinges?"

"All," he said. "Everything."

"How did you age the wood?"

He smiled. "It's my secret."

On one wall hung a portrait of a rough-coated chestnut foal with upstanding crest and ears. "The colt that was born while you were here," Mme Hamel said. "The foal of the mare the Cossacks abandoned."

There had been Cossacks in the region before we came, part of the Vlasov Army of Russian prisoners of war, who had consented—under threat of death, they inevitably said when captured by us—to fight for Hitler. They were an anomaly in the German Army, since the Germans never trusted them sufficiently to issue them any armament that dated from later than the First World War. They had therefore been used principally to garrison and overawe regions where nothing much was expected to happen, and they had a nasty reputation for pillaging. The German soldiers had as low an opinion of them as they had of their Italian allies in the Mediterranean, and when the Allies landed in Normandy, the Russians fought only until it was apparent that the debarka-

tion was no mere raid. Then they quit. Prisoner-of-war pens were full
of them well before we began to get genuine Germans in quantity. The
Cossack horses wandered through the pastures and mixed in with the
herds of cattle. I remembered the mare and her foal, a pair of tolerated
free boarders among Mme Hamel's cows. She didn't have the foal any
longer, she said, but the old mare was still around. Young Mme Hamel,
the daughter-in-law, had painted the picture.

Mme Hamel brought out a bottle of muscat de Frontignan, a cloy-
ingly sweet white wine from the south of France. Wine is a ceremonial
drink in Normandy, where none is grown or made. It is not expected
to taste good. M. Hamel came to my rescue by bringing out a carved
wooden bottle of Calvados. "I remember you always preferred this," he
said. "It's some of our own make, ten years old." I reflected bitterly on
the greed of all the Americans, including me, and all the British who
had passed through in the war years and accepted the one-or-two-drinks-
at-a-time hospitality of the Hamels, drying up the prewar stock. This
1945 Calvados was merely promising, but I got a couple of glasses down
in order not to offend my hosts. While I was tasting the Calvados and
Michel was sipping the horrid wine with the air of a connoisseur, madame went to the armoire and returned with a great black scrapbook of
clippings, like a grand old lady of the theater; she resembles one. These
were her clippings of things that had been written about her, unfortunately all in English.

"This is by M. Beyle," she said, and I looked at the by-line and saw
that it was not by the M. Beyle who took the nom de plume of Sten-
dhal but by M. Hal Boyle, the Associated Press columnist and an old
tenter in the pasture, who wrote how glad he was that madame was
alive and well and nicer than ever. There were other clippings of the
same tenor; the authors, or other Americans who saw them in print,
had evidently sent them to her. On pages where no clippings had been
pasted, former guests had written appropriate sentiments and their
names and addresses. One of these entries was by Col. Monk Dickson,
the G-2, or head intelligence officer, of First Army, dated a couple of
days after the fall of St. Lô. It said, as nearly as I can remember now,
"To the good family of the Château de Vouilly, which was the reposi-
tory for a week of the secret of Cobra." Cobra was the code name of the
breakthrough, on the road that stretched west from St. Lô to Périers,
that stove in the left wing of the German Seventh Army. It led to the
great hooking movement that rolled the Germans up like a window
shade.

Dickson's name reminded me of an incident at the Château that I had forgotten. A bit after the capture of St. Lô, Gen. Omar Bradley came there to see the correspondents and tell us about the next move, so that we could prepare to cover it. The tall, long-jawed, gravely humorous Missouri General who was so great a soldier that he never felt compelled to bark to prove it, arrived by jeep with his aide, Maj. Chet Hansen, and Dickson. Hansen carried a map under his arm. The lecture room in which he chose to announce the impending doom of the German Seventh Army—"I may be sticking my neck out in predicting it," he said, to soften any hint of cockiness—was a shed that had been extended forward with canvas tent sides and roofing to serve as a movie theater for the troops. General Bradley said that he hadn't wanted to trouble us to come over to his headquarters—there were so many of us. It had also been a far better idea, from the point of view of security, for him to disappear from headquarters for an hour than to convoke fifty correspondents and their jeep drivers, which would have given an always possible enemy agent a decided notion that something was up. But Bradley did not mention this second consideration; it was as if he shrank from encouraging the idea that anything he did could be important. General Collins' VII Corps, so reinforced that it virtually constituted an army—four infantry and two armored divisions, I think—was to make the strike, amputating the arm that Gerhardt had bound off. Then Patton's Third Army was to come into official being—it already existed incognito, behind the First Army line—and race through the hole south and west into Brittany. (The plan worked even better than that, of course, but a fighter starting a combination of blows can't know in advance the other fellow's capacity to absorb them.) I suppose that if I had heard Scipio, before the Battle of Zama, describe how he was going to cancel out Hannibal's elephants, I would have thought it a historic occasion, but it took Monk Dickson's handwriting in Mme Hamel's book to remind me that I had heard Bradley call his shot.

"Do you remember when General Bradley came here and spoke in the shed?" I asked madame.

"Yes," she said. "There were no movies that night."

The breakthrough, I remembered, was originally scheduled for July 21. It was aborted by soaking rain, which spoiled the ground for armor and made it impossible for the bombers in the preparatory air strike to see their targets. So Collins didn't jump off until July 25, when, aided by perfect visibility, the Air Corps inflicted heavy casualties on our 30th Division. I remembered that because I had watched the planes, not knowing where their bombs were falling. We had wondered why the 30th didn't get along and let us move.

I felt that it was time to go, because there was not much left to say. I answered all the usual biographical questions: How was my family? Did I continue to occupy myself with journalism? It was superfluous to ask madame how she occupied herself: the fifty cows, the hay crop, the chickens answered that. Her son, I was sure, was an excellent farmer, but she would never dissociate herself from any of his farming. Seeking a question slightly less idiotic, I asked her how she amused herself.

"Ah, well, there is always fishing," she said brightly.

This was a side of madame's personality I had never divined. She scarcely seemed the type to put on waders and dangle feathers at the end of a line.

"Where?" I asked.

"But here, in the dining room," she said. "Look."

She led me to a window, and we looked down at the moat, covered with lily pads, beneath which the water barely moved. It was originally formed by diverting a stream and leading it around the house, but the stream was no Mississippi to begin with.

"It is full of carp," Mme Hamel said. "Every day, I throw bread and bits of potato out the window. The carp accustom themselves to the snack. Then I put a hook in a potato and drop my line from the window. Instantaneously, I have a magnificent carp. You cannot make yourself an idea how good really fresh fish is."

I gazed at her with an admiration whose extent I could not express. No sunburn, no squint from looking at the shimmer on water, no bony shins sticking out of Bermuda shorts—she displayed none of the usual stigmata of the sports fisherwoman, yet her technique was of an intellectual refinement that my friend Col. John R. Stingo would have appreciated. The Norman carp is a conservative investor, not to be taken in, like a trout, by the flash of an obviously spurious insect flourished under his nose like a prospectus for Montenegran carbuncle mines. The kind of chump who is really worth taking has to be encouraged by a series of unwarranted dividends. "When the habituation is achieved," Colonel Stingo once said to me, describing a parallel process, "the chump, ascribing his success to his own talents, demands a further opportunity to invest. He is then ready for the *coup de grâce*."

I did not wish to take time to explain to madame who Colonel Stingo is, so I did not call her attention to their affinity. Instead, I asked another question: "Are there pike?"

"Not here, but in the pond," madame said. The pond is behind the house, at a distance of perhaps a hundred yards. It is a large pond, shadowed by great willows, and in 1944 we used to swim in it. "My son goes out there," Mme Hamel said. "I don't often have the time. He has also arranged a pair of shooting holes, with sliding shutters, in the back of the carriage house, which is turned toward the pond. When the wild fowl settle on the pond, he goes into the carriage house, slides back a shutter, and shoots them."

It sounded to me like the only shooting and fishing preserve I ever wanted to lease.

The Hamels, *mère et fils,* entreated us to stay for dinner, but I had it in my mind that I wanted to get back to Bayeux before dark.

"Come back soon," madame enjoined me as we departed. "I am getting old, and who knows?" She looked imposingly durable.

As Michel and the Versailles and I headed back up the avenue of trees, I composed in my mind the text of an advertisement I meant to insert in the *Times* when I was next in London: "Syndicate of keen guns being organized to fish Merovingian carp moat, hunt Gallo-Roman duck bath in attractive country surroundings."

A cow, perhaps a daughter of L'Anglaise or La Nitouche, stopped eating to watch us as we passed, then again put her head down in the grass.

Westbound Tanker

A TANKER is a kind of ship that inspires small affection. It is an oilcan with a diesel motor to push it through the water, and it looks painfully functional. Its silhouette suggests a monster submarine with two conning towers. A destroyer's clipper-ship ancestry is patent in the lines of its hull, but neither tankers nor submarines betray any origin. They seem to have been improvised simultaneously by some rudely practical person and then put in the water to fight each other. A submarine scores a point when it sinks a tanker, and a tanker when it completes a voyage. When the oil reservoirs of the Allied bases are full, the tankers are beating the submarines. They have been doing that since the beginning of this war, but few people think of a tanker as a fighting ship. When a tanker gets sunk you read about it in the paper, but when it docks safely nobody hangs any flags in the streets.

The *Regnbue,* on which I made a voyage from England to the United

States this winter, is a Norwegian tanker. It is not remarkable in any way. Norway has a tanker fleet second only to that of the United States, and Norwegian tankers have carried 50 per cent of the oil that has gone to Britain since the war began. The *Regnbue*—the name means "Rainbow," as you may have surmised—was built at Gothenburg, Sweden, in 1930. She displaces nine thousand tons, a good, middling tanker size, and can do eleven knots loaded, a fair, medium speed. Her lead-gray hull was streaked with rust and her masts and funnel and deckhouses showed only a trace of paint the first time I saw her. A grimy Norwegian flag, ragged at the edges, flapped from her mizzenmast, and there was a cowled four-inch gun on a platform raised above her poop. I was joining her as a passenger, but I didn't learn her name until I got close enough to read it on a small sign on the side of her bridge. This was because the Norwegian Trade Mission in London, through which I had booked my passage, believes in secrecy about ship movements. Since the German invasion of Norway, the Norwegian government in exile has chartered most of the Norwegian ships in the world to the British Ministry of War Transport. The ships still fly Norway's flag, have predominantly Norwegian crews, and are, for the duration, in the custody of the Trade Mission.

An official at the Trade Mission, knowing I was ready to leave on short notice, had called me up at my hotel in London one Saturday morning and said that if I didn't mind sailing from London instead of a west coast port, they had a ship for me. I said I didn't mind, although this would add several days to the voyage. Next morning I took a taxi to the Mission offices on Leadenhall Street and there handed over my passage money. The man who had telephoned me said that the ship was bound for New York in water ballast to take on cargo there. He gave me a sealed envelope addressed to one Capt. W. Petersen and a slip of paper bearing written instructions for getting to the ship. I was to take a certain train at Fenchurch Street station early Monday morning and travel to a small station near the Essex shore, a ride of an hour and a half. A taximan would meet me at the station and drive me to a pier, where I would find a boatman named Mace. Mace would put me aboard Captain Petersen's ship.

Shortly after eleven o'clock on Monday, December 1, I found myself in Mace's launch, moving through the water of the Thames Estuary toward the tanker, which lay about a mile offshore. The only other passenger in the launch was a Norwegian port engineer who was going out to examine the ship's motors.

"Look at that paintwork!" the engineer said as we neared the *Regn-bue.* "Tankers make such quick turnarounds the crews have no chance to paint. Discharge in twenty-four hours or less, take bunker and water, and out to sea again. Oil docks are always in some place like *this,* too—miles from the center of the city. The men don't get a chance to see the town. I know. I was in tankers in the last war."

Before he had time to tell me more about them, we were under the rope ladder leading to the *Regnbue's* main deck. It was an extremely uninviting ladder, but the engineer went up it as if it were an escalator. A seaman dropped a line to Mace, who made a loop through the handles of my suitcase and portable typewriter, which then rose through the air like Little Eva going to heaven. I went up the ladder in my turn with neither grace nor relish. My style must have amused one of the several men who were leaning over the rail, because he looked down at me, then turned to the man next to him, and said, "Commando."

This fellow, who was wearing a white jacket, was obviously a steward. He was of medium size but had long arms, so the jacket sleeves ended midway between elbow and wrist, baring the tattooing on his wide forearms. On the right arm he had a sailor and his lass above the legend, in English, "True Love." The design on the left arm was a full-rigged ship with the inscription "Hilse fra Yokohama," which means "Greetings from Yokohama." His head was large and bald except for two tufts of red hair at the temples, looking like a circus clown's wig. He had a bulging forehead and a flat face with small eyes, a turned-up nose, and a wide mouth. As soon as I got my breath, I said, "Passenger," and he took me in charge with a professional steward's manner, which, I afterward learned, he had acquired while working for a fleet of bauxite freighters that often carried tourists. The bauxite freighters had operated out of a port the steward called Noolians, and most of the tourists had been vacationing schoolteachers from the Middle West. Fearing emotional involvement with a schoolteacher, he had switched to tankers. "Tankers is safe," he said. "No schoolteachers." His name was Harry Larsen.

The steward led me along the rust-stained steel deck to the ship's forward deckhouse. The main deck of a tanker is simply the steel carapace over the tanks. In rough weather the seas break over this deck. The human activities of the ship are concentrated in two deckhouses, fore and aft. The forward one is like a four-story house rising from the main deck and contains the bridge and the captain's and deck officers' quarters. A long catwalk ten feet above the main deck serves as the highroad between the deckhouses, and even on the catwalk you are likely to get doused when there is a sea running. The engine room and the galley, the ship's one funnel, the cannon, the refrigerator, the crew's quarters, and the cat's sandbox are all jammed in and around the stern deckhouse.

The steward showed me to my cabin, which was the one called the owner's, although the owner had never used it. It was next to the captain's office. His bedroom was on the other side of the office, and we were to share a bathroom. It was a fairly good cabin, with two portholes, a bed, a divan, and a desk. The steward said that the captain was still ashore but I should make myself at home.

I went out on deck to look around and was pleased to see one of the British Navy's barrage-balloon boats alongside. A balloon boat is a lighter with a half-dozen or so bright, silvery balloons floating above it, each attached to a slender wire. The *Regnbue* dropped a wire cable aboard the lighter, and a couple of naval ratings rove the end of a balloon cable to ours. They let go the cable, and the balloon rose above our foremast, securely attached, as we thought, to the *Regnbue*. It wasn't, though. It blew away two nights later, but it was a pretty embellishment as long as we had it. While I was watching the transfer, a little man in a blue uniform came over and stood next to me. I asked him when he thought we would get under way. He said that he was the pilot and was going to take the ship a short distance farther down the river that afternoon. The captain was coming aboard after we got downriver. The pilot was a black-haired, red-faced Londoner with a habit of laughing nervously after practically everything he said.

"Good thing about a tanker in water ballast," he said. "She's just a box of air, what? Tanks half full of seawater, all the rest air—wants a long time to sink if she's torpedoed. Much as forty minutes, perhaps, eh?" He laughed. I said that I thought this was very nice, and he said that now you take a loaded tanker, it was just the opposite—the very worst sort of ship to be torpedoed aboard. "Flaming oil all about. Rather depressing, what?" he said. I agreed.

The steward came along and told us that dinner was on the table in the saloon, so the pilot and I followed him down a flight of stairs into a large, rectangular room with paneled walls and a dark-green carpet. The most impressive feature of the saloon was a portrait, nearly life-size, of an old gentleman with a face the color of a Killarney rose and a bifurcated beard that looked like two blobs of whipped cream. The artist had used plenty of paint of the best quality. I could imagine a jury of boatswains giving the picture grand prize at a *salon*. "The founder of the line that owned this ship," the pilot said.

"Capitalist!" the steward said, simply and with distaste.

"Rum thing on Norwegian ships," the pilot said, "the captain doesn't eat with the other officers. As a passenger, you'll mess down here in the saloon with the captain, and there'll be just the two of you at every meal. But in every other respect they're more democratic than our ships. Odd, what?"

The pilot had been at Dunkerque, he told me a bit later on. "I was in command of seven motorboats," he said, with his laugh, "transferring troops from the beach to destroyers. I lost the boats one by one. A motorboat doesn't take much smashing, does it? When the last one foundered, my two ratings and I swam to a destroyer's boat. What I shan't forget," he said, after a pause, "is the motorbike races on Dunkerque beach. Chaps waiting to be taken off, you know. Never saw better sport. There were soldiers making book on the races. Couldn't leave the beach until all bets were settled or they'd be known as welshers."

The dinner of pea soup, corned beef, and baked beans, ending with a double-size can of California peaches for the pilot and me, was big by London standards. The portions were on a scale I had almost forgotten, and there was a lot of butter. The steward said the food had been loaded at Corpus Christi, Texas, in October.

"We don't take any food in England," he said. "I hope we get to New York for Christmas. I got nothing to make Christmas at sea—no newts, no frewts, no yin for drinking."

"We ought to make it," I said, with the confidence of inexperience.

"It depends what kind commodore we get," the steward said. "If we get slow commodore, old man retire from Navy fifty year and only come back for the war, we lucky to get New York for New Year's. I don't care much for New York anyhow," he added loftily. "Too much noise, too many Norweeyans in Brooklyn, argue, argue, argue! I like better Camden, New Yersey, go with the Polish girls."

The ship moved slowly down the estuary during the afternoon. We dropped anchor again before dark at a point where the Thames had definitely ceased to seem like a river and where half a dozen other ships already rode at anchor. Our men looked at them curiously, as one surveys the other occupants of the lounge car at the beginning of a long railroad journey. There were a couple of British tankers with fancy Spanish names, a gray, medium-sized Dutch freighter, and a big, boxlike Elder Dempster boat that had once been in the West African service. I have seen the Dutch freighter's name in a newspaper since. She had shot down a German plane. There was also a stubby, soot-black Norwegian steamer of not more than three thousand tons, which had a single funnel so narrow and long that it reminded me of an American riverboat. The third officer, a husky blond chap who wore an orange turtleneck sweater, pointed to the stubby ship and said to me, "That is the slowest ship in the world. Once she made one trip from Cape Town in four convooeys. They started two weeks apart and she kept on losing one convooey and getting into the next. She was going full speed the whole time." All the ships were, like ourselves, light and bound for America to get a cargo.

The pilot came down from the bridge and joined me when the ship was at anchor. I asked him when he thought we should get to New York, and he said that with luck we ought to make it in about twenty days. It depended a lot on what connections we made at the assembly ports, he said. The *Regnbue* was going all the way around Scotland to get to the west coast of Britain. We would spend the first few days of our voyage in a small convoy sailing up the east coast of England to our first assembly port. From there, we would go to the west coast in a larger convoy, but we might have to wait a couple of days while this larger convoy was being assembled. Then we would proceed to the second assembly port and go through the same business there. We might be just in time to leave with a transatlantic convoy or we might have to wait a week. There was no way of telling. "The most ticklish bit in the trip begins about twelve hours above here," the pilot added consolingly. "If we get off tomorrow morning, you'll be in it by night."

Captain Petersen came aboard shortly before nightfall. He was a small, stoop-shouldered man. His brown shoregoing suit was carefully pressed. He had a long, curved nose and lank, sandy hair, and he spoke English slowly but accurately, using American idioms. He had lived in Philadelphia, where he worked in an oil refinery, during part of the last war, he told me, and then had moved to Hoboken, where he had roomed in the house of an Irish policeman. After the war he had gone back to Norway to enter navigation school with the money he had earned in America. All the reminiscences of the United States that he politely introduced into our conversation dated from before 1919. He gave detailed accounts of several Chaplin comedies, like *The Count* and *The Cure*, which he had seen then. We went down to supper with the pilot, and Captain Petersen, pointing to the whiskered portrait, said to me, "That is a man who once owned eighty sailing ships. Even when he was ninety-two he combed his beard for one hour every morning. I remember seeing him in my hometown when I was a boy. The company owns only a couple of ships now. It belongs to an old lady, who lives in my town also."

His town is a sleepy little city in southern Norway which in the nineteenth century was a great port for sailing ships. The *Regnbue,* the captain explained to me, is emphatically a ship from his town. Not only is she owned there—although, as he explained, owners captive in Norway had no control over their ships for the duration of the war—but skipper, chief officer, and second officer all came from there and had known each other as schoolboys. Both the captain and the chief officer, a man named Gjertsen, had even been married aboard the *Regnbue.* Their brides had joined them on the ship at Antwerp and Constanţa, Romania, respectively. Petersen had been second officer and Gjertsen third officer then, and they had honeymooned in turn in the captain's suite. The wives were at home now. "The second and third officers have wives in Norway, too," he said, "and so has the chief engineer. I was lucky enough to have a vacation in December, 1939, so I saw my wife and boy only a little while before the Germans came."

Petersen told me that when the Germans invaded Norway, the Norwegian government had commandeered Norwegian ships all over the world, ordering those at sea to put into neutral or Allied ports. A radio message had been sufficient to accomplish this. Only a small part of the merchant marine had been caught at home. Now the exiled government's income from ship hire not only supported it but provided a surplus, which is to be used for the nation's reconstruction after the Germans are driven out. He didn't show any doubt that they would be driven out, nor did anyone I talked to on the *Regnbue.* The boatswain, a weathered gnome of a man, once said to me, "I couldn't sleep at night if I didn't believe on it." The owners of the ships were nearly all caught in the invasion. The government has promised that after the war they will receive compensation for the use of their ships provided they pay allotments to the sailors' families in the meanwhile. So the captive families have been receiving small amounts of money, but even with money there isn't much food.

There was a door at each side of the saloon. One led to the pantry and the steward's cabin, the other to the deck officers' quarters. The officers had their mess aft, in the other deckhouse. After supper on a normal evening aboard the *Regnbue,* I was to learn, the captain and the steward visited the deck officers. Then, at about eight o'clock, everybody visited the steward and drank coffee, made in a big electric percolator which the steward brought in from the pantry. I suppose a torpedo would have disrupted this routine, but nothing less could have. This evening marked my initiation into the ship's social life. Since we were still in port, it was a *soirée de gala;* none of the officers had to stand watch, and it was all right to use the short-wave radio in Gjertsen's cabin. Such sets are sealed at sea because they cause a radiation which can betray a ship's position. For news of the outside world you depend on what the wireless operator picks up on long-wave.

Around seven o'clock, the captain, the pilot, the steward, and I marched into Gjertsen's cabin, where the other officers already were gathered. Gjertsen, a tall, dark man who looked something like Lincoln, was stretched out on his berth halfway between floor and ceiling. His wedding picture hung just above the berth. Gjertsen had not been home since 1937. Haraldsen, the second officer, who was small and jolly, turned the dials of the radio, with occasional professional counsel from Grung, the wireless operator, a serious young fellow whom the others considered something of a dandy. He came from Bergen, which is almost a big city. Bull, the third officer, the big fellow in the orange sweater, sat on the divan looking at a picture of the backsides of thirty-two bathing girls in *Life*. He didn't turn the page all evening. Nilsen, the gunner, sat on the floor and said nothing. He hardly ever said anything to anybody. The captain explained to me later that it was because Nilsen was a whaler. Whalers talk themselves out on their first voyage, the captain said. They exhaust all possible topics of conversation, then fall silent for life.

"It isn't like a lighthouse keeper," Petersen said. "He hasn't had a chance to talk in months, so he is bursting with it. But a whaling man is talked out."

Gjertsen hated the radio, but he insisted on keeping the set in his cabin because he liked company. No matter what kind of music Haraldsen got, Gjertsen said it was rotten and Haraldsen should turn to something else. Whenever they got a news program he just fell asleep. He said there was enough trouble on the ocean without dialing for it. They were all low that evening because of a broadcast by the Norwegian radio of the news that the Germans were planning to cut off the money for their families.

"I wonder how long people in the old country will be able to keep from starving," Haraldsen said helplessly.

"Why don't the British start the invasion?" Grung demanded, looking sternly at the English pilot. "All the fellows who escape from Norway say there are only a few thousand Germans there."

"Full moon tomorrow night," the pilot said pleasantly, by way of changing the subject.

"Yes, fine moon for dive bombers," the radioman said resentfully. "We'll be right in the middle of E-boat Alley then."

"Maybe there'll be fog," the pilot suggested helpfully. "Fog is no good for bombers."

"Fog is fine for E-boats," Grung said. "Can't see them coming."

Grung, I was to learn, liked to have something to complain about; actually, he worried little about enemy action. Danger at sea is like having a jumpy appendix: men can live with it for years, knowing in an academic way that it may cause trouble but forgetting about it most of the time.

Haraldsen said that the *Regnbue* had always been a lucky ship—fourteen crossings since the war began and never a conning tower sighted. Everybody banged on wood.

"The *Meddelfjord* always was a lucky ship, too, before the last time," Grung said, insisting on his right to grumble. "I lost a good pal on her, the second engineer. Burned to death in the sea. The oil was blazing on top of the water and the fellows had to swim in it. That was a nice joke!"

"We didn't miss that by much ourselves," the captain said to me. "We were together with the *Meddelfjord* at Newcastle, both bound for London. We stayed to discharge some of our oil. The *Meddelfjord* and eight other ships went on. Three of them were sunk by planes and motor torpedo boats."

Bull put down his magazine and said in a matter-of-fact tone, "I like to catch a Yerman. Bile him in ile."

Unexpectedly, Nilsen, the silent, spoke up. "I have no respect for them," he said.

Before coming aboard I had calculated roughly that the chances are at least ninety to one against being torpedoed on any one crossing. Incidentally, the American marine-insurance companies now charge a premium of 1 per cent to insure tanker cargo, which indicates that they think the odds are considerably longer than a hundred to one. It is not a great risk to take, once. The men in the *Regnbue* lived continually with this risk, which is quite a different thing. They seldom talked of danger except when they were angry about something else, like no shore leave or the British failure to invade the Continent.

Bull started turning the dials of the radio set again and got a program of jazz music from Stockholm. A woman was singing something that sounded like "Klop, klop, klop! Sving, sving, sving!" Bull and Haraldsen laughed so hard they could barely stand it.

"I can't explain it to you," Haraldsen said to me, "but to a Norwegian the Swedish language sounds always very funny."

We had three or four cups of strong coffee apiece in the pantry and then went to our cabins. Norwegians use coffee as a sedative.

Long before I got up next morning I could hear the anchor chain coming in, and when I got out on deck we were moving along in a column of eight ships. The strings of signal flags looked like holiday bunting, and each ship had its own bright new balloon. Half a dozen sloops and corvettes in pink-and-green camouflage milled around our column. The convoy was probably not moving better than eight knots, so the corvettes looked lightning-fast. Machine guns were being tested on all the ships, and the intermittent bursts of gunfire added to the gaiety. The tracer bullets from the machine guns are fun to watch as they skitter over the water; they seem a superior kind of flying fish, with electric light and central heating. We had a pair of Hotchkisses mounted one on each side of the bridge. If we were attacked, they would be manned by the two seamen on lookout. We also had two British machine gunners, who manned a small fort on the poop deck, where they had a couple of Lewis guns. There was not enough open space around for our gun crew to try out our four-inch gun, but an antiaircraft battery on shore was practicing. Its guns went off at one-minute intervals, and the shells made a straight line of white smoke puffs across the sky, like pearls on a string. A couple of minesweepers dragging magnetized floats went ahead of us, in case the *Luftwaffe* had planted any magnetics during the night.

We dropped the pilot at noon. Life on the ship picked up its sea rhythm. The crew consisted of the usual three watches, each of which was on duty four hours and then rested eight. Haraldsen, the second officer, was on the bridge from twelve to four, Gjertsen, the chief, from four to eight, and Bull, the third officer, from eight to twelve, when Haraldsen relieved him. I had a chance to get to know some of the sailors, because they came forward to stand their watches on the bridge. However, the engineer officers and the rest of the crew, down at the other end of the ship, remained relative strangers.

When the men came forward they wore life jackets. The officers, when they went up to the bridge, carried their life jackets with them and tied them to a stanchion. I had bought a kapok-lined reefer from Gieves, the naval outfitter then in Piccadilly, a swank garment that purported to double as an overcoat and life jacket. It was supposed to close with a zipper, and each clash with the zipper presented a completely new tactical problem. The zipper changed its defensive arrangements to meet my attacks; I could never throw it twice with the same hold. Sometimes I could close it in a couple of minutes, but on other occasions it beat me. I was sure that if a torpedo ever struck us, I would go down in a death grapple with my zipper. I had an ordinary life jacket in my cabin, of course, but I had paid good money for the reefer. I was also given a huge, one-piece rubber suit, so stiff that it stood up in a corner of my cabin like a suit of armor. It was a Norwegian invention, Captain Petersen said, and everybody on the ship had one. The idea was to climb into its legs and tie yourself into the rest of it, so only your face showed. The air in the folds of the suit would both hold you up and insulate you from the cold of the water. This consoled me until Grung, the radio-man, told me that a crew had once demonstrated the invention for the Norwegian Minister of Shipping and that while all of them had floated for hours, a couple of fellows who went in head first had floated upside down. Grung was a man of few enthusiasms. For example, we had a large escort for such a small convoy, and this made him unhappy. "There must be trouble expected or there wouldn't be so many," he said.

Late in the afternoon we reached the bad spot about which the pilot had told me. This is a lane along the East Anglian coast that London newspapers have named E-boat Alley. The Commodore of the convoy was in the ship ahead of us, a British tanker. Commodores are usually commanders in His Majesty's Navy; they carry a pair of aides and a squad of signalmen with them and communicate their orders by flag signal or flash lamp. This Commodore would go with us only as far as the first assembly port; he was an east-coast specialist.

I was in the saloon just before suppertime, reading Hakluyt's *Principall Navigations, Voiages and Discoveries of the English Nation*, when I heard a noise that sounded exactly like a very emphatic blast during the excavation of a building site. The ship quivered, as if she had taken a big sea. Larsen, the steward, was the only other man around; he was laying out a few plates of salami and ham and herring salad as table decorations.

I took it for granted that the noise was a depth charge and said, "My, my!" to show how calm I was.

Larsen winked and said, "Mak raddy der bahding suit!"

Both of us, I imagine, wanted to run out on deck and see what had happened, but since we had only recently met, we tried to impress each other.

Captain Petersen came down to supper ten minutes later and said that a mine had gone off a hundred feet from the Commodore's ship and almost knocked her out of the water. "Gjertsen was on the bridge and saw it," he said. "He says it threw a column of water higher than the ship's masts. She was hidden completely. Then, when the water settled, Gjertsen could see the ship was still there, but she had only a little way on. Then she hoisted two red lights to signal she was out of control. The blast must have damaged her rudder. So she has to go back to port."

"Goodbye, Commodore," Larsen said unfeelingly.

"It must have been one of those acoustic mines," the captain said, "but it didn't work well. It went off too soon." There was a certain wonder in his tone, as if he felt that the Germans must be overrated.

The explosion of the mine was the only evidence of enemy action we were to encounter during the whole trip.

Larsen had it figured out that in order to get to New York by Christmas, we would have to leave the west coast of England by December 7.

"We get off with lucky seven and in seventeen days we come to New York," he said. "Get there Christmas Eve, the immigration officers ain't working, and we stay on the ship until December twenty-sixth."

This was a sample of what I got to know as Scandinavian optimism. We didn't reach even the first of our two assembly ports until December 5, so it looked certain that we would spend Christmas at sea. We were seventy-two hours going up the east coast from London, anchoring each night because of heavy fog. The second time we anchored, Larsen began getting out and repairing the green-and-red paper Christmas decorations that formed part of the tanker's stores. He went about his work during the day muttering a sad little refrain that I sometimes caught myself repeating: "No newts, no frewts, no yin for drinking."

The crew looked forward to spending its shore leave in Brooklyn, even if we got to New York after Christmas. To a Norwegian the finest part of the United States is Brooklyn. For the duration of the war it is the Norwegian fatherland. When a Norwegian seaman meets an American, he usually begins the conversation with "I got a cousin in Brooklyn." Haraldsen, the second officer, had two brothers there. Larsen pretended to be supercilious about Brooklyn, but he fooled nobody on the *Regnbue*. The *Regnbue* had been in the Thames for only a couple of days, and few of her men had gone into London. The ship had been anchored at such an awkward distance from the city that it had hardly seemed worth the journey. Some men had got drunk at a hotel not far from the oil dock. Others had not even set foot on land. Corpus Christi, Texas, the ship's last American port of call, had not been exactly a Brooklyn, either.

Olsen, the carpenter; Grung, the radioman; and I were visiting the steward and drinking coffee on one of the foggy nights and Olsen said, "The last time I was in Brooklyn I didn't take my shoes off for three weeks. My feet was so swollen I had to cut my shoes off." Olsen was a man who liked to startle people.

"It must have been good liquor you were drinking," I said.

This was just the kind of opening Olsen wanted. He put his head on one side and looked at me fixedly for a full half-minute, as if I were a dangerous lunatic. "Good liquor!" he finally said, contemptuously. "A man is a fool to drink good liquor. I never drink liquor that tastes good." He stared at me again, as if expecting me to leap at his throat, and then said, "Because why? I get drinking it too fast. Then I get drunk too quick. The best thing is whiskey that tastes bad. Then you stop between drinks about ten minutes, until you need another one. Then you can keep on drinking for a month." The carpenter was a solid, rectangular fellow of fifty, with blue eyes set wide apart in a boiled-ham face. He could make a davit out of iron pipe or reseat a rattan chair with equal competence. He was the ship's delegate of the Norwegian Seamen's Union, to which all the men belonged.

The steward lay in his berth at the summit of a stack of drawers. There was no other place for him, because the rest of us occupied all the chairs. He said, "In Brooklyn I live in Hotel St. Yorge. Yentleman! I don't go on Court Street in Eyetalian saloons. I yust buy good old bottle aquavit and go to my room and drink like yentleman. Go to Norweeyan church Sunday and put five dollars in collection. Brooklyn women too smart. Better leave 'em alone."

The radioman said that once he and some shipmates had been in a taxi-dance hall near Borough Hall and had asked a couple of hostesses to sit down and have a drink. The hostesses had charged them four dollars apiece for their time. "You got more for your money in Constanța," he said. Constanța, in Romania, used to be a great port for Norwegian tankers before the war.

"We had a man on one ship going down to Constanța," the carpenter said, "and he wouldn't believe all we told him about it. He said he had been in every other port in the world and he wouldn't lose his head in Constanța. So he went ashore one night, and two days later we seen a man walking down on the dock with nothing on but his socks, and it was him. Always lots of fun in Constanța."

The steward found this so amusing that he reared up on the back of his neck and kicked the ceiling. He had been a leading light of the gymnastic society in a small town in southern Norway, and he liked to use the edge of his berth as a gymnastic bar. He spent a good deal of time composing letters to English and American girls on a portable typewriter he had in his cabin, and when he was at a loss for an English phrase he would get up, face his berth, and jump high in the air, twisting in time to land in a sitting position. Usually three or four jumps would bring him the phrase he wanted and he would return to his typewriter. The steward called his cabin Larsen's Club, and the atmosphere was congenially ribald except when Captain Petersen was there. The skipper came in every night for his three cups of coffee. Captain Petersen was a friendly man who did not stand on formality, but he was a Methodist and a teetotaler. He didn't try to deter anybody else from drinking or talking randy, but Larsen seldom kicked the ceiling when the skipper was around. All the men were cut off from their home country and lonely, and the captain was the loneliest of all. Once he said to me, "It isn't so bad for a man who drinks and—" He stopped suddenly, as if just understanding what he had said, and went off to his cabin looking miserable.

At meals with Captain Petersen I had plenty of time for eating, because there was not much conversation. Once he said, as he began on his first plate of cabbage soup, "I have an uncle in New York who has been fifty-two years with the Methodist Book Concern." Twenty minutes later, having finished his second helping of farina pudding, he said, "He came over in a wind-yammer."

On another occasion he said, "We had a Chinaman on the ship once. When we came to Shanghai he couldn't talk to the other Chinamen." After an interlude during which he ate three plates of lobscouse, a stew made of leftover meats and vegetables, he explained, "He came from another part of China."

And once, taking a long look at the shipowner's portrait, he said, "I went to see an art gallery near Bordeaux." After eating a large quantity of dried codfish cooked with raisins, cabbage, and onions, he added, "Some of the frames were that wide," indicating with his hands how impressively wide they were.

Once, in an effort to make talk, I asked him, "How would you say, 'Please pass me the butter, Mr. Petersen,' in Norwegian?"

He said, "We don't use 'please' or 'mister.' It sounds too polite. And you never have to say pass me something in a Norwegian house because the people *force* food on you, so if you said 'pass' they would think they forgot something and their feelings would be hurt. The word for butter is *smør*."

It was morning when we reached our first assembly port, and the captain went ashore to see the naval authorities. He returned with word that we would sail next evening. In the afternoon a boat came out from shore and a naval officer climbed aboard to tell the captain that our destination had been changed from New York to Port Arthur, Texas. Luckily, the *Regnbue* had enough fuel for the longer journey or we would have lost more time taking bunker. The captain told me of the change and said he was sorry I would be carried so far from New York, but things like that happened all the time. The changes weren't made for strategic reasons, because no one could tell three weeks or a month in advance how the U-boats would be distributed off the American coast. It was just that there probably weren't enough "dirty" tankers to handle all the heavy oils from the Gulf of Mexico. A "clean" tanker handles only gasoline. A "dirty" tanker has tanks equipped with heating coils to keep heavy oils liquid. The *Regnbue,* the captain said with pride, was a first-class dirty tanker.

News of the change of destination quickly got about among the crew. There isn't much point in secrecy aboard a ship anchored offshore if none of the men are allowed to go ashore. Port Arthur is a dismal place compared to Brooklyn, and the seamen were disappointed. There are no Norwegians in Port Arthur and no taxi-dance halls. Mikkelsen, the electrician, said that you couldn't even buy whiskey in a saloon in Port Arthur; you had to buy a bottle at a package store and take it into a soft-drink joint to get a setup. Perhaps the most disappointed men on the ship were the British machine gunners, Ramsay and Robinson. They had been out to India and Australia with other ships but never to America.

"Where is Texas?" Robinson asked me. "Will I be able to get up to New York for a weekend?"

Ramsay, who was a lance bombardier, laughed derisively. "You haven't got money enough to get that far," he said. "It's all of two hundred miles."

Robinson earned three shillings and threepence a day, of which the War Office sent one and three to his mother in Salford, slap up against Manchester. Ramsay drew ninepence more for his single chevron, and he was always boasting to Robinson about his opulence.

The Britishers belonged to the Maritime Anti-Aircraft Regiment, generally called the Sea Soldiers at home. The Sea Soldiers ride on merchant ships in the manner of old-time American stagecoach guards. They have had more training with automatic arms than the seamen who man machine guns and are supposed to steady the seamen in a fight. Robinson and Ramsay had been partners on other ships and had been in a long running battle with some Axis submarines off the west coast of Africa just before they joined the *Regnbue.* Convoys are nearly always attacked off the African coast, they said. There is a belief among seamen that the Germans have a submarine base at Dakar, no matter what Pétain may say. Robinson was a quiet lad who said, "A odn't been sottisfied i' infantry, so thought A'd try summat else, and this was fair champion—nowt to do." Ramsay was a Glaswegian, a hyperenergetic type who was always shadowboxing on deck and shouting "Pooh!" or "Coo!" for no apparent reason. He used to brag about how many German planes he had shot down, although it is hard to apportion credit for bringing down a plane when a whole convoy is blazing away at it. One day he said that if we captured a German submarine—not a likely prospect—he would personally kill all the prisoners. Gjertsen, the chief officer, said to him seriously, "You can't kill anybody on this ship without the captain say so." This made Ramsay sulk.

There were three other Britishers on the ship—a man in the engine room, a seaman, and a messboy. English seamen like to get on Norwegian ships when there is an opportunity, because the pay is better than the British scale. Nearly all seafaring Norwegians speak English, so there is no trouble about understanding orders. The only fellows on the *Regnbue* who knew no English were five youths who recently, and separately, had escaped from Norway by crossing the North Sea in small boats. They were all studying a textbook on Basic English. They had received word that after they had escaped, their parents had been put in prison. News from Norway reaches England quite regularly by boat. There are even motorboats that smuggle mail between the two coasts.

Most of the men grew thoughtful when we cleared the first assembly port. We were within three hundred miles of Norway now, and they could not help thinking about it. Otherwise the tension, which had never been great, seemed to have completely vanished. There was no further danger from motor torpedo boats and not much from dive bombers. The big Focke-Wulf Kuriers and the submarine packs generally operate farther to the west, where the large convoys form, so we felt relatively safe. We had parted company with a couple of ships at the assembly port and picked up a couple of others. What bothered me was the weather. Captain Petersen advised me to chew on dry crackers and drink no water. The steward said, "Don't use nothing yuicy. Yust dry stuff."

The prescription of "a brisk walk around the deck," classic on passenger liners, is not much good on a tanker, because deck space is so limited. You can take a few steps on the bridge or make a circuit of the forward deckhouse, picking your way among ropes, slings, boats, and the entrances to two companionways. If you go aft, you have a slightly longer promenade around the after deckhouse, although you have to crawl under the gun platform once on each lap to complete the circuit. The main deck, between the two deckhouses and forward of the bridge, is low and lashed by spray. There is a catwalk, an elevated pathway between the two deckhouses, but men with work to do are constantly passing back and forth on it, so there is no room for a *flâneur*.

At the beginning of the voyage I had decided to let my beard grow until I got home again. The boatswain, who came from a port in the far north of Norway, counseled me to shave my beard, on the ground that it would bring fine weather and then the ship wouldn't rock. The boatswain was a small man who looked as dry and tough as jerked meat. He had ice-blue eyes and a long, drooping, ginger-colored mustache, and he repeated his joke about the beard every morning. Then, later in the day, he would manage to ask me the time and say, "I had two gold watches but they're on the bottom now." His last ship had been bombed and sunk at her dock in Liverpool and he had lost all his gear on board. Fortunately, he had been spending the night on shore with a respectable lady friend—the widow of an old shipmate, he was always careful to explain when he told the story. He had a French wife in Caen, but he had not seen her in seven years, because big ships seldom went there. I once tried to talk French with him, but he said with a sigh, *"Ya goobliay toute."* The boatswain was aware that he said the same things every day, but he said them to be friendly. After all, nobody can think of something new to say when he sees the same shipmates daily for weeks on end. The quip about the beard contented the boatswain, and he laughed every time he said it. His laugh sounded like cakes of ice knocking together.

On December 7, we were in a gale. I turned in early and put my watch and fountain pen in the desk drawer, where they rattled like dice in a nervous crapshooter's hand.

There is a difference of thirteen and a half hours between the time in Hawaii and Great Britain, and I was asleep before Grung, the radioman, picked up the first bulletin about the attack on Pearl Harbor. I heard the news when I went up on the bridge next morning. Bull, the third officer, pumped my hand and said, "We both allies now!" It felt more natural to be a belligerent on a belligerent ship than that anomalous creature, a neutral among belligerent friends.

I tried to visualize New York. People at home must be frightfully angry, I imagined. I kept telling the Norwegians, "Americans aren't like the English. They get mad much quicker and they stay mad." (I was to feel pretty silly about that after I got back to New York.) We all wondered why the fleet had been in Pearl Harbor and how the Japs had got there. The B.B.C. bulletins received by the radioman were skimpy. We were actually near the base of the British Home Fleet, but suddenly we felt far from the war.

The ship had sailed with two neutrals aboard and now it had none.

The other neutral had been an ordinary seaman named Sandor, who was a Romanian. Great Britain had declared war on Romania a few days after we cleared, so Sandor had become an enemy alien. He took the news calmly. "Can't send me back now," he said. He had stowed away on the *Regnbue* at Constanța in the early summer of 1939 and had stayed with her ever since. He had learned Norwegian and English on the ship.

We were glad to get to our second assembly port, where we were permitted to turn on the short-wave radio in the chief officer's cabin. We sat around it for hours, listening to the B.B.C., the Norwegian broadcasts from London and Boston, and even Radio-Paris, the Quisling station in Oslo, and Lord Hawhaw. We got some of our best laughs from an Italian English-language announcer who used to sink Allied shipping in astronomical quantities twice a day. It was a Norwegian broadcast from Boston, I remember, that told us Lindbergh had endorsed the war and a Free French announcer in London who said Senator Wheeler had done the same thing. The steward was amused. "Next thing, Quisling against Yermans!" he shouted.

As soon as we arrived at the second assembly port, the captain went ashore. When he came back, he said that we were starting for America early the next morning. The port was at the head of a deep and narrow bay. The *Regnbue* and nine other ships were to start just before dawn and go to sea to meet vessels that would simultaneously leave other assembly ports. There would be from fifty to a hundred in the combined convoy, which was to be a very slow one. It would make only eight knots, because it included a lot of ships like the Norwegian steamer that Bull, the third officer, had pointed out to me some days before as the slowest ship in the world. We had lost her in the gale on December 7, but she had steamed into the second assembly port twelve hours behind us. She was called the *Blaskjell*, which means "mussel." An eight-knot convoy takes a long time to get across the ocean, Captain Petersen said, but going that way was better than hanging about waiting for a ten-knotter. Fast ships go alone, on the theory that they can run away from any submarine they sight, but the *Regnbue* was not nearly that fast.

It was about seven o'clock when we hove anchor next morning, but the moon was still high in the sky. The other ships that were going out showed one light apiece, and a corvette was talking to us in Morse code squawked out on a whistle that sounded like Donald Duck. A westerly wind was howling, and I remembered that we had received a gale warning the evening before. The moon slipped into a cloud abruptly, like a watch going into a fat man's vest pocket, and didn't come out again.

When it is as dark as it was that morning, it is hard for a landsman to tell if a ship is moving, because he can't see her position in relation to anything else. But after a while I was sure. When it began to get light, I went up on the bridge and looked at the ships in front of us and astern. They were already plunging about. When you look at other ships in a heavy sea, the extravagance of their contortions surprises you. Your own ship is going through the same motions, but you wouldn't believe they were so extreme unless you saw the other ships. The farther we got down the bay, the worse the weather grew. The Commodore's ship, about a mile ahead of us, sent up a string of flags; the ships between us repeated the signal. Bull, who was on the bridge, said, "Commodore wants us slow down, says he can't hold his position." He threw the engine-room telegraph to "Half Speed." In heavy weather the *Regnbue* steered well only at full speed, and the men at the wheel had an unhappy time from then on. Now and then her bow came clear out of the water—from watching other tankers I could see exactly how it happened —and the sea gave her a ringing slap on the bottom. I felt that this was an impertinence, precisely the sort of thing a German would do if he were running the ocean.

By noon we were getting away from land. I went down to the saloon to have dinner with Captain Petersen and found him already ladling his third plate of milk soup out of the tureen. Milk soup is made of condensed milk and water, heavily sugared and full of rice, raisins, dried apricots, canned peaches, and anything else sweet the cook can find about the galley. It is served hot at the beginning of a meal, and only a Norwegian can see any sense in it. It appeared on the table regularly twice a week, and at each appearance the steward said, "Fawny soup today, Liebling." At the beginning of every meal, without exception, he would say to me, *"Vaer so gọd"* ("Be so good"), and bow. I would say the same thing to him and bow, and we would both laugh. It was like the boatswain's joke about the beard.

On the bridge that afternoon, the captain was preoccupied. He said that unless we could go at full speed, he didn't see how we could get to the rendezvous before dark, but only about one other ship in our lot could keep up with us at full speed. Our entire escort was one eight-hundred-ton corvette, and if we left the convoy, we left the escort. Sometimes you have a big escort and sometimes you have a small one. It's like going into a shop in England: you get what they have in stock.

Haraldsen, the second officer, who was also on the bridge, was as jolly as usual. "By-and-by Florida!" he would shout when water whipped across the front of the wheelhouse and splashed in our faces. That was *his* standard joke. The corvette seemed to stand on its head every time it went into a wave, and Haraldsen got a lot of fun watching it. "The little feller is doing good," he would say. "I hope they got a good belly."

By three o'clock we had lost the *Blaskjell* and two of the others, and a half hour later we could see the Commodore's ship turning. The Commodore was signaling us to return to port. He had judged that there was no chance of reaching the rendezvous before nightfall, and he didn't want us to be out on the ocean alone when morning came. "We made about thirty miles in nine hours," Captain Petersen said. We turned, and on the way back to the assembly port we picked up the *Blaskjell* and passed her. At nine o'clock we were again at anchor in our old berth.

The boatswain was not the only one who looked suspiciously at my beard after the return. "This has always been a lucky ship," the carpenter said. "I think we got a Rasmus on board now." A Rasmus is the equivalent of a Jonah.

The next day the weather was fine. The carpenter said that this was just what you might expect now that we had missed the convoy. Captain Petersen put on his brown suit and went ashore. He came back with word that we were stuck for at least a week. We had already been at sea for a fortnight. It was not entirely bad news to the boatswain and the steward. The boatswain could now put the men to work painting the ship. When a ship's paint gets streaky, a boatswain becomes melancholy and embarrassed, like a housewife who has not had time to wash the curtains. Griffin, the English seaman on board, once said to me, "If the bos'n ain't a bastard, the ship's no good." He added that the *Regnbue* was quite a good ship.

The steward saw a chance to get the supplies he needed for Christmas. About all that the captain and I had been hearing lately at our meals was a monologue by Larsen about the horrors of Christmas at sea without newts or frewts or yin. Once a ship has left the port of origin, Navy people permit only the captain and the radioman to go ashore—the radioman for a single conference before a convoy leaves—so Larsen gave the captain a list to take to a ship chandler. The captain found no nuts or fruits, but in a couple of days a lighter brought out a case of gin and two cases of whiskey, which the steward put away in the pantry closet. Ordinarily, I was told, no liquor was served on the ship except to pilots and immigration officers, but Christmas was always an exception.

The days at anchor were tranquil. Every morning the captain went ashore and the rest of us painted and theorized about our false start for America. The officers worked alongside the men, and I daubed a bit for company. Some of the men argued that we should have started for our rendezvous at midnight instead of just before dawn, and others said that with a wind like that against us we shouldn't have started at all. Haraldsen said why complain, maybe the convoy we had missed would be attacked anyway. (A couple of days later we heard that all but fourteen ships out of seventy had had to turn back because of the weather.) Evenings, we listened to the radio and talked about the war. The men talked a lot about what they were going to do with Quislings in Norway after the war. They used Quisling as a generic term, just as we do. Some of the men wanted to put them on Bear Island, up north of Norway. Others just wanted to kill them. Even the messboys were angry at Knut Hamsun and Johan Bojer for having betrayed Norwegian culture. The ship had a library of four hundred volumes. None of the seamen would read Hamsun or Bojer now. Norwegians seem more interested in books than music, and the captain was the only one who mentioned Kirsten Flagstad to me. He said Wagner had gone to her head.

Often, when Captain Petersen sat down to a meal, he would look at the customary plates of cold meat on the table and say, "I wonder what they have to eat in the old country now" or "I wonder what my wife has to eat." When we had fish he would say, "My wife never liked fish. Her father was a butcher" or else "My father-in-law always said, 'Fish is fish, but meat is nourishment.' " Once he heard me humming that old barroom favorite, "m-o-t-h-e-r." He said, "I heard a fellow sing that in vaudeville in Philadelphia. He had his wife on the stage and their six children. When he sang it, one kid held up a card with 'm' on it. The next kid held up 'o' and so on until the smallest one held up 'r'. It was the cleverest thing I ever saw on the stage." Often he showed me photographs of his wife and their little boy.

We put to sea again a few days before Christmas. Just before we left, a naval man came out to say that our destination was now Baton Rouge. Nobody even speculated about the reason for this second change. We took it for granted that there was some kind of muddle. Despite my beard and the carpenter's forebodings, we had normal North Atlantic winter weather this time. Early in the afternoon we sighted a huge fleet of ships on the horizon. This was to be a ten-knot convoy, so we had left the *Blaskjell* and a couple of other tubs behind. "Now we'll have something to look at," Haraldsen, the second officer, said as the courses of the large group and our small one converged. Every ship in a convoy has a number. No. 44 had been assigned to us at the assembly port, and as we joined the others we hoisted the "4" flag and the pennon that corresponds to a ditto mark. All we had to do was find the 43 ship and fall in behind her.

The small convoys we had traveled in along the coast had gone in either single file or a column of twos. This one was in a column of eights. We had ships to port and starboard as well as ahead but only an escorting corvette behind us, as we were a file-closer. This tickled Haraldsen, because we wouldn't have to repeat any of the Commodore's signals. A signal is passed down a file of ships, each repeating it for the benefit of the one behind. All the file-closer has to do is run up the answering pennon to acknowledge the message.

Grung, the radioman, came out of his shack to look at the escort. There were only four corvettes for fifty-six large ships. "It's a bad yoke," he said bitterly. "Those English lords are sitting with girls behind drawn curtains on large estates, and we can go to hell." When we had had a large escort on the east coast, Grung had said that was a bad sign.

Haraldsen said, "Oh, boy, I wish I had one of them girls here! Some fun." He had worked as a carpenter in New York during the building boom from 1924 to 1929 and talked of this as the romantic period of his life. "I got fifteen dollars a day," he said. "Fellows would wait for you in front of your yob—Yews, you know—and say, 'Listen, come with me. I give you a dollar more.' I like Yews." He had been on sailing ships during the last war, but he did not recall them with the same affection as, for example, John Masefield or Lincoln Colcord. "A sailing ship is hell in cold weather," he once told me.

It takes a combination of keen eyes and accurate navigation to keep a ship in its proper position in a convoy during the night, and the fleet is usually rather jumbled in the morning. This situation helped to kill time aboard the *Regnbue*. In the morning everybody was eager to see how badly the convoy had broken ranks.

Bull, the third officer, was always on watch at dawn, and every morning he would say, with a sort of pride, "Dis der vorst convooey I ever see. Every morning all over der Atlahntic."

The *Regnbue* nearly always held its position in relation to the Commodore; either we kept to our course accurately or there was a telepathy which made him and us commit the same errors. Some of the other ships, however, would be far off on the horizon. This would always amuse Bull and the lookouts. The 43 ship, which was supposed to stay just ahead of us, was nearly always miles to starboard, and when she tried to get back into her place we would, for the fun of it, speed up so that she couldn't edge in. She was an old tanker and slower than the *Regnbue*. Her skipper must have been a rather fussy sort; she would break into an angry rash of signal flags and her radioman would bring out his signal flash lamp and deliver a harangue in Morse. Finally we would let her ease into the column. It usually took an hour or so to get everybody aligned. The ships always reminded me of numbered liberty horses forming sequences in a circus.

After the convoy was reformed, we could kill another half hour trying to count the ships. There were a few less every day. Ships drop out with engine trouble or get so far off the course during the night that they lose sight of the convoy. These run a bigger risk than the ones that keep pace, but most of them turn up in port eventually. Two ships carried catafighters; that is, Hurricane fighters that could be shot into the air from catapults if a Focke-Wulf appeared. In profile, the catapults look like cocked pistols. We used to find comfort in looking at them, even though Grung said that the pilots were probably seasick and the planes would break away from their lashings in a storm just before we were attacked by an air fleet.

Sometimes ships in convoy talk to each other out of boredom, like prisoners tapping on cell walls. One morning I found Bull, signal lamp in hand, carrying on a parley with a British tanker in the column to starboard. When at last he put the lamp down, I asked what it was all about, and he said, "Oh, they invite us to come aboard for lunch."

"What did you tell them?" I asked.

"Oh," Bull replied, "I say, 'If you got a drop of yin, I wouldn't say no.'"

When you are in convoy, it is sometimes impossible to remember whether a thing happened yesterday or the day before yesterday or the day before that. You watch the other ships and you read whatever there is to read and you play jokes on the ship's cat. You go to the pantry and slam the refrigerator door, and the cat runs in, thinking you are going to give him something to eat. Then you pretend to ignore him. Finally, when his whining becomes unbearable, you throw him a few bits of crabmeat.

I had brought three books along with me on the *Regnbue,* but I had finished them in the three weeks we spent idling off the British coast. After that I read several ninepenny thrillers by Agatha Christie and Valentine Williams that happened to be aboard, and then a copy of *Pilgrim's Progress,* donated to the ship by the Glasgow YMCA. Eventually I was reduced to looking at September numbers of *Life.* Once I found an early 1939 issue of *Redbook.* I read every page of it gratefully, though it contained six stories about husbands who strayed but found that they liked their wives best after all.

There was a strict blackout every evening, but I didn't mind it as much as I had in London, because on the ship there was no place to

go anyhow. One of the lifeboats had a fashion of working loose from
its fastenings in heavy weather, and then the boatswain would summon
a gang to heave on the ropes until he could make it fast again. I used
to look forward to the chance of pulling on one of the ropes. Whenever
the crew had to make the boat fast while I was napping in my cabin,
I felt slighted.

Some of the men were always speculating about our destination,
Baton Rouge. It didn't show on any of the maps on the ship. If it had,
they figured, the size of the print might have given them an idea of
how big the town was. My own guess was that it was a city of 100,000.
Actually, the population was 34,000. American cities weren't listed in
Hvem, Hvad, Hvor, the Norwegian equivalent of the *World Almanac*
and the favorite reference work on board. *Hvem, Hvad, Hvor* means
"Who, What, Where." The book contains street plans of every city in
Norway, even places of as few as 5,000 inhabitants. The men used to
mark the locations of their houses and show them to each other and to
me. Once, Gjertsen, the chief officer, showed me where he lived in his
hometown. The next day he came into my cabin looking for me, with
Hvem, Hvad, Hvor in his hand. "I made a mistake," he said, pointing
to the plan of the place. *"Here* is where I live," and he showed me a
dot about a quarter of an inch from the one he had made before.

As Christmas drew near, Larsen, the steward, was often missing from
his cabin during the evenings. He was aft in the valley with the cook,
constructing great quantities of "fat things" and "poor men," the Norwegian terms for doughnuts and crullers, respectively. On his journeys
aft he carried with him a thick, calf-bound Norwegian cookbook. Larsen
had formerly been a cook; he sometimes regretted his changeover from
creative to executive catering. The cook was a tall, thin young man who
looked as if he were built of paraffin. Together they elaborated on the
plans for the Christmas Eve dinner. Rumors were spread by one of the
British machine gunners, who had talked to the third engineer, who
had it straight from a messboy, that there would be turkey. While the
convoy moved along at its steady ten knots, nobody aboard the *Regnbue*
talked of anything but the coming dinner.

On the great night, the table was laid for a dozen persons in the
saloon, where ordinarily the captain and I dined alone. We were lucky;
the sea was reasonably calm. The steward and the boy who helped him
in the saloon, which was forward, would have had a hard time in a gale,
for the galley was in the after deckhouse and they had to carry all the
food over the long catwalk between. Promptly at six o'clock, the engineer
officers came forward to dine with us. Larsen, the chief engineer, who

was not related to Larsen the steward, was a girthy, middle-aged man who resembled Hendrik Willem van Loon. If I looked aft on a fair day, I could generally see him standing by a door of the engine room with his hands in his pockets. He was a fixture in the seascape, like Nilsen, the gunner and ex-whaler, who silently paced the deck near the four-inch gun, and like whichever of the British machine gunners was on duty, wearing a pointed hood and sitting inside a little concrete breast-work on the poop deck, looking like a jack-in-the-box. Chief Engineer Larsen and his officers seldom came forward to visit us. To mark the occasion on this night, they were wearing collars and neckties. They looked scrubbed and solemn, and so did Captain Petersen and the three deck officers and the gunner and the radioman, all of whom were at the table.

Steward Larsen had set three glasses at each place—one, he told me, for port, one for whiskey, and a third for gin. He had no aquavit for the Christmas dinner, and gin was supposed to replace it. To get the meal started, the steward brought in some porridge called *jul grøt*, which is traditional and practically tasteless. Engineer Larsen said "Skoal" and emptied a glass of gin. We all said "Skoal" and did likewise. Then Steward Larsen served a thick soup with canned shrimp and crabmeat and chicken in it. We all drank again. The steward next served fish pudding and there was more drinking of skoals. Then he brought in the turkey with the pride of a Soviet explorer presenting a hunk of frozen mammoth excavated from a glacier. The turkey had been in the ship's cold room since the September equinox, and ship chandlers' turkeys are presumed to have been dead for quite a while before they come aboard. We had plenty of canned vegetables and, above all, plenty of gin.

The teetotaler Methodist captain, who stuck to his principles and didn't drink, brought out a couple of songbooks that he had got from a Norwegian church and suggested we sing some Christmas hymns. His guests sang them, without much pleasure, it seemed to me, and we ate a lot of Jello covered with vanilla sauce and drank some more gin. All the men's faces remained rigid and solemn.

Engineer Larsen said, in English, "Merry Christmas to our American friend."

The captain whispered to me, "You can tell he's from Oslo. He talks too much."

The steward then brought in mounds of doughnuts and crullers, and some fancy drinks in tall glasses. He called the tall drinks Larsen's Spezials. They were triple portions of gin with lump sugar and canned cherries. Everyone said, "Thank you, steward. Very good." The whiskey was served straight, as a dessert liqueur. We all began drinking it out of jiggers and saying "Skoal" some more. The singing got fairly continuous, and the choice of numbers gradually grew more secular. Most Norwegian songs, I noticed, have many verses, and the men who are not singing pay no attention to the one who is. They look as if they are trying to recall the innumerable verses they are going to sing in their turn. We all got together on one patriotic number, though. The last line, translated into English, was "If Norway goes under, I want to go too." We clasped hands on that one.

The captain asked me to sing "My Old Kentucky Home," which I couldn't remember many words of, but fortunately three other fellows started to sing three other songs at the same time.

The steward, considering his official duties over, drew up a chair to the table and received congratulations. The cook, looking taller and more solemn than ever, came in and was hailed as a great man. The drinkers still made intermittent efforts to remain grave. They yielded slowly, as if they were trying to postpone their pleasure. Now the dignitaries of the crew, who had finished a dinner with exactly the same menu in their own quarters, began to appear in the saloon and take seats at the table—first the argumentative carpenter, then the boatswain with the cackle, and finally the pumpman, a tall fellow who looked like a Hapsburg and spent his life shooting compressed air into clogged oil tanks. The carpenter arose to sing a song. He had the same argumentative, deliberate delivery that he had in conversation, and he paused so long between verses that the chief officer, who had come down off the bridge and entered the saloon just after the carpenter had finished a verse, thought the all clear had sounded and began a song of his own. The usually timid cook, buoyed up by one of Larsen's Spezials, thundered, "Shut up, Chief Officer! Let the carpenter sing!" As the chief officer and the fourth engineer joined the party, the third officer and another of the engineers left to stand their watches. The machine gunner from Glasgow arrived to wish the Captain a Merry Christmas and snitch a bottle of whiskey. Two seamen, lads of about eighteen, came in to convey the respects of the crew. They had, I imagine, thought of this mission themselves. One, a small, neat boy with a straw-blond mustache, sang a long song with the refrain *"Farvel, farvel"* ("Farewell, farewell"). It appeared to make him very unhappy.

Nearly all the seamen on the *Regnbue* were youngsters, which would have been true on a Norwegian ship even before the war. After three and a half years at sea they are eligible to take a course at a mates' school if they can save or borrow the price.

Boys who don't like the sea quit after a couple of voyages.

Presently Steward Larsen pulled me by the arm and took me off with him to visit the rest of the crew. Before leaving the saloon, he had handed out a bottle of whiskey to each four men, and on the whole they were doing all right with it.

"I am a Commoonist," he kept saying to me on our way aft, "so I want you to love these fellers."

Everybody on the ship had received as a Christmas greeting from the Norwegian government a facsimile letter signed "Haakon, Rex." The letters, which had been put aboard at London for the captain to hand out, told Norwegian seamen that they were their country's mainstay. The "Commoonist" read this letter over and over again and cried every time. The government had also sent the crew a set of phonograph records and patriotic songs. The favorite was called *"Du Gamle Mor"* ("Thou Old Mother"), which means Norway. The boys aft were all wearing blue stocking caps, which had come in a Christmas-gift bundle with a card saying that they had been knitted by a Miss Georgie Gunn, of 1035 Park Avenue, New York City.

By the time Larsen and I staggered back over the catwalk to the saloon, everybody but Captain Petersen was unashamedly happy. It was very close in the blacked-out saloon with all the ports shut, and I went up to the bridge for air. Bull, the third officer, was on watch up there. He was a big, fair-haired fellow who had sailed for several years between United States and West Indian ports. He had been moderately dizzy when he had gone on watch at eight o'clock after eating his dinner, he told me, but now he felt only a sense of sober well-being. "I see ships all around," he said, "so ve must be in de meddel de convooey." Sandor, the Romanian seaman who had stowed away on the ship in 1939 and remained aboard ever since, was on lookout duty. He said, "This makes three Christmas on ship since I left home. No good. On ship you see thirty, thirty-five peoples. On shore you see hoondreds peoples. I like to get one Christmas ashore." Sandor's chances were not bright. The British immigration officers at our second assembly port had told him that since he was now an enemy alien, he would not be allowed on shore in Britain for the remainder of the war. They had added that the Americans would probably also refuse to let him land, so he might have to remain afloat indefinitely. Griffin, the English seaman, was at the wheel. When Sandor spelled him, Griffin came out of the wheelhouse and we wished each other Merry Christmas. I had heard so much talk about hometowns and traditions that night that I asked Griffin where he was from. "Blowed if I know," he said cheerfully. "Sandor don't know where 'e's going and I don't know where I come from."

When I went down to my cabin, a row that would have done credit to an early convention of the American Legion was going on in the saloon. I looked in, but everybody was shouting in Norwegian and no one looked sufficiently detached to translate for me, so I didn't hear what it was all about until the next day, when I was told that someone had been trying to get subscriptions to the Norwegian Air Force Spitfire Fund and that Grung, the radioman, had protested that the Norwegian government, even in exile, was giving $300,000 a year to missionaries in China and Africa. "Let them spend the missionary money for Spitfires before they bother workingmen," he had said. The steward had called Grung a bad name and Grung had pushed him over a case of empty whiskey bottles. Later, when I happened to see Grung coming out of the radio shack, I asked him what Larsen had called him. "He called me a Commoonist," Grung said.

The party gave us something to talk about for a couple of days afterward. The carpenter went around repeating a line he had memorized from the label of a whiskey bottle: "Yentle as a lamb." He would say it and roll his eyes and then exclaim, "Yeezis!"

On Christmas morning an English ship signaled to us, "Merry Christmas. Keep your chins and thumbs up." Grung and Bull had a consultation and then, not being able to think of anything witty, just ran up the answering flag meaning "Message noted."

One morning, when we were about halfway across the Atlantic, I found Bull in a particularly good humor. "Look around," he said, handing me a glass. "Vare is escort?"

I had a good look around and there wasn't any. The corvettes had disappeared during the night. "Does that mean we've reached the safe part of the Atlantic?" I asked.

"Safe yust so long ve see no submarine," Bull said.

Captain Petersen, who came up a half hour later to look around, said, "Maybe the escort from America was supposed to meet us here, and it didn't, and the British corvettes had a date to meet an eastbound convoy off Iceland. We don't count as much as eastbound ships, because they're loaded."

We went on all day without an escort. Grung came out of his shack and stared at three hundred and fifty thousand tons of valuable shipping moving placidly on, unprotected and unattacked. "Admiral Raeder must be lousy," he said at last.

Next morning a force of Canadian destroyers met us. No harm had been done. It wasn't the only time the *Regnbue* had traveled in an un-

convoyed convoy, Bull said. Once she had left Halifax in a convoy
escorted by a battleship that was returning from an American dockyard.
A couple of hundred miles out, the battleship had been summoned to
help hunt the *Bismarck,* so she had moved off at thirty knots and left
the merchantmen to push on by themselves to England. There are never
enough vessels for convoy duty, Bull said, but luckily there never seem
to be enough submarines, either. The Battle of the Atlantic sounds imposing, but it is rather like a football game with five men on a side.

A few days after we met the Canadians, the ships bound for Gulf
ports split off from the convoy. We were one of them. Each ship was
to proceed as an individual, the theory at that time being that waters
within a few hundred miles of the American coast were fairly safe. We
had always cherished a notion that we were one of the fastest ships in
our convoy. When dispersal day came, however, most of the others
bound for the south quickly left us behind. Twenty-four hours after
the split we were alone in the ocean, without another ship in sight.
We steered southwest within a couple of hundred miles of the coast
for nearly two weeks and saw only two vessels, neither of them a war-
ship. Nor did we sight a single patrol plane. We hoped that no hostile
aircraft carrier would ever have the same luck. The *Regnbue,* now that
she was alone, zigzagged in a constant series of tangents to her course.
This lost a mile an hour, which still further delayed my homecoming.

The weather stayed seasonably rough. We never ran into the kind
of storm that sends smashed ships to port to make pictures for the newspaper photographers, but for days on end we couldn't see the sun long
enough to get a position, and on New Year's Eve, when we were
thirty-one days out of London, we had a sixty-mile gale, which made
a second holiday party impossible. The day before we left the convoy
I had been standing at the wheelhouse window watching the extraordinary antics of the tankers around us. A tanker in water ballast is
a good sea boat but not a comfortable one. It rides the waves like a canoe,
but it has a tendency to twist from side to side as it comes down. As I
have already noted, this is even more disconcerting to watch than to
endure. I was thinking about this when Mikkelsen, the electrician, a
big, snaggletoothed West Norwegian, came up and stood next to me.
He looked at the ships for a while, then said quietly, "Fine weather."
According to his lights, it probably was.

After you leave your convoy you may have no other ships to watch
and discuss, but you have a chance to fire your gun. That is an event
to look forward to for days. Admiralty regulations require a ship to fire
at least two shots on each trip. The captain gave Nilsen, the gunner,

the order to prepare to fire these ritual shots. A day was set for the performance—not too soon, because, on account of a scarcity of ammunition, we couldn't afford such pleasures more than once and we wanted
to prolong the period of anticipation. The ordinarily silent Nilsen became the embodiment of the busy-executive type. The other members
of the gun crew were the Hapsburg pumpman, two diesel motormen,
the fourth engineer, and the little sailor who had sung *"Farvel."* They
assumed new dignity among their fellows during the days before the
gun practice. Everybody on the *Regnbue* told jokes about the last time
the gun had been fired. Some said that Larsen, the chief engineer, had
been asleep in his cabin when the gun went off and had been knocked
off his divan. Others told the same story about the cook, the steward,
or the second officer. All of this was invention, because nobody on a
merchant ship sleeps when the gun is to be fired. One might as well
expect a small boy to sleep late on Christmas morning.

On the big day the raised gun platform served as an excellent stage
for the gun crew and the protagonist, the gun. The boatswain had distributed pounds of cotton batting and we had stuffed our ears with wads
of the stuff. The little sailor, a romantic chap, had carefully smudged
his forehead with grease so that he would look like one of Admiral Tor-
denskjold's powder monkeys. An empty oil drum would serve as target.
A couple of sailors threw it off the stern. Nilsen's crew loaded the gun.
Then, after the ship had gone an estimated two thousand meters, they
fired. There was a great spat of flame from the gun's muzzle, a satisfactory roar, and something splashed in the water a long distance away.
I could not see the oil drum, but Haraldsen, the second officer, who
had once been an ensign in the Norwegian Navy, said that the shell
had not missed by much. We all shouted "Hurrah!" It was better than
the Fourth of July. The gun was reloaded and fired again. After the
second shot we all felt much safer, because we knew that the gun would
not burst until the next trip.

The days continued alike as we went on, but they had a different
feeling. After we had passed Hatteras, even the carpenter and the radioman, the ship's leading grousers, began to admit it was probable we
would make port. And all through the ship men made plans for whatever shore leave they might get. Larsen, the steward, who had once
worked out of the port of "Noolians," proposed to the cook and a couple
of others that they hire a taxi at Baton Rouge and drive straight to the
French quarter in New Orleans. "I always say I'm going to save money,"
he told me, "but when I get near land I can't keep my temper." Captain
Petersen looked forward to renewing acquaintance with the pastor of

the Norwegian church in New Orleans, where he planned to go by train. A few of the men owned electric flatirons, and these were in heavy demand by shipmates who wanted to press their pants. Grung, the radioman, was in charge of the pay list. All the men had fairly large sums coming to them, and each signified to Grung the amount he wanted to draw at Baton Rouge. Usually a man changed his mind several times, raising the ante each time. The cook and the steward held long conferences about stores, occasionally asking me how to spell "bitterscots pewding" or "tomates cetseps." The steward said that he would send the list ashore to a ship chandler in Noolians when we went through customs and have the stuff trucked up to Baton Rouge.

The ship had not taken stores for more than three months now, and the eggs caused a daily argument between the steward and me. For several mornings he had served them hardboiled, a sign he had no real confidence in them. Each morning I would open my first egg and say, "*Dårlig,*" which is Norwegian for "bad."

The steward would protest, "*Naj, naj.*"

"But this one has green spots inside the shell," I would say.

"Ex like dot sometimes," he would maintain.

The captain always ate his eggs without any remark; his silence accused me of finicking. At last, one morning toward the end of the voyage, he opened an egg and looked at the steward. "*Dårlig,*" he said. The steward looked embarrassed. Then the captain ate the egg; a bad hardboiled egg is probably as nourishing as a good one.

Next morning the steward brought me an amorphous yellow mass on a plate. It tasted mostly of sugar, but he offered me a jug of maple and cane sugar syrup to pour on it. I took a spoonful, fancying it some Norse confection, and said, "Not bad. What do you call it?" The steward said, "I call it ummelet. Same ex."

Once the captain opened up a bit more than usual and talked about the Oxford Movement. The Movement had been strong in Norway, he said, and had frequently coincided with Quislingism. "A shipowner in my town," he once said to me, "got crazy about the Oxford Movement. He took his wife and children to a public meeting and then he got up in the meeting and said that when he went to Antwerp on business he used to use bad women. His wife fainted. I don't call that a Christian." Several times the captain talked about his native town. "It has two fine hotels and the harbor is full of beautiful little islands," he said once. "You can take your family in a boat fishing and then have a picnic on an island. In the winter we go skiing. My boy is three years old and he has his second pair of skis. In the summer we used to have lobster parties, or dumpling-and-buttermilk parties. But it probably isn't like that now."

"By-and-by Florida" had been a gag line with Haraldsen, the second officer, throughout the voyage, but one day we really got there. It was the first land we had sighted since leaving Britain, and it looked exactly like the newsreels, with fine, white hotels and palm trees and scores of spick-and-span motorboats in the blue water offshore, fishing for whatever people fish for in Florida. The weather was clear but cold. When we got close to shore, we were permitted to use the radio receiving set in the chief officer's cabin again, and one of the first things I heard was an announcer saying, "There is no frost in Florida. This morning's temperature was thirty-seven." I tried to get some war news and heard another announcer saying, "The slant-eyed specialists in treachery continue their advance toward Singapore. One, two, three, four, five seconds. You could not employ them better than by making a lather of creamy Sweetheart Soap."

We sailed along the shore. There were plenty of airplanes overhead now. They swooped almost to our masthead and looked us over every five minutes. It made all the men happy just to see the coast. From the bridge we kept looking through our glasses for bathing girls, but the weather was too cold for them. We wondered what the people in the Palm Beach and Miami hotels thought of our rusty ship, with its wheelhouse fortified with concrete slabs and its ragged red flag with the blue cross. Fellows kept making attempts at jokes, like "There's the dog track; let's go" or "Grung, get out the flash lamp and signal women that want a date yust wait on the beach. I going to swim in."

That afternoon the steward came into my cabin and said that the captain and the officers were giving me a farewell supper that evening. As on Christmas Eve, it was formal dress—collars and neckties. The occasion itself was solemn; Norwegians are not effusive. My companions just sat there, talking Norwegian among themselves and ignoring me. Nobody made a speech, but at the end of the meal the cook carried in a cake about the size and shape of the Aztec calendar stone. It was encrusted with slightly damp sugar. He held it out to me and I stood up and reached for it. It nearly pulled me forward on my face, and as I looked down on the top, I saw, written in icing, *"Farvel."*

A few nights later we were at the mouth of the Mississippi, waiting for a pilot. A northerly gale howled down at us straight from Lake Michigan. There were plenty of lights visible on the shore, more than I had seen at a comparable hour since leaving New York in the summer. Somehow I had expected our lights to go out when we entered the war.

It seemed strange coming in our blacked-out ship to a country that was neither neutral *nor* dark. A boy in a rowboat brought out the pilot, a heavyset, shivering man in a leatherette jacket, who announced as soon as he came aboard that it was the coldest damn winter he had ever known in Louisiana. He brought aboard a copy of the New Orleans *Times-Picayune,* containing a lot of basketball scores and society notes and a few stories about a war that seemed to be on some remote sphere. A naval party came aboard and sealed the radio shack. The pilot took us seventeen miles up the river and then was relieved by a second pilot, who was going to take us the eighty remaining miles to New Orleans. I turned in.

We dropped anchor off quarantine in New Orleans at about ten o'clock on the morning of the forty-second day out of London. It was Sunday. We had to pass the immigration and public-health officers' inspections before the *Regnbue* could continue up the river. I had my suitcase packed before the government officers arrived, hoping that I would be able to go back to shore with them. It was the sort of day we had had off Florida, chilly but bright, and the city looked good in the sunlight. The *Regnbue's* men, lining the rails, talked about how fine it would be to be going ashore again. I had been at sea for only six weeks, but few of them had set foot ashore in four months.

The immigration-and-health boat came out soon after ten with a party including a doctor and a rat inspector. The immigration men brought five armed guards to post about the ship to see that none of our allies would try to land too soon. Soon a customs officer came aboard and asked the captain if any man on the ship had more than three hundred cigarettes. Seamen buy their cigarettes in America, and our men had started to run short a fortnight before. Captain Petersen did not seem astonished by the question. He sent Grung to take a census of the cigarettes on board. Grung came back after a half hour with word that only the second engineer had more than three hundred cigarettes. He had three hundred and twenty-five. The customs man asked if the twenty-five were loose, and Grung said that five of them were. The customs man said he thought he could let the second engineer keep the other twenty, although, he pointed out, he was making an exception. I pictured a large convoy missing a tide while the United States Customs counted cigarettes. Then the customs man asked about liquor, because he would have to seal up what we had on board. Grung went on a search for liquor and reported back that we had had two bottles of whiskey and one of gin but that one of the public-health men had drunk about half of one of the bottles of whiskey.

Next the immigration men came to the consideration of me. They said that since I had a good passport and had apparently been born in New York, I probably had a right to land in the United States, but not until my baggage had been passed by a customs appraiser. Unfortunately, they said, no appraisers had come along. "The last thing I expected to find on this ship was a passenger," the head immigration man said, giving me a rat inspector's look. He said that unless I wanted to stay on the ship for twenty-four hours longer, I would have to pay two days' wages for the appraiser myself. Double pay for Sunday work. I said that would be all right and they sent for an appraiser. It cost me $13.33. While waiting for the appraiser, I went out on deck. Captain Petersen came out too, and we stood looking at the shore. He was quiet, as usual, but he seemed to be struggling with an unusual emotion. At last he said, "Say, is it true the Hippodrome has been torn down?"

I said, "Yes, and the Sixth Avenue 'L,' too."

Again he looked troubled, and I thought he was going to say he would miss me, but he said, "*The Big Show* were a wonderful play." That was an extravaganza that had played at the Hipp in 1917, when the captain had lived in Hoboken.

I said, "Yes, with Joe Jackson."

"A very funny man," Captain Petersen said.

A shabby motorboat came toward us from the left bank of the river. Captain Petersen said, "It must be a ship chandler after our business."

There was a man on the forward deck with a megaphone and as the boat came under our bow, he called up inquiringly, "Captain, Captain?"

Petersen pointed to his peaked cap, his emblem of office.

The fellow shouted, "We got orders to send you on to Curaçao! You got enough bunker?"

Curaçao is nine days from New Orleans for a ten-knot boat. Petersen showed no sign of surprise or disappointment. "We need bunker," he shouted back, "but we can get out in twenty-four hours!"

An hour later, when I was in a boat going ashore, I could see most of the *Regnbue* fellows on deck, leaning over the rail. There was the carpenter, with his square head and his obstinate shoulders, and the tall pumpman, and the electrician, and the two British gunners in their khaki uniforms. I could make out the bearish form of Sandor, the Romanian, who would not have to stay on board alone now, because the others would stay with him. And there was Larsen, the steward, in a belted, horizon-blue overcoat and a bright-green hat, his shoregoing uniform. He wouldn't go ashore, after all.

Antebellum

Apology for Breathing

※ ※

PEOPLE I KNOW in New York are incessantly on the point of going back where they came from to write a book, or of staying on and writing a book about back where they came from. Back where they came from, I gather, is the American scene (New York, of course, just isn't America). It is all pretty hard on me because I have no place to go back to. I was born in an apartment house at 94th Street and Lexington Avenue, about three miles from where I now live. Friends often tell me of their excitement when the train on which they are riding passes from Indiana into Illinois, or back again. I am ashamed to admit that when the Jerome Avenue express rolls into 86th Street station, I have absolutely no reaction.

I always think of back where my friends came from as one place, possessing a homogeneous quality of not being New York. The thought has been well expressed by my literary adviser, Whitey Bimstein, who also trains prizefighters. I once asked him how he liked the country. He said, "It is a nice spot." I have been to the country myself. I went to a college in New Hampshire. But I seldom mention this, because I would like to be considered quaint and regional, like William Faulkner.

The finest thing about New York City, I think, is that it is like one of those complicated Renaissance clocks where on one level an allegorical marionette pops out to mark the day of the week, on another a skeleton Death bangs the quarter-hour with his scythe, and on a third the Twelve Apostles do a cakewalk. The variety of the sideshows distracts one's attention from the advance of the hour hand. I know people who say that, as in the clock, all the exhibits depend upon the same movement. This they insist is economic. But they are the sort of people who look at a fine woman and remind you that the human body is composed of $1.62 worth of chemicals.*

* The author has not checked on this figure.—The Editor

I like to think of all the city microcosms so nicely synchronized though unaware of one another: the worlds of the weight lifters, yodelers, tugboat captains and sideshow barkers, of the book dutchers, sparring partners, song pluggers, sporting girls, and religious painters, of the dealers in rhesus monkeys and the bishops of churches that they themselves establish under the religious-corporations law. It strengthens my hold on reality to know when I awake with a brandy headache in my house, which is nine blocks due south of the Chrysler Building and four blocks due east of the Empire State, that Eddie Arcaro, the jockey, is galloping a horse around the track at Belmont while Ollie Thomas, a colored clocker of my acquaintance, is holding a watch on him. I can be sure that Kit Coates, at the Aquarium, is worrying over the liverish deportment of a new tropical fish, that presently Whitey will be laying out the gloves and headguards for the fighters he trains at Stillman's gymnasium, while Miss Ira, the Harlem modiste, will be trying to talk a dark-complexioned girl out of buying herself an orange turban, and Hymie the Tummler ruminates a plan for opening a new nightclub. It would be easier to predicate the existence of God on such recurrences than on the cracking of ice in ponds, the peeping of spring peepers in their peeperies, and the shy green sprigs of poison ivy so well advertised by writers like Thoreau.

There are New Yorkers so completely submerged in one environment, like the Garment Center or Jack and Charlie's, that they live and die oblivious of the other worlds around them. Others are instinctively aware of the wonders of New York natural history, but think them hardly worthy of mention. My father was a New Yorker of the latter sort. In separate phases of his business life, he had occasion to retain Monk Eastman, a leading prewar gangster, and the Rev. Charles Parkhurst, a notorious crusader against vice. This seemed to him no more paradoxical than going to Coward's for his shoes while he bought his hats of Knox. When Father was president of an association of furriers during a strike, he hired Eastman to break up a strikers' mass meeting. His employment of Dr. Parkhurst was more subtle. In about 1910 Father bought some real estate in West 26th Street on which he purposed to put several loft buildings. He believed that the fur industry was going to move up in that direction from below 23rd. But 26th Street between Sixth and Seventh Avenues was full of brothels, and there was no hope of getting tenants for the new buildings until the block was made respectable. First Father dispossessed the hook shops from the houses which he had acquired with his building lots. But the watchmen rented the empty rooms to the drabs for fifty cents a night. Then Father made a substantial gift to Dr. Parkhurst's society, enclosing with his check a letter that called attention to the sinful conditions on West 26th Street. Dr. Parkhurst raised hell with the police, who made the girls move on to another block, and then Father put up his buildings. Father always said Monk and Dr. Parkhurst gave him his money's worth, but he never liked either of them. He became labor-conscious after he retired from business, and toward the end of his life often said that unions were a fine thing, but that they had doubtless changed a lot since the time he hired Eastman. He died a staunch Roosevelt man.

Even though he made his home during the second part of his life among middle-class enterprisers with horizons slimmer than a gnat's waist, Father lived in other milieus in retrospect. He liked to talk of the Lower East Side in the eighties, when the carters left their wagons in the streets of nights and the small boys would roll the wains away and burn them on Election Day, and of how he, a workingman at ten, boxed with the other furriers' apprentices using beaver muffs for mitts. He would even tell of the gay life of London and Paris and Leipzig in the late nineties when he was a bachelor buyer, although, he always protested, he had finished with that sort of thing when he got married. And he early introduced me to those worlds into which one may escape temporarily for the payment of a fee, the racecourse and the baseball park. These have their own conflicts that do not follow scenarios predetermined in Hollywood.

Since this is a regional book about people I met back where I came from, I should like to say something here about the local language. This is a regional tongue imported from the British Isles, as is the dialect spoken by the retarded inhabitants of the Great Smoky Mountains back where *they* come from. Being spoken by several million people, it has not been considered of any philological importance. Basically, New Yorkese is the common speech of early nineteenth-century Cork, transplanted during the mass immigration of the South Irish a hundred years ago. Of this Cork dialect Thomas Crofton Croker in 1839 wrote, "The vernacular of this region may be regarded as the ancient cockneyism of the mixed race who held the old city—Danes, English and Irish. It is a jargon, whose principal characteristic appears in the pronunciation of *th,* as exemplified in *dis, dat, den, dey*—this, that, then, they; and in the dovetailing of words as, 'kum our rish' for 'come of this.'" New York example, "gerradahere" for "get out of here." The neo-Corkonian proved particularly suited to the later immigrants who came here from Continental Europe—the *th* sound is equally impossible for French, Germans, and Italians. Moreover, it was impressed upon the latecomers because it was the talk of the police and the elementary-school teachers, the only Americans who would talk to them at all. Father, who was born in Austria but came here when he was seven years old, spoke New Yorkese perfectly.

It is true that since the Diaspora the modern dialects of Cork and New York have diverged slightly like Italian and Provençal, both of which stem from vulgar Latin. Yet Seán O'Faoláin's modern story of Cork, "A Born Genius," contains dialogue that might have come out of Eleventh Avenue: "He's after painting two swans on deh ketchen windes. Wan is facin' wan way and d'oder is facin' d'oder way.—So dat so help me God dis day you'd tink deh swans was floatin' in a garden! And deh garden was floatin' in trough deh winda! And dere was no winda!"

There are interesting things about New York besides the language. It is one of the oldest places in the United States, but doesn't live in retrospect like the professionally picturesque provinces. Any city may have one period of magnificence, like Boston or New Orleans or San Francisco, but it takes a real one to keep renewing itself until the past is perennially forgotten. There were plenty of clipper ships out of New York in the old days and privateers before them, but there are better ships out of here today. The Revolution was fought all over town, from Harlem to Red Hook and back again, but that isn't the revolution you will hear New Yorkers discussing now.

Native New Yorkers are the best-mannered people in America; they never speak out of turn in saloons, because they have experience in group etiquette. Whenever you hear a drinker let a blat out of him, you can be sure he is a recent immigrant from the South or Middle West. New Yorkers are modest. It is a distinction for a child in New York to be the brightest on one block; he acquires no exaggerated idea of his own relative intelligence. Prairie geniuses are raced in cheap company when young. They are intoxicated by the feel of being boy wonders in Amarillo, and when they bounce off New York's skin as adults, they resent it.

New York women are the most beautiful in the world. They have their teeth straightened in early youth. They get their notions of chic from S. Klein's windows instead of the movies. Really loud and funny New Yorkers are invariably carpetbaggers. The climate is extremely healthy. The death rate is lower in Queens and the Bronx than in any other large city in the United States, and the average life expectancy is so high that one of our morning newspapers specializes in interviewing people a hundred years old and upward. The average is slightly lowered, however, by the inlanders who come here and insist on eating in Little Southern Tea Roomes on side streets.

The natives put up with a lot back here where I came from. If the inhabitants of Kentucky are distrustful of strangers, that is duly noted as an entertaining local trait. But if a New Yorker says that he doesn't like Kentuckians, he is marked a cold churl. It is perennially difficult for the New Yorker who subscribes to a circulating library to understand how the city survived destruction during the Civil War. When he reads about those regional demigods haunted by ancestral daemons and festooned in magnolia blossoms and ghosts who composed practically the whole Confederate Army, he wonders what happened to them en route. I asked Whitey Bimstein what he thought of that one. He said, "Our guys must have slapped their ears down." Whitey does not know that we have been paying a war indemnity ever since in the form of royalties.

Another, later, better hymn to New York is by my friend Col. John R. Stingo:

"Some Friday nights I sit up in my room at the Dixie," he said, "working away on my column. I finish, and it is perhaps one o'clock. I always keep an old felt hat by my bedside," he said, "because I like to sleep with my windows wide open, and bedclothes make no provision for the protection of the thinly veiled cranium. The brain, like Rhenish wine, should be chilled, not iced, to be at its best. Women, however, are best at room temperature.

"Up there in my retreat I feel the city calling to me," he said. "It winks at me with its myriad eyes, and I go out and get stiff as a board. I seek out companionship, and if I do not find friends I make them. A wonderful grand old Babylon."

The difference between the Colonel's tribute and mine is that between a poet's and a cataloguer's. He is a wonderful grand old Colonel.

Getting By

THE CHIEF INDUSTRY in my part of the country is getting by. You can get by in several million ways. I know a professional faster and a professional eater, and both were getting by all right when I last saw them. The faster weighs 260 pounds when he isn't working. The eater weighs only 180 pounds. The faster, as you might expect, has to eat a lot when he is laying off so he will be in condition to fast when he gets an engagement. But the eater trains by eating. He says appetite comes that way.

The faster is named Ben Green. He is not a mere passive non-eater. He fasts for fifty days at a clip, lifting a hundred-pound weight on the first day and adding two pounds to the lift on each succeeding day, so that on the last morning of his fast he hoists two hundred pounds. He does this to advertise swimming pools and department stores, on the same principle as a flagpole sitter. During the course of each of his fasts Green studies geometry, algebra, chemistry, and accounting, and sometimes he sings.

Tony Di Laurentis is the professional eater. I met him when he was doing a stint for Billy the Oysterman's restaurant a few years ago. It was September 1, and Tony was eating a couple of hundred oysters to signalize the opening of the season. After eating the oysters, he was going to meet all comers in an eating contest.

"Have another dozen, Tony," Billy the Oysterman urged. Billy the Oysterman has a voice like a foghorn and a bluff, hearty, grasping manner.

"Maybe some challenge comes," argued Mr. Di Laurentis. "I don't want to get full before the contests. I don't need to eat these. I just eat them for show how good sport I am."

There is something more ingratiating about a professional eater than a professional faster. Most people are prejudiced in favor of eating. But Green is a more intellectual fellow than Di Laurentis. Mrs. Green is a chiropractor.

It was the economic depression that led Green, like so many others, to discover his talent for fasting. Not directly. It did not actually cut him off from lunch money. But when the laundry he had established in Belle Harbor, one of our most charming suburbs, failed in 1929, he had time to consider his figure. It was shocking, he says.

"At the age of thirty-eight I weighed two hundred and seventy-eight pounds," he told me once. "I was in a fair way to become a laughing-stock.

"I tried dieting and then I tried exercise. Neither seemed to help, so I decided to try both together. One day when my wife called me to dinner in our home at 74 Beach 132nd Street, I put on my hat. 'Instead of eating further viands,' I told her, 'I am going for a nice nourishing twelve-mile walk.'

"I went, and I went to bed afterward without having eaten. The next day I got up feeling fine, and instead of breakfast I took a five-mile walk. For lunch I had a juicy eight-mile hike, and for dinner I ran a luscious marathon on the Rockaway boardwalk.

"During the fast my wife and I went down to Philadelphia, and on the thirty-seventh day I said I had to return to New York on business. She said I was too weak. My wife weighs a hundred and thirty pounds, and I picked her up in my arms and tossed her up and down in the air like a rubber ball.

"I went back to New York, and might have continued my fast indefinitely had I not been tempted with a herring. I never could resist a broiled herring with onions. So I ended my first fast after thirty-eight days. I had lost forty-one pounds, but felt improved physically by the reduction of my obesity, and mentally by the absorption of large quantities of algebra, geometry, chemistry, and accountancy." The extemporaneous fast was the beginning of a career.

Di Laurentis, who, like many another worthy fellow, is an immigrant from out of town, discovered his talent while he was working as a barber in Hatboro, Pennsylvania, where he speedily became known as Old Quicklime.

"I train hard for this contess," he told me at Billy's. "For lunch I take just a steak and a couple of eggs and three or four glasses of whiskey and some fried potatoes. And I walk around the block twice. Yesterday is the first time I eat oysters. I like them fine. No seeds in them. I guess you read about the Lion's Club picnic in Hatboro. I eat a hundred and thirty apples in one hour, thirty-four minutes. You would say I am the most popola fellow in town. This is my first big-money shot. I am not nervous. I don't sweat, huh?"

Mr. Di Laurentis was square shouldered and blocky, but not overly fat. He stood five feet eight inches, weighed 180 pounds, and was thirty-seven years old. His black hair was pomaded, and he wore a wrist-watch on a gold link bracelet. His jaw was broad at the base and he bent dimes with his teeth.

"Don't tell anybody I do this," he said, as he demonstrated on Billy the Oysterman's favorite ten-cent piece, a family heirloom. It seems somebody had once told Mr. Di Laurentis it was against the law.

"I start in this way to make pleasure to my friends," he stated when asked for an account of his career. "Nine of us went down to Atlantic City once for a picnic. We got plenty dinner, chicken and spaghetti and fruit, and a gallon of wine in the car.

"While they swim, I go back to the car, eat up the nine dinners and drink the wine. They come back, they say, 'You hog!' I say no, to prove I eat nothing, we all go to the restaurant and I eat as much as anybody. Which I did."

"I don't restrain myself unless I got a good competition," said the man who was known in Hatboro, Pennsylvania, as The Maw. "I risk my life for my championship. The doctor he say not one man in thousand could eat them hundred and thirty apples and live. I don't eat against any bum that ain't eat for three days, maybe. He gotto got a reputation, and been eating regular, like me. You blame me?

"I can make a lot of money if I get the breaks. After I make popola the oyster business, maybe the pork butcher hire me for eat how many pigs I can. Maybe the apple-pie business, the spaghetti business, the mozzarella in carozza business, they all need advertising. I got a reputation."

"The man's a wonder!" shouted the oysterman.

"You bet my life," conceded Mr. Di Laurentis.

It is harder to get by as a professional drinker, but I have heard of a fellow who did very well that way. Patrolman Bill Finn of the Poplar Street station, who pounded a beat outside the Brooklyn Navy Yard for thirty years, told me about this fellow. He was a Marine stationed at the Yard. "Whenever any ships was in and men with money to spend," Patrolman Finn said, "this Marine would walk into them sailors' rendy-views and bet anybody there that he could drink a half barrel of beer and eat eight pounds of raw potatoes. He wouldn't drink the beer without eating the potatoes—he thought they brought him luck. He done so well with the betting that he bought himself out of the service and set up his own saloon over on Prospect Street. There was some very talented men in the Navy in them days."

Beginning with the Undertaker

IN THE MIDDLE of any New York block there is likely to be one store that remains open and discreetly lighted all night. This is the undertaker's. The undertaker or an assistant is always in attendance, waiting for something to turn up. Undertakers are sociable men; they welcome company during their unavoidable periods of idleness. High-school boys study for their state Regents' examinations in undertakers' offices on hot June nights. The door is always open, the electric fan soothing, the whole environment more conducive to reflective scholarship than the crowded apartment where the boy lives. Policemen going off duty sometimes drop in for a visit with the undertaker before climbing into the subway for the long trip home to another part of the city.

There is no merchandise in the front part of an undertaker's store. Usually there are a few comfortable chairs for bereaved relatives, and policemen sit in these chairs. During the day, the undertaker acts as a referee in the disputes of children. Housewives tell him their troubles; priests appeal to him to head church committees. Ten to one he becomes the biggest man in the neighborhood, like my friend Mayor Angelo Rizzo of Mulberry Street. Some New York streets have mayors, but they are not elected. A man lives on a street until the mayoralty grows over him, like a patina. To Mayor Rizzo, Elizabeth Street, although but two blocks east of Mulberry, is an alien place. For the feast of San Gennaro, who is the Mulberry Street saint, Mayor Rizzo usually heads at least three committees and festoons his shop front with electric lights. A celebration on Elizabeth Street leaves him unmoved. "Just one of them Sicilian saints," he says.

Once Mayor Rizzo told me he was hard put to keep track of his constituents' baths. "I think I will have to get a secretary," he said, as he improved the taste of a casket salesman's gift cigar with a swig of iced *barbera* wine. He sat in front of 178 Mulberry Street, enthroned upon one of the elegant portable chairs which he is prepared to furnish in any number for correct funerals. "They should call this cigar a La Palooka," he remarked on the side.

"Mrs. Aranciata is getting crazy because she don't remember whether

Jimmy has been to Cooney* Island twenty-two times or twenty-three times. So she come to me and said I should tell the kid not to go no more, because maybe that will make it an even number of times and he will get rheumatism. So I said to her, 'But suppose he has been only twenty-two times? Then by keeping him home you will be preventing him getting on the odd number again, and the rheumatism will be your fault.'

" 'Oh, *Madonna mia*,' she says, 'and what will I do?'

"So I says, 'Why don't you forget all about it and purtend this is a new year. Start all over again and when he goes to Cooney tell me, and I will keep track of it on a piece of paper.' So she is delighted and the next thing I know she tells all her friends, and now I got about fourteen women coming in wanting me to keep score how many times the family goes swimming.

"It is like when I feed one cat spaghetti a couple of winters ago and in a week I got a waiting line of five hundred and ninety-eight cats, including a lot of Sicilian cats from Elizabeth Street."

"But what difference does it make how many times you go swimming —at Coney or anyplace else?" I asked.

"What difference does it make?" shouted Mr. Rizzo. "Do you mean to tell me that you, an educated man, do not know that saltwater baths are only good for you if you go an odd number of times? Any old woman on Mulberry Street knows that much."

To prove his point Mayor Rizzo called the cop on the beat.

"You are an Italian," said His Honor. "Which is it lucky to take baths, an odd number or an even number?"

"Odd number," answered the officer promptly. "My mother-in-law, she keeps count on her fingers. She would never go in the water two times, or four times, in an afternoon, but always three times or five times."

The argument became a little involved here. Some of the folklore hydrotherapists held that each immersion counts as a bath, and if you go in the drink an odd number of times at each visit to the beach, your health will not suffer.

Others maintain that you must keep track of the total number of days' bathing, and be sure to wind up the season on an odd.

"I remember when I was a kid an old lady from Calabria made me go in fifty-one times one summer," said Al Gallichio, the restaurant man.

* This is the New York pronunciation of Coney Island. It seems to me as noteworthy as the Texas fashion of saying "Hughston" for Houston.

An antique and gracious lady waddling past with a bag of zucchini was invoked as a superior authority.

"Pardon me, madam," said Mayor Rizzo, "but I would wish to request a word with you."

"Voluntarily," she replied.

"When you are accustomed to go bathing, which is the more auspicious, to go an even or an uneven number of times?"

"Childish," said the dame. "It makes no difference. But once you have begun to go, you must go at least fifteen times, else your bones rot. It is for that reason I have not gone to the sea, this year, because I might not be able to afford fifteen visits."

She was an exception, because the odd-and-even belief, in one or other of its two forms, is prevalent all the way from Bleecker Street down to Park Row.

"It is very important this year," said the Mayor, "because we got no public bath in the neighborhood. There used to be a bathhouse on Center Market Place where the fellow would let you take a shower for a nickel. Of course, even the old-timers do not count whether a shower is odd or even. But now the Broome Street Tamanacle* Church has bought the building. A lot of these old houses have no bathtubs even, so the nearest place the people can get a bath is Allen Street, and they figure they might just as well go out to Cooney.

"Do I believe in this odd-and-even business?" he said. "Well, I tell you. I went swimming off the Battery just once, which is an odd number, and a kid pushed my head under and nearly drowned me, so I figured if I went back, that would be an even number and even worse luck and I probably would remain drowned, so now I do all my swimming in a bathtub."

* A regional pronunciation of Tabernacle.

Tummler

❦ ❦

To THE BOYS of the I. & Y., Hymie Katz is a hero. He is a short, broad-shouldered, olive-complexioned man who looks about forty-two and is really somewhat older. In his time he has owned twenty-five nightclubs.

"Hymie is a tummler," the boys at the I. & Y. say. "Hymie is a man what knows to get a dollar."

Hymie at present is running a horse-race tipping service in an office building on Longacre Square. "What is a nightclub made of?" he sometimes asks contemptuously. "Spit and toilet paper. An upholstered joint. The attractions get the money and the boss gets a kick in the pants." His admirers understand that this is only a peevish interlude. Soon he will open another nightclub.

The tipping service requires no capital. Hymie reads out-of-town telephone books for the names of doctors and ministers fifty or a hundred miles from New York. Then he calls them, one by one, asking the operator to reverse the charges. Hymie tells the operator, let us say, that he is Mr. Miller whom Dr. Blank or the Reverend Mr. Doe met at Belmont Park last summer. If the man accepts the call, Hymie knows he has a prospect. The man probably hasn't been at Belmont, and certainly hasn't met a Mr. Miller there, but thinks he is the beneficiary of a case of mistaken identity. Hymie tells him about a horse that is sure to win. All the doctor or minister has to do, Hymie says, is to send him the winnings on a ten-dollar bet. Sometimes the horse does win, and the small-town man always remits Hymie's share of the profits. He wants to be in on the next sure thing. Doctors, Hymie believes, are the most credulous of mortals. Ministers never squawk.

Hymie picks his horses very carefully from the past-performance charts of the *Morning Telegraph*. He usually tips three or four entries in each race. Naturally, the physicians and clergymen who get bad tips send him no money, but the supply of small-town professional men is practically unlimited. Hymie says it is an ideal business for a man satisfied with a modest, steady income. Personally, he is resigned to opening another nightclub. "If I wasn't ashamed," he says, "I would put a couple of hundred dollars in it myself." The investment of his own money, according to Hymie's code, would be unethical.

All Hymie needs to open a nightclub is an idea and a loan of fifty dollars. There are fifteen or twenty basements and one-flight-up places between 45th and 55th Streets that cannot economically be used as anything but nightclubs. They have raised dance floors, ramps, numerous light outlets, kitchens, and men's and women's washrooms. Because they are dark during the day, or can be reached only by staircases, they are not adapted to ordinary restaurant use. Such a place may be worth $600 a month as a nightclub. Dismantled, it would bring only $100 or so as a store. The owner of a nightclub site makes out pretty well if his space is tenanted for six months of the year.

Hymie has been around Broadway since 1924. He is a good talker. In the past, some of his clubs actually have made money, although none of it has stuck to him. As a matter of ritual he always tells the owner of the spot he proposes to rent that he is going to spend $40,000 to fix it up. The owner does not believe this, but the sound of the words reassures him. If Hymie said less than $40,000, the landlord would sense a certain lack of enthusiasm. If more, the landlord would feel derided. It is customary to mention $40,000 when talking about redecorating a nightclub. If the owner appears to be hooked, Hymie goes out and spends the borrowed $50. He pays it to a lawyer to draw up a lease. The lawyer Hymie patronizes is the only man in the world Hymie has never been able to put on the cuff. But he draws a fine lease. It contains all sorts of alluring clauses, like "party of the first part and party of the second part agree to share equally in all profits above $10,000 a week, after reimbursement of party of the second part for outlays made in equipping the Dopey Club (said outlays for this purpose not to exceed $40,000)." It makes provision for profits of Aluminum Trust magnitude.

Hymie takes the lease to a hatcheck concessionaire. This is the really critical phase of the enterprise. He must convince the concessionaire that the place has a chance to do business ("Look at the figures in the lease, you can see what we're expecting"). He must fill the concessionaire with enthusiasm for the entertainers, who have not yet been engaged. For it is up to the concessionaire to provide the cash that will make the enterprise go—$3,000 in advance, in return for the hatcheck and cigarette concession for six months. Hymie is a great salesman. He does impersonations of his hypothetical acts. He tells about the Broadway columnists who eat out of his hand and will give yards of free publicity. While Hymie talks, the concessionaire distills drops of probability from his gallons of conversation. In his mind he turns Hymie's thou-sands of anticipated revenue into fifties and hundreds. If the club runs three months, the concessionaire knows, he will get his money back. If by some fluke it runs six months, he will double his money. If nobody financed nightclubs, there would be no concession business. So the con-cessionaire lets Hymie have the $3,000.

Hymie goes back to the landlord, signs the lease, and pays him a month's rent in advance—say $600. That leaves $2,400 for the other expenses. If possible, he saves himself from headaches by renting out the kitchen. The kitchen concessionaire provides the food, cooks up a stew on which all the nightclub help feed every night, and even pays half of the cost of the table linen. (Linen is rented, not bought.) The proprie-tor of the club gets from 12 to 20 per cent of the gross receipts for food. Since nightclub food is absurdly high, the food concessionaire, like the hatcheck man, is bound to make a good profit if the place lasts a few months.

The club may contain tables, chairs, and any amount of miscella-neous equipment abandoned by a former tenant in lieu of rent. If it doesn't, Hymie goes to a man named I. Arthur Ganger, who runs a Cain's warehouse of the nightclub business on West 45th Street. Ganger can provide out of used stock anything from a pink-and-onyx Joseph Urban bar to a wicker *smörgåsbord* table. Some of his silverware has been in and out of ten previous clubs. Usually Ganger will accept a 25 per cent down payment, which for one of Hymie's clubs amounts to a few hundred dollars. He takes notes payable weekly for the rest. Ganger is amenable to reason when the notes fall due. He has a favorite joke for customers like Hymie. "Your mother carried you only nine months," he says, "but I been carrying you all your life." The supply man retains title to his things until they are entirely paid for, and if the club folds, he carts them back to his warehouse. Ganger decorates some clubs, but Hymie would not think of hiring him for such a job. Hymie gets a girl-ish young man to perform a *maquillage* for $150, including paint.

Of the $3,000 received from the concessionaire, Hymie has now dis-bursed at most $1,200. He pays another $600 for a liquor license good for six months, and puts the rest of the money in the bank as profit in case the club flops. The remaining preparations are on the cuff. Hymie hires acts for his new club on the understanding that he will pay off a week after the place opens. He engages a band on the same terms. If there is to be a line of girls in the show, the girls rehearse free. But Hymie is not a bad fellow. He sends out for coffee and sandwiches for the girls during rehearsals. Once or twice he has been known to lend a girl $5 for room rent before a club opened.

Liquor is harder to buy on credit these days than before repeal. Mob credit was flexible, and if you bought from a bootlegger independent of the gangs, Hymie says, you never paid him at all. Wholesalers now are allowed to extend only twenty-one days' credit, according to the regulations of the State Liquor Authority. But matters sometimes may be arranged by paying a bill on the twenty-first day and then borrowing most of the money back from the wholesaler on the twenty-second.

A few days before the opening Hymie effects a deal that always puts him in especially good humor. He sells twenty waiters their jobs. The headwaiter pays $400, two captains pay $200 each, and ordinary waiters $50. Waiters like to work for Hymie because he lets them take what they can get. He wastes no time watching his employees. "Most of the stealing they do is from the customers, so what do I care?" says Hymie.

Despite all his forethought, exigencies sometimes arise which demand fresh capital. Perhaps an unusually stubborn landlord demands three months' security, or a police official must be heavily greased before he will let the club stay open after hours. In some places, especially black-and-tan or crudely bawdy spots, all the money comes in during the illegal early hours of the morning, after the bigger clubs have closed. In such emergencies Hymie sometimes has to take in partners. He usually bilks his partners for the principle of the thing. He is not avaricious. Dollars, Hymie thinks, are markers in a game of wits as well as a medium of exchange. He refuses to let his partners keep any markers.

Once he had to take a partner in a roadhouse he was running near Babylon. He sold the fellow 50 per cent of the place for one season. It happened to be a very good season, so Hymie built a sliding metal roof over a garden one hundred feet square, installed a swimming pool, and presented all his employees with a large bonus out of the receipts.

"I thought I would make some improvements and build up good will for next year, when Milton would be out," he says.

Some persons may wonder why even a concessionaire would trust Hymie with his money. But concessionaires know that he will not skip before the club opens, for he is under a compulsion as strong as the drive of a spawning salmon to swim upstream. His clubs satisfy his craving for distinction.

A week before an opening, Hymie gets out a mailing list of exhibitionists which he has accumulated through a decade of nightclub operation, and sends out his announcements. Then he makes the entertainers write letters to their friends inviting them to buy ringside tables. He insists on the attendance of every salesman who has ever sold him anything for the club, even if it all was on credit. The costumer who has dressed the show is expected to take part of his pay in trade. Since this may be the only part of it he will ever collect, the costumer usually brings a large party. It is a nice arrangement for Hymie, because he pays off on the costumer bill with Scotch at about 6 cents on the dollar. The costumer has made a profit of about 95 cents on the dollar, so this makes them both feel good. The band leader, if he has any considerable reputation in the trade, forces music publishers' pluggers to reserve tables. If the pluggers don't spend money, the leader slights their tunes.

A week after the opening, if it was profitable, Hymie gives his entertainers three days' pay. He tells them he is holding something back so they won't run out on him. Of course they never get it. If the opening has been bad, the entertainers and the concessionaire are likely to find the door locked the next night. In the event of a sour opening, Hymie takes the $1,000 or $1,500 of concession money remaining to him out of the bank and lays it on a ten-to-one shot at some obscure racetrack. He shares the weakness for betting common to most nightclub people, but he has it in an exaggerated form. He has never played a horse at less than eight-to-one in his life, because he is sure that every race is fixed. When a favorite wins, he attributes it to a double-cross. Hymie almost always loses.

Occasionally the personality of one of Hymie's entertainers catches on, or the *décor* hits the fancy of the Broadway high-life crowd, and the club begins to make money legitimately. Under these circumstances Hymie sells it to a corporation called Hymie-club, Inc. As manager for the corporation, he kicks out the hatcheck concessionaire and sells the concession over again for a higher price. The entertainer who draws the crowd gets a manager and demands more money. Hymie pays blackmail in the form of weekly raises. He spends a great part of his receipts in competitors' clubs to show how prosperous he is. He stalls off all creditors on general principles.

"Sometimes you can hold them off for six months," he says. "Meanwhile everything that comes in is profit."

Finally the creditors close in, or the entertainer either loses his brief vogue or goes on to a larger club. Hymie returns to the horse-tipping business. He has written one more chapter in his saga; he has been in the money again.

Hymie admits readily that it was vanity that drew him into the nightclub business in the first place, and that keeps him at it.

"Take a fellow who is born in Brooklyn," he says, "and he is a cloak-and-suiter or a shoe clerk, which he would feel honored even to talk to a trumpet player in a famous orchestra. He goes into this business and in two years celebrities like Rudy Vallee and Harry Thaw are calling him Hymie. It makes him feel wonderful. But it don't mean nothing."

Take, more specifically, Hymie Katz. He was born in Brooklyn, in the Williamsburg district. The record of his early days is shadowy, but he says that once he was a fur stretcher, and once he drove a taxi, and once he was married to a wealthy woman who died and cut him off with a dollar in her will because she didn't want him to spend anything on other dolls. Hymie got his start in the nightclub world as a singing waiter in a pseudo-Bavarian joint where people drank spiked near-beer at 50 cents a glass and sang *"Ja, das ist ein Schnitzelbank."* He had not been there long before he had invented a new technique for reaming the customers. When one of the parties he was serving asked for a check, he would delay bringing it, if possible, until he had a similar request from another party of about the same size. One check might be for $16, say, the other for $12. Hymie would put the $12 check in the hip pocket of his leather pants and collect the $16 check from both parties, one after the other. The customers seldom became aware of the mistake.

After he got used to late hours, Hymie decided to open a nightclub for himself. That was in the winter of 1924, and many buildings between Longacre Square and Sixth Avenue had a joint on every floor. There would be a shabby nightclub at street level, a speakeasy-restaurant on the second floor, and two or three ratty bars on the levels above. Hymie picked a second-floor loft that had a dance floor ten by ten and forty tables with pink lampshades on them, left by a former proprietor who had not paid his beer bill. Hymie put down $200 for an option on the place—he could not then afford his present scruples against using his own cash. He dropped in at the I. & Y., where he was beginning to be known, and sold 20 per cent of the club for $1,000 to a fellow we will call Johnny Attorney. Johnny came from Attorney Street originally, but he was quite a big beer man by then, and had moved uptown.

Hymie and Johnny were able to sell the hatcheck concession for another $1,000 because Johnny was in on a couple of speakeasies where the hatcheck man did business. Then they took in the no-good brother of a famous nightclub hostess who was the surest draw in town. They gave the brother 20 per cent, and all they asked was that he stay away from the place as much as possible. The hostess was working for a man named Denny Boylan, who had a large, elaborate club (for those days) about five doors up the block from their place. The Boylan club was on the street level, with a uniformed doorman and a marquee, and it had to close at two or three o'clock in the morning. Drawing her ermine wrap about her and jiggling her headdress of egrets two feet long, the hostess would then suggest to the best spenders present that they accompany her to a little intimate spot down the street, where the party could continue. Down the street they would stagger, and up the stairs to the Daylight Club, as Hymie and Johnny called their stuffy loft. After the second week the hostess demanded a share for herself, so Hymie sold her half of his 60 per cent for $5,000.

"The prices we got for liquor those days were brutal," Hymie recalls happily. "Twenty-five dollars for a bottle of champagne a guy made for us down on Mott Street. But the price didn't mean nothing. It was the bottles you could stab in on a customer's check that really counted. I mean the bottles you charged him for that he had never had at all. I remember a big patent-medicine man from Baltimore that used to come into the place that once paid me twenty-eight hundred dollars for one bottle of wine. He ordered the wine and then he fell asleep with his head on the table. I had the sense to have empty bottles in ice buckets put next to every table. When he woke up, I slipped him the check. 'What's this?' he says. 'Well,' I says, 'you ordered wine for everybody in the house. A hundred and twelve bottles at twenty-five a copy. The one on your table is on me.' He couldn't remember whether he had or not, but the money didn't mean nothing to him, so he paid."

After the Daylight Club was fairly launched, Hymie devoted late afternoons to the manufacturing department. Hymie doesn't mind work when it's fun.

"I made Black and White so good those millionaires wouldn't drink nothing else," he says. "There was a big towel man from North Carolina who would take cases of my Black and White home with him every time he come to town. Once a fellow in another joint gave him some of the McCoy straight from St. Pierre, and the towel man spit it out. 'You trying to poison me?' he says. 'This don't taste nothing like the genuine Black and White I buy from Hymie.' He would never go back to the joint."

Hymie thinks most of his customers in those days were temporarily insane. There was, for example, a wholesale whiskey exporter from Canada who, on his business trips to New York, had the quaint conceit of carrying only fifty-dollar bills. He would toss one of them on Hymie's bar and order drinks for everybody. If there were thirteen drinkers in the house, Hymie would charge him for about twenty-nine drinks at a dollar apiece. The Canadian never counted. He would leave his change for the bartender.

"When he come in," Hymie says, "I used to go behind the bar myself."

Hymie thinks that many of his former customers still have money, but have been afraid to throw it around in public since the depression. In a select spot like the Daylight Club, he says, "they knew they was among their own kind."

The end of the Daylight Club came when a squad of twenty prohibition agents raided the place and padlocked it.

"The reason you couldn't do nothing about them big raids," he says, "is that there was never twenty Feds who would trust each other. Each one would think one of the others in the squad was trying to put him in the bag, so you couldn't talk business. But when just one fellow or two or three come in, you knew they was on the shake. If you felt good-natured, you slipped them fifty. If you didn't, you kicked them down the stairs."

Hymie likes harness cops, but not detectives. He says the latter are like Feds, always on the shake.

"The cop on the block was a kind of doorman," Hymie explains. "When you threw a drunk out, the cop picked him up and walked him down to the corner to sober up, so he wouldn't remember where he was thrown out of." Each place on the block paid the policeman on beat from $2 to $5 a night, according to its volume of business. On a good block, Hymie estimates, it might have run to as much as $100 a night. He doesn't believe that the cop on beat was allowed to retain all this, but he says he never paid money to a police official higher up. His guess is that it was divided in the Department.

Hymie always enjoyed bouncing people in a nice way. When a big tough fellow heckled the hostess, Hymie would go to the cashier and get a roll of quarters. He would hold it in his right hand, with one end of the roll protruding, and he would lean over the fellow's table and slug him on the side of the jaw with it. Then a couple of waiters would carry the gentleman out and lay him on the sidewalk, where the cop would find him.

Mickey Finns, the pacifying pills slipped to obstreperous customers in many places, do not amuse Hymie. "Any fool can go into a drugstore for a dollar and buy a box of Mickeys," he says. Mickeys are purgative pills designed for horses, and act so drastically that one may kill a drunk with a weak heart. "But even with Mickeys, there is an art in the way to serve them," says Hymie. "Some fellows wait until the customer orders another drink, which may be too long, and others offer him a drink on the house, which maybe makes him suspicious. The best way is to tell the waiter, 'A little more ice in that glass, please.' The waiter has the ice on a spoon and the Mickey under the ice. He drops them in the drink together."

The Daylight Club ran fourteen months, during which, Hymie says, the partners earned about a quarter of a million dollars. The racetracks got most of Hymie's share. He remembers days when he went out to the track and lost $5,000 in an afternoon, then came back and delivered a case of bathtub gin to make $6. "Money don't mean nothing to me," he says. "Maybe I'm crazy."

After the Daylight was padlocked, Hymie and his associates opened a far more pretentious place on 50th Street, which he called the Club Chez Nous. He pronounced it the Club Chestnuts. The partners continued to make money. The place went out of existence because of the hostess's sense of humor. The adolescent son of a statesman then prominent came into the club drunk one night. She persuaded him to go out on the floor and do imitations of his father, who was flirting with a Presidential nomination. The father used his influence to have the place padlocked.

Hymie's third place, the Club Monastery, was a hard-lucker. It had been open only three weeks when a party of mobsmen dropped in and began shooting at Johnny Attorney and some friends. Two men were killed and Johnny Attorney disappeared. It is popularly supposed that his body was run through a rockcrusher and that he is now part of the roadbed of the Pulaski Skyway in New Jersey. The police, however, hadn't heard about this and thought that Hymie knew where Johnny was, so they gave him a terrific beating. Hymie was not the kind who would appeal to the American Civil Liberties Union. When the police let him go, some of the gangsters took him for a ride. Fortunately they forgot to gag him, and he talked so fast that they brought him back to his hotel and loaned him $20. It is one of his proudest memories. But the Monastery was "out on the street." Whenever there was a shooting in a speakeasy, the New York police closed it. That was the reason patrons about to shoot each other were always asked to leave.

The cares that might be expected to attend such a frenzied existence have left no mark on Hymie Katz. There are scars on his face from the beating the police gave him when they questioned him about Johnny Attorney, but no worry lines. He is not as handsome as he was twenty years ago, before he began to put on weight, but he has nice white teeth and pleasant features that wear a habitual unforced smile.

Hymie is unmarried at present. Wives, with Hymie, are symptoms of prosperity, like tailored shirts. His father is still living and owns a small jewelry shop on the Bowery near Canal Street. When Hymie visits him, the old man comes out to meet his son and locks the door from the outside. Then they talk on the sidewalk. Hymie is not offended by his parent's caution; he is flattered. Whenever he meets anybody new, he tells him about his father.

Hymie is living in a hotel on West 49th Street on a due bill. He pays the due-bill broker with due bills for entertainment at his next club, which he hasn't opened yet. When the club does open, the broker will sell the accumulated due bills for half their face value to couples who arrive via the bus lines and want to see New York night life.

Shortly before noon every day Hymie goes to his office, which he shares with a man who puts on stag shows, to see if any money has come in by mail. If there is any, Hymie spends the afternoon in a poolroom betting on races. If there is no money, he puts in a hard day at the telephone as Mr. Miller of Belmont Park. Generally he has dinner at an Italian Kitchen on Eighth Avenue, where he gets spaghetti, meatballs, and coffee for 25 cents. He smokes six cigars a day, five nickel ones and a 50-center, buying them all at the I. & Y. He smokes the 50-center after his 25-cent dinner, so he will feel prosperous. Evenings he usually leans against a stack of cases in the cigar store and discusses his plans—never his real plans, of course, but vast enterprises like taking over the Paramount Theater and turning it into a nightclub with a ski slide and a $5 minimum. With ribald arguments he maintains the feasibility of projects which he improvises on the spot. The other habitués of the I. & Y. listen with respect.

"You know who was in here?" Izzy asks friends who come in after Hymie has departed. "Hymie Katz." Izzy shakes his head admiringly. "He's a real tummler, that Hymie. He knows to get a dollar."

Achille and the Madonna

❧ ❧

THE MOST resourceful man I know is my friend Achille, who is a painter of religious pictures. During his mornings, from seven until noon, Achille paints with bitter energy. Sometimes his commissions are for Stations of the Cross or Holy Families, but Madonnas are his staple product. Almost all his Madonnas are copied from those of the late Renaissance, a period which he detests but which is a universal favorite with the parish priests who are his chief patrons. It takes a good salesman to strike a bargain with a priest, and Achille likes to brag of his expertness in ecclesiastical psychology. Yet in spite of his secular business acumen, he always disclaims irreverence.

"I paint my Lord, but not depressing," he sometimes says, "and also Madonna with modern appeal. But don't think that I don't love my Lord. I do love Him, you bet. If I didn't, it would be goodbye Charlie. Without faith it would be impossible to support painting so many copies of Guido Reni."

In the thirty years since he came to this country from Nantes, his native city, Achille has never improved his broken English or permitted his accent to lapse. He considers the latter one of his most important assets, and he has gone to much trouble to preserve it. "If I ever lose that," he says, "oh boy, goodbye Charlie!" He thinks he can say without undue complacency that his speech today is even more formidable than when he landed. The richly exotic sound of his "Ex-*cell*-ency" as he straightens up after kissing an episcopal ring has been known to overcome a prelate's sales resistance right then and there.

The back of each of Achille's canvases bears the inscription "Guaranteed to be a genuine oil painting, painted with the best of oil paint on canvas of the first quality, and will not fade. Signed, Achille Gambade." His sales talk to a prospect includes the recitation of a fifteen-page lecture on the history of religious art, which he has memorized in French, English, and Italian.

Achille keeps always by his easel a current copy of the *Catholic Directory,* containing the names, affiliations, and addresses of every Roman Catholic cleric in the country. He reads church necrologies with passionate interest, for a new pastor often likes to add to his church some adornment which will distinguish his regime from his predecessor's in the parishioners' minds. Achille has a library of about ten thousand reproductions of European religious paintings, mostly on postcards, and can copy any of them on demand, but he has a steady call for only about one hundred numbers, without exception versions of sixteenth- and seventeenth-century Italian pictures.

In competing with the representatives of the great religious houses on Barclay Street, who ordinarily secure most of the orders for church paintings, Achille must match his resourcefulness against the firms' prestige with the priesthood. Every spring and every fall he goes on the road with a few samples. With a wide black hat pulled down over his eyes and the ends of a Windsor tie peeping from beneath his curly red Breton beard, he presents an appearance of art incarnate, unmistakable even to a young priest in rural New Jersey or Rhode Island. Achille times his appearance at the rectory for about eight-thirty in the morning. At that hour, he explains when he is in a confidential mood, the priest is likely to be feeling good. The good Father has said his Mass, had his breakfast, made his usual matinal jest, at which his housekeeper has registered the proper degree of amusement, and probably is smoking a cigar when Achille drives up. Then, if ever, he will be in a mood to buy a fine Madonna, for which Achille will allow him to pay in installments as his parishioners contribute the money.

There was a time a dozen years ago, however, when despite all Achille's tact a crisis arose in his business. Madonnas simply weren't going. There was no particular way to account for it, although some of the younger priests were indulging in the fantastic theory that it might be well to spend more on basketball equipment for the parish boys' clubs than on a devitalized church art, even in genuine oil paint. It was then that Achille evolved his masterstroke of salesmanship. This is a trade secret which he never divulges except to people with whom he is on terms of the most cordial intimacy.

Attending a moving-picture show one afternoon during the period of depression in sacred art, Achille observed a party of young priests who appeared to be much interested in the feature. That gave him his great idea. When he came out, he wrote fan letters to a dozen feminine movie stars, requesting their photographs. When he got them, he set to work painting a Madonna with the face of a film star—"but ideal*ize*." He reasoned that the young priests were so used to seeing moving pictures that the faces of the leading ladies were impressed on their unconscious, but that the priests would never associate them with church art and would therefore not realize whose faces they found so charming when Achille painted them into his Madonnas.

"My first movie Madonna," says Achille, "was Priscilla Dean, and I sell fifty-four Madonna with 'er feature." Achille defends this practice because, he says, the painters of the Renaissance—for example, that pig of a Reni, whom he deplores—all used female models who were no better than they should have been. It's the concept, not the model, that counts, Achille says. His second Madonna was Agnes Ayres, who was a hit. He even got her into a couple of minor cathedrals. He had a bit of a flop with Joan Crawford—not the type, he decided—and a moderate success with Loretta Young.

Merle Oberon is his mainstay today. *"Une merveille,"* Achille says with rapture that partakes of astonishment. *"Regardez cette p'tite femme-là!* You wouldn't think she was the type at all, but take out a liddle bad from the face, put in a liddle good, turn up the eyes a liddle bid, put on her the robes—and oh, boy, she's the Madonna of 1938!"

P.S. The original of Achille killed himself in 1946, leaving $26,000. He was a good water-colorist (impressionist) but nobody would buy his secular work. The Madonna broke his spirit.

The Cow, He Roared . . .

THE STORY of the sea cow is Capt. Bob Forsythe's masterpiece—the choicest fruit of a long experience in steam navigation, and well he knows it.

Captain Forsythe is a limber and lean-faced towboater from Kingston on the Hudson, "which has produced more steamboat men than I daresay any town in the United States." ("Canawler," snorts Tom Wilson.) But he has plied the waters of the harbor and the Sound so long that he feels at home in the office of the Kennedy Line.

"It was during prohibition," Captain Forsythe always begins, as one who would say, "It was during the Civil War."

"We was lying at the foot of Sackett Street, Brooklyn, when I seed the man that owned the boat coming along with what I thought was a big Newfoundland dog, and then I made out this bull, whatever t'hell he was—a cow."

Captain Forsythe pronounced "cow" with a quality of bitterness such as towboat men generally reserve for the pilots of ferryboats, and he also got into his tone a suggestion that he had moved all his life in a different social sphere from cows, that he hardly knew what a cow was, and that he would feel himself degraded by the acquisition of such knowledge.

"We had a big open lighter that had belonged to the Navy," he said, "and we had it loaded with provisions and coal and slops that we was to take out to a rum boat at sea east of Block Island, and bring back four thousand cases of booze.

"Well, all would have been well, but the bootlegger conceived the idea to send this cow out to the ship so he would give the boys fresh milk, and then when they wanted meat they would kill him. The minute the cow seed me he let a roar out of him, and we had a big time making him walk down a plank into the lighter. Then when we got him aboard, he liked to kick our brains out, but we made his legs fast and stowed him by the rail.

"We even shipped a bale of hay, which is fuel for them damn animals.

"We cast and went out by Hell Gate, and there was a fog in the Sound that you couldn't see a hundred yards in front of you, it was perfect. She was so deep in the water with coal, and no deck onto her, just an open lighter, the sharks come swimming right up on the side to visit with the cow. If we had good sense we would have thrown him overboard. But we amused ourselves feeding loaves of bread to the sharks instead. She shipped some water, but everything would have been all right if it wasn't for this cow.

"He began to beller so we didn't need no foghorn. I bet you could hear him in Boston. And sure enough we get a hail—one of those Coast Guard four-stackers out of New London. They send an officer aboard and I give him a line that I am taking provisions to an Isthmian Line boat at Boston, but he says the Isthmian does not run any boats to Boston.

" 'Turn her around and folly us into New London,' he says.

" 'You're only a public servant,' I says. 'This is piracy and damn impudence, and if you want to take her into New London you can run her yourself.' So I called up my engineer and the firemen, and we sat with our arms folded on top of the canned goods, and cursed the cow who continued his impersonation of a whistle buoy. They put the crew aboard, but so much water came over the side that they couldn't keep steam on her. The steering gear locked, and she nearly rammed the destroyer.

"They had to tow her into New London, and the further they towed the madder they got, until by the time they docked her the only one in the party that was pleased with himself was the cow.

"Of course they didn't really have anything on us, because we had not been out there to get the rum yet, and there wasn't a drop aboard, but still and all, nobody would acknowledge ownership, fearing some kind of a tangle with the law, and meanwhile me and my crew was stranded. The bootlegger that owned the boat wouldn't send us a penny. The Coast Guard wouldn't release the boat until some owner turned up, and we stayed aboard hoping to collect our pay.

"To keep going, I sold the coal off her, and then the provisions, and at last there was nothing left but this here bull, whatever it was, a cow, and I hated him more every time I looked at him. We were tied up at a dock in the Thames River, a high dock, and it was low water, and we were way below level. I goes ashore and looks for a farmer, and sure enough, the second field I look into I find one."

Captain Forsythe pronounced "farmer" in much the same manner as "cow," but with slightly less acerbity.

" 'Do you want to buy a cow?' I asks him.

" 'Maybe,' he says. 'Where is it?'

" 'Come with me,' I says. He follies me onto the dock and I show him the cow in the lighter.

" 'How much do you want for him?' he says.

" 'Fifty dollars,' I asks him, guessing at the value.

" 'I'll give you fifty dollars for him,' he says, 'delivered on the dock.'

"I says, 'Give me the fifty and I'll have him on the dock in five minutes.' So he gives me the fifty and I went aboard and we made a couple of belly bands and put them around the cow and lifted him with the steam hoist, meaning to put him down on the dock, but when I got the cow up and started to lower away, the power stopped, and there was the cow dangling a good fifteen feet above the dock. Up comes my engineer. " 'I stopped her,' he says, 'because there's no more rope on the drum. She's block to block. How will we get rid of the cow?' he says. 'I'll show you,' I says.

"With that I grabbed an axe and cut through the cable with one wallop. The bull, whatever t'hell he was, a cow, came flying through the air and landed on his four feet like a cat, and up the hill into New

London, making a good eighteen knots, and the farmer after him. And that was the last I seed of either one."

Animal Husbandry

NORMAN BERNSTEIN, my rabbit breeder, raises mice and guinea pigs, too. He would like to get an AAA crop limitation on all of them, but the rabbits, mice, and guinea pigs will not stand for it.

"Overproduction broke the price of white mice and guinea pigs," he said to me, explaining why he would not bid on a city contract for nine thousand white mice. "Rabbits, too, although I won't say that we won't throw them a bid on the sixteen hundred rabbits and two thousand guinea pigs they want for the hospitals.

"What was the cause of overproduction? Overcapitalization, just like among bulls and bears.

"You see, a lot of fake small-stock schemes sprang up in the beginning of the depression—small livestock, I mean. The rabbit racket, we called it. Companies with impressive names—the Pink Eye Imperial Universal Rabbitries, or such names—started out selling individuals, say, ten rabbits or ten mice for breeding.

"They picked mostly on people who were out of work but who had some savings. They would sell these people ten rabbits with a hutch and one month's food for five hundred dollars or three hundred dollars or whatever they could get. Then the company would give a contract to buy back all the future rabbits at a fancy price.

"Well, at first they would buy back a few rabbits. The rabbits they bought back at thirty-two cents a pound, say, they would plant on new suckers at five hundred dollars for ten. It was like the Ponzi business. Then they would begin to shut down, buying the rabbits back at market prices, fourteen cents a pound, say, but not cash. They would dump those rabbits in the market by the thousands, breaking the price to four cents a pound, and grab the cash.

"So all over the country there are too many white mice, too many guinea pigs, too many white rats, too many rabbits.

"The millionaires who used to endow research foundations every time their wives had birthdays have quit, so there is less demand for laboratory animals. That is why I expect mice may go for a nickel on these sealed bids for the city."

The Breeder Company, Bernstein's firm, occupies a barnlike, white-washed building which resounds with the continual *eek-eek* of cavies (the correct name for guinea pigs) and mice. Even with the checked production, there are about ten thousand mice, one thousand rats and one thousand cavies and rabbits in stock.

There is a large white Angora cat, which feeds on mice. Not the fifteen-cents-straight mice, but the house mice who appear at night.

"They carry mouse typhoid," Mr. Bernstein explains. "They might start an epidemic.

"We don't need the city's business," he said. "We got quality customers like the Rockefeller Institute and hospitals all over the East.

"Kill Mrs. Horowitz today, Jerry," he directed a helper. "How is Mrs. O'Shaughnessy?

"You see," he explained, "doctors come here to make tests on rabbits.

"They inject the rabibt with urine taken from a patient, and in a certain number of hours they know from the condition of the rabbits' ovaries whether the patient is pregnant or not.

"Naturally, we can't afford to get those rabbits mixed or it would come out that one woman was going to have a baby when, as a matter of fact, she had some kind of other trouble altogether. So we put each rabbit in a separate box labeled Mrs. Grossman or Mrs. Schmidt, according to the patient's name. Then we refer to the rabbit by that name as long as it lives, which is not so long, of course."

Handspring Hall

To KEEP the rest of the country happy, New York maintains an ever-normal granary of acrobats in hotels in cross streets off Eighth Avenue. These hotels have succeeded the theatrical boardinghouses of the 1890s.

My favorite is one named Irvington Hall, on West 51st Street, in the halls of which I used to encounter a pair of magnificent Mexican sisters. They were hand-balancers, and used to take turns carrying each other, with the top sister's toes pointed at the ceiling. When they were doing a head-to-head, Rosita, the younger sister, would wave in response to my greeting. But when they were doing a hand-to-hand, she could only smile.

Irvington Hall was the home of the Braatz family, excellent friends of mine. Mickey, the daughter, was a genius. She could turn seventy-five successive pinwheels without pausing. I well remember the first time I visited her.

"The greatest inventions come by accident," said Harry Braatz, her proud but modest father. "Like the time I was rehearsing headstands with an understander and the boss of the troupe said to another fellow, 'Let him rest his feet on your head, instead of coming down to the ground every time he gets tired.' I bridged back with my head on the understander's head, until my feet were on the head of the third fellow —and we had made the first human bridge!' Mr. Braatz sighed with pleasure.

"So when my daughter tried her first tinsika—she was four years old —and she fell in so natural—right there I knew she would be a credit to the family. But never did I imagine—seventy-five! If I would measure my words carefully, I would say it was superhuman."

Daughter Mickey, a straight and sturdy blonde of seventeen, with level eyes in a boyish, pugnacious face, accepted the adjective without delight or demurrer.

"I don't get out of breath," she said. "Not a bit. I could do pinwheels all night on a dime."

She used the layman's word for the trick—her father preferred the more erudite "tinsika."

"The trick was named after Tinsika, the Arab who invented it," he says, "and he should have credit."

But he was not angry with his daughter, who, by combining a tap dance with her seventy-five successive head-over-heels revolutions on one spot (that is what makes it a "spotted" tinsika), had moved out of the acrobats' world and into music show business.

"There used to be a great future in acrobatics," he said, "but no more. If I had a son, I would not teach him further than a backbend."

"I like flip-flops," said Mickey. "But I like pinwheels better. Every year I can do more pinwheels, but I think seventy-five is enough. One might injure one's heart."

"Yes," said Mrs. Selma Braatz, the champion lady juggler of the world, Mickey's mother. "Remember Ernst, the handstander? He jumped from four tables down on his hands. He was on his hands more than his feet and finally he became religious crazy and ran around nude. Too much is too much."

Mrs. Braatz, although about to leave the house when I called, consented to doff her furs and balance a wheel on her forehead on the end of a long stem. She made the wheel revolve, with a red ball in its inner rim, and juggled four balls through and around the whirling circumference.

"There," she said, allowing the apparatus to crash to the floor. "Practice, practice, always you got to practice. That is what I always tell Mickey. When I was a little girl, my father made me practice twelve, fourteen hours a day. Now sometimes when I sit down in a restaurant, absentminded I begin to juggle the knife, the fork, soon a plate—it's very embarrassing."

"Her brother used to juggle cannonballs on the back of his neck," Mr. Braatz confided as his wife departed, with a commission from Mickey to bring back "any kind of cake but not apple cake."

Although Tinsika was a man, the pinwheel has become an exclusively feminine trick, Mr. Braatz says, because women are quicker and more supple. Three is about the limit for male tinsikas, and they are not spotted.

"I speak lines in the show," said Mickey. "I met Rudy Vallee at a party, but he has a terrible voice. I do not like the way his left eye droops."

It was a matter of dispute in the hotel, although naturally nobody told Mickey, whether she or Bozo, who lived two floors above the Braatzes, was the more prodigious prodigy.

Bozo is the greatest canine hand-balancer of all time, the only dog to circumambulate Madison Square Garden arena on forefeet exclusively, a feature of Ringling Brothers' and Barnum and Bailey's combined circus.

He is the property of Shorty Flenn, a clown who works in a rube outfit, with white chin whiskers.

Bozo weighs four pounds, and in relation to his bulk, one circumference of the ten-lap arena is equivalent to four miles for a human acrobat walking on his hands.

He is nine years old, nearly ten, an age which would entitle him to rank as a DeWolf Hopper among canine performers, but he acts more like a juvenile.

If you pretend to ignore him, he goes into his act spontaneously, sitting up, waltzing on his hind legs, imitating a crippled dog, and finally, for the sock, going into his hand-walk. If you still ignore him, he scratches at your knee and raises a squawk like a columnist whom nobody reads.

He is a native of Iowa, and, like most bright Iowans, an *émigré*. Mr. Cameron, the manager of the state fair, perhaps ashamed of such a small dog in a fiesta devoted to such large hogs, presented him to his present owner, who was appearing with a refined divertissement known as "Peck's Bad Boys and Girls," doing a rube character bit.

Bozo is black-and-tan, and his brain capacity is so phenomenal in proportion to his body weight, Shorty reports, that a professor from the University of Iowa asked him to appear before a university course in psychology during one of his triumphal tours.

"They had him away from me for nearly an hour," Shorty recalls, "and he nearly died for lack of some intelligent conversation. Intelligent? Do you know how I trained him to live in an apartment? I clapped my hands once, and he has never done anything wrong since."

Shorty has a cauliflower ear, a legacy from a boxing kangaroo which he once owned and which hit him after the bell rang. He says all kangaroos are punchers, but none of them can take beating around the head.

Chesty, the Boxing Clown, who shares Shorty's suite, agrees fully as to Bozo's "qualities *magnifiques, extraordinaires*." Chesty is a Belgian, whose gestures of a pantaloon (he has been a clown from childhood) ill accord with the melancholy grandeur of his thought.

Chesty is a clown by profession, and in Europe a clown wears beautiful clothes, like a matador. The fellow who gets slapped around by the clown is the Auguste. Here nobody knows the difference; it is give and take. The audience distinguishes not even a contortionist who is a front-bender from a contortionist who is a back-bender. But Bozo—he is better than the Fratellinis, Chesty says.

Bozo has never been sick. He never overeats. When left alone, he spends hours rehearsing.

"I don't think a dog trainer could ever do as well," says Mr. Flenn. "I have just one animal at a time. There was the kangaroo, a good fellow even if he did sneak a punch on me. He died of pneumonia. And then I had the smallest mule in the world, but a llama fell on him with the Wallace show."

"Cut Yourself a Piece of Throat"

※ ※

IT IS UNLIKELY that the names of Adelman and Millman will figure conspicuously in the annals of the American theater. Yet they are the authors, producers, and cast of "Cut Yourself a Piece of Throat," a drama which is undoubtedly the run leader of the century (more than twenty years), and which must have earned gross receipts comparing favorably with *Tobacco Road's*.

Adelman and Millman put on their show in the window of a vacant store. Since there are always vacant stores, this custom frees Adelman and Millman from the necessity of dickering with the Shuberts. Their production is audience-proof. I have caught them on the road, in the notoriously unenthusiastic city of Providence, as well as back where I came from. They always click.

Adelman and Millman are, with Charlie Chaplin, the sole surviving exponents of pure pantomime.

"The show is a wow," the senior partner admits. "Every time you see it, it is as if you had never seen it before. But it is exhausting, so we can only put it on every other week. If we did it in two successive weeks, we would go stale and lose our punch. We alternate it with the thirty-nine-cent fountain-pen demonstration, and consequently we never give a dull or indifferent performance."

The act is set in a show window, and this is important, because, as Mr. Adelman says, "You see a man selling something on a street corner, and right away the mental reaction is 'faker.' You see him in a store window and you think 'businessman.'" Never does the Adelman-Millman Consolidated Show play a street engagement.

The setting, the finesse of the performers, the breathtaking qualities of the scenario, and a ton of cheese a year combine to prolong the run of the performance.

The act starts when the partner in the window picks up a fair-sized kitchen knife, pounds the edge of the blade with a hammer, and then presses the knife against his throat, draws it past his ears, and pushes it against his wrists, showing how thoroughly it has been dulled. He then picks a Belgian whetstone from a stack by his side, sharpens the knife with a few strokes, and drops a page of a magazine or newspaper from shoulder height. As the paper falls, he slices it into shreds with the newly sharpened knife.

Next he produces a bread knife with a serrate edge like a Malay kris. When he draws this across his throat, grimacing like a policy collector being put on the spot, the crowd outside his window comes as near applause as a street crowd ever does. He sharpens it and slices some more paper.

Then comes a scissors, with which he earnestly tries to cut his nose off. He fails, sharpens the instrument, moistens it with his tongue, and shaves hair off his arm with one blade. Then comes a butcher's cleaver and then, if he is in fettle, the big punch. This is a monster cleaver with a blade three feet by two.

The pantomimist leans his weight upon it. He is unscathed. A few deft strokes of the stone, he whirls the monster chopper through the air and cuts page 156 of *The Saturday Evening Post* to confetti.

The partner who is not acting stays inside the store and sells whet-stones, fifteen apiece and two for a quarter. Fifteen minutes in the window is enough—then they change roles.

The fountain-pen act consists of drawing in the style of various cartoonists, then writing out in fancy script, "You can do it, too," or something of that nature. It is lucrative, because, as the partners explain, nobody has the price of a dollar fountain pen any more.

But their hearts are in whetstones—long, ship-shaped articles that weigh at least half a pound. That is why they carry the cheese.

"You see," said Mr. Adelman, "the market for whetstones is not limitless. They don't wear out, and they are hard to mislay. Yet we must sell several thousand a week to pay our way. So what do we do?

"We distribute this cheese where young mice will get it. The mice eat it, flourish, and multiply. They grow fat and dull-witted, not having to hunt for their food. Cats feed upon the mice and they, too, multiply.

"The cats go out on back fences and express their high spirits. House-holders cannot sleep. They go to their windows, and what is so handy to throw as a cheap, hard, heavy whetstone? In this way millions of stones pass into oblivion, every year."

"What Do You Expect for Two Dollars?"

THERE NEVER WERE many people in the finest restaurant I ever discovered within the city limits (it was at one of New York's bathing beaches), and most of those there were seemed unwanted. Sometimes a party of four sunburned adults and maybe three children would sit around a table uneasily for half an hour, the men in shirt-sleeves, the women in cotton dresses, and no waiter would come near them. Three or four waiters, old, acrid fellows, would be standing in the farthest corner of the vast room, talking and laughing bitterly, and looking over at the people at the table. The waiters wore black alpaca coats and round tin badges with numbers on them. Once we saw a man at a table grow angry and bang on the water carafe with a knife. There was only yellow, tepid water in the carafe. A waiter shuffled to his table from the far corner. He seemed to take an interminable time getting there, and the *slup-slup* of his broken old shoes on the floor sounded loud in that almost silent place. The man said something to him, and then the waiter said in a loud, contemptuous voice, "We don't serve sandwiches or soft drinks here." The party went out, the men looking ashamed, the women scolding their males for subjecting them to such embarrassment.

"Some of them turf-cutters," our waiter said, flicking crumbs off our table with the end of his napkin. " 'Turf-cutter' is a word we use for cheap Irish," he said, knocking most of the crumbs into my girl's lap. He looked Irish himself. "The Beach is full of them," he said. "Let them go down to the Limerick House."

The restaurant must have been built shortly after the Columbia Exposition. It was an imitation of a cake-frosting exposition building, with seven senseless minarets on it. Most of the white paint had flaked off, or turned gray with age and sea air. The signs about specialties of the house were painted right on the building, in what had once been silver lettering, on what had once been a maroon ground. Evidently the lettering had not been changed since the restaurant was built. Most of the signs said RHODE ISLAND CLAMBAKE, $1.75 or ROAST CHICKEN DINNER,

$1.50. In the state to which the Beach has declined, these are high prices. They must have been high forty years ago, too, but then the Beach was a fashionable resort, with a clientele of hot sports. It cost a dollar just to get there from Manhattan, in a steamboat. Now the most dashing attractions are a couple of tired carrousels and a few saloons that advertise in the Irish-American newspapers, but most of the people who come to the Beach do not patronize even them. They just change into their bathing suits under the boardwalk and go swimming, and when they come out, they eat at hot-dog stands. The swimming is good.

The floor of the restaurant sloped like a ship's deck in a big sea. Like all the older buildings at the Beach, it had been built without a foundation, and it had settled in the sand unevenly. The dish covers, the soup tureens, and the rest of the tableware had an antiquarian interest. Each piece bore the name of an old, vanished restaurant: Shanley's, Churchill's, or Jack's.

The restaurant was so obviously decadent and unprosperous that we had not ventured into it the first few times that we went to the Beach to swim. It was only after investigating the possibilities of the Greek lunchrooms, the Japanese waffle shops, and the saloons that we had dared that ghostly pavilion, deciding that we had nothing to lose. The food in the old restaurant had astonished us. The steamed clams were small, clean, and accompanied by a stiff sauce of butter with tarragon vinegar and curry powder blended into it. The chicken fricassee was not smothered in a white flour paste, but yellow and succulent. The $3.50 steak, for two, was perfect. As long as we ordered substantially, took cocktails before dinner, and drank plenty of beer with the meal, the waiters tolerated us.

One evening I ordered a "combination" of steamed clams and a broiled lobster, with potatoes. It had seemed to me that included in this offering, on the menu, was a green salad. Having finished the lobster, I asked for this salad.

The waiter said, "What do you expect for two dollars? A *gold* watch?"

It was this same waiter, however, who on another evening began to talk to me, almost without condescension. It is true he had been drinking.

"The place is a hundred years behind the times," he said. "It's a summer home for broken-down waiters."

He put one hand on our table and leaned his weight on it.

"The cook is forty-nine million years old," he said. "Some day he'll fall into the clam chowder. At the end of every season the old man says to him, 'I never want to see you no more. You're as dead as a doornail.' And at the beginning of the next season he sends a taxicab for him. He used to cook at Burns's. The old man is in his second childhood. That's him setting up on the high stool by the bar. He ain't got no cash register, only an old wooden cashbox. He sets there from ten o'clock in the morning until closing time, to see that no waiter gets away with a glass of beer."

The waiter pointed his chin angrily toward the figure on the stool, diagonally across the room from us. The old gentleman was dressed in a black broadcloth suit, such as a conservative undertaker might wear in winter. The upper part of the vest looked very big for him, but his lower abdomen ballooned out like a spider's. On top of his head he balanced on old Panama hat, colored like a meerschaum pipe. Even from there we could see how badly he needed a shave.

"He's had that Panama hat for twenty years," the waiter grumbled. "Every spring he has it cleaned, and I think painted, and he brags to everybody he knows about it. 'See,' he says, 'the Panama hat is good for another season.' He's in his second childhood. But try to take a dime off him," the waiter said, "and he ain't in his second childhood no more. You can't do it."

The old man came down off the stool, reluctantly, like a boy sliding into a too-cold swimming pool. He shuffled toward our end of the room, glaring suspiciously over the tops of his spectacles. He had a long, pointed nose. Fifteen feet from our table the old man stopped and stared at us for a minute. Then he turned and went away. Laboriously he climbed up on the stool.

"He was just coming over to see there wasn't too many customers in the place," the waiter explained. "The other night they was lined up two deep at the bar, for once, so he says to the bartender, 'Come out from behind that bar, Joe, and take a walk around the block until they clear out of here.' He don't like no customers. It's second childhood. Do you know what worries him the most? The fear that somebody would park at the curb here. He hates automobiles. So he puts a stepladder in front of the curb and a pot of green paint on top of it. So anybody that drives in will knock the ladder over and get paint on his car. 'Oh, he-he-he,' the old man laughs the last time that happens. 'Look at the damn fool! Too bad he didn't get it on his clothes,' the old man says."

The dining room opens onto a terrace on a level with the sidewalk. We looked out and saw the ladder, with the paintpot perched on the top step.

Another waiter, even older than ours, who was pretty old himself, edged up to our man. "I don't like to say nothing, Murph," he said, "but them people over at that table over there says they give you their order half an hour ago."

"Tell them it's a two-mile walk to the kitchen and back," said our waiter. The people, two men and two women, had been watching him right along, and knew he had not been to the kitchen. When they saw he was not going to do anything about it, they got up and left.

"Deaf as a post the old man is," the waiter went on. "You should hear him talk on the telephone with his sister that lives at the Plaza. 'I'm fine,' he yells as soon as he picks up the phone. He thinks she's asking him how he is. No matter what the hell she calls up to talk to him about, he just says, 'I'm fine,' and hangs up. But if you drop a dollar bill on the floor, he hears it hit."

Perhaps the old man sensed that we were talking about him. Hesitantly, he got down off his stool again and walked over toward us, then stopped, irresolute, at the same point as before, and turned and went back.

"It's on account of him that the Beach is going to hell," said our waiter. "He owns all the property for a mile around, and he won't put a coat of paint on a building. Last year four blocks of his stuff burnt up, the damned old tinderboxes. 'It don't do me no good anyway,' he says. 'I couldn't get no insurance on them.' The papers says, '$500,000 Fire at the Beach,' but he couldn't get five cents for them buildings."

"Why does he keep the place open if he doesn't want any customers?" my girl asked.

"So he can lose money and take it off his income tax," Murph told her. "And now for God's sake don't order no pie à la mode like the last time, for I have to walk down to one end of the old shack for the pie and then I have to walk to the other end to the icehouse for the ice cream. Before you can get an order together in this place, you got to get a letter from the Pope. And then before you can find a dish to serve it in, you got to go through all that heap of old tinware, like a junkshop."

My girl meekly ordered watermelon, but Murph did not start to get it. He felt like talking.

"Before his wife died sixteen years ago, it wasn't so bad," he said. "Sometimes she would buy a round of drinks for the house. She was always soused. Twenty-four seasons I've worked here, God help me, and now it's too late to get fired. He'll die next winter surely."

He did.

The Press

❧ ❧

Elijah and Sinbad: 1961

❧ ❧

As AN OBSERVER from outside, I take a grave view of the plight of the press. It is the weak slat under the bed of democracy. It is an anomaly that information, the one thing most necessary to our survival as choosers of our own way, should be a commodity subject to the same merchandising rules as chewing gum, while armament, a secondary instrument of liberty, is a government concern. A man is not free if he cannot see where he is going, even if he has a gun to help him get there.

One alternative to an informed people making right decisions from choice is a correctly informed government making decisions on the basis of information it cannot communicate to the people. That would be competing with private industry, even in the squalid form that a number of publishers represent, and the preservation of private industry is the principal reason for having a country at all. To make this alternative system work requires a people imbued with, or cowed into, the habit of blind obedience. We are not ready for it.

The other alternative, a badly informed government leading a badly informed people, is not an ideal, although it has happened here at times, notably during the Cuban repatriation episode last April.

As an observer from inside, since most of my work has been journalism, I have a rather different view. I am a chronic, incurable, recidivist reporter. When I am working at it, I have no time to think about the shortcomings of the American or world press; I must look sharp not to come too short myself. Sinbad, clinging to a spar, had no time to think of systematic geography. To understand perfectly a new country, new situation, the new characters you confront on an assignment, is impossible. To understand more than half, so that your report will have significant correlation with what is happening, is hard. To transmit more than half of what you understand is a hard trick, too, far beyond the task of the so-called creative artist, who if he finds a character in his story awkward can simply change its characteristics. (Even to sex, *vide* Proust and Albertine. Let him try it with General de Gaulle.) It is possible, occasionally, to get something completely right—a scene, or a pattern of larceny, or a man's mind. These are the reporter's victories, as rare as a pitcher's home runs.

A good reporter, if he chooses the right approach, can understand a cat or an Arab. The choice is the problem, and if he chooses wrong he will come away scratched or baffled. (There is a different approach to every cat and every Arab.) The best reporters occasionally fail badly, and the fair ones half-fail often.

I suspect, from my own few shallow dips below the surface of news, that it is reported superficially. I felt, after Suez and Gaza in 1956-7, and Earl Long's Louisiana in 1959, for example, that I might just as well not have read about them before going, because what I found was different. My point here is not that what I see is always exact, and that the harried press-association men are always wrong, but that different reporters see different things, or the same things differently, and that the reader at home has a right to a diversity of reports. A one-man account of a crisis in a foreign country is like a Gallup poll with one straw. The same goes for national news.

The critic of other reporters therefore takes a mighty risk when he goes out to work with them. I take a humbler tone about reporters than about publishers. There is a healthy American newspaper tradition of not taking yourself seriously. It is the story you must take that way. This applies, of course, equally to the relation between doctor and patient, or soldier and enemy. And if you do take yourself seriously, according to this sound convention, you are supposed to do your best not to let anybody else know about it. (Like bed wetting.)

The outside-observing and inside-observing Lieblings consequently speak in different tones. One is Liebling-Elijah and the other Liebling-Sinbad. (Sinbad was the very prince of reporters, and he always went back to take a second look. Up he would get, from those comfortable banquets at which he could have squatted indefinitely in an executive capacity, and back to sea to see what the world looked like. He was interested in money, but more in people. He would never have made a publisher. The publisher in what the *Post* would call The Sinbad Story is symbolized by the Old Man of the Sea.)

What reporters can do when an Old Man turns benevolent and gets off their necks was illustrated in Little Rock in 1957, when Gov. Orval Faubus staged his successful bid for a third term, at the small expense—

to him—of making "Little Rock" a symbol of hypocrisy and intolerance everywhere outside the national boundaries.

John Netherland Heiskell, the proprietor, and his son-in-law Hugh Patterson, the publisher, allowed Harry Ashmore, the editor, and his staff to fight the good fight. Their performance, before an audience of journalists drawn to the scene from all over the literate world, saved whatever shreds of prestige the United States salvaged. It confirmed the golden legend of a free and fearless press, and so did more for our prestige abroad than all the Eisenhower-Nixon globe-trotting of the unfortunate administration.

Mr. Heiskell, Mr. Patterson, and their merry men received a number of triffling unofficial honors, such as Pulitzer prizes, from conscience-stricken colleagues, but they got no recognition from the Federal government in the shape of citations in orders of the day, special medals, letters from the President, or even ¼ of 1 per cent rebates on their income taxes. Yet they did more to brake the deterioration of our foreign relations than any dozen political ambassadors who retired with tear-bedewed letters of gratitude from the Chief of State.

Little Rock, incidentally, is not a one-ownership town. The *Gazette* held with Law and Order—recognition of the validity of the Fourteenth Amendment as interpreted by the Supreme Court—while the *Democrat*, the other paper, took up for Peace and Harmony, which is not the same thing when the going gets rough. The *Gazette* lost, and the *Democrat* gained, in circulation and advertising. The publishers of the *Gazette* therefore made a sacrifice which, in their caste, is comparable to that of a Brahman who permits himself to be run through a sewing machine in order to achieve virtue.

In my orientation to the press I resemble the late Robert Benchley, who began The Wayward Press department in *The New Yorker*, and carried it on from 1927 to 1937. Benchley, in a passage I cannot forget, told of his joy every morning, when he got up that early, at padding to the front door in his pajamas, opening it, and finding all the morning papers lying on the doormat with the milk. The milk had been delivered by mistake. There were seven New York morning papers up until 1931, instead of our measly four. Benchley was, and I am, addicted to papers, as I was then—I cannot speak for him—to needled beer. This was a delectable drink that disappeared like a newspaper with the repeal of prohibition. The 20 per cent of alcohol that the bootleggers added to this beer will never be replaced in my affections by the picture of Miss Rheingold. Taking the newspapers inside with him, Benchley was quit of the need of thinking for several hours.

Newspapers always offer something to be delighted or concerned or enraged over. Some reporter has done a good job, some editorialist shown a flash of unsuspected spirit. And there is always at least one astonishing story—for example, an octogenarian recluse has starved to death, and nobody has found $212,000 in dirty one-dollar bills hidden in the foul straw of his dingy mattress. In such cases I always figure the cops have stolen the money. Newspapers can be more fun than a quiet girl.

Sometimes I write my own occasional Wayward Press pieces. I write a case history of how the New York papers—or once in a while out-of-New York newspapers—have handled a story that interested me. If I choose one that they have kicked around the infield, it is not done out of malice but from a hope to instruct. It is true that I get few letters of thanks from editors, but readers sometimes send them. In this I take example from my friend Whitey Bimstein, the educator, who never intervenes when a pair of his professional pupils are going along all right in a sparring bout at the Eighth Avenue Gymnasium, but is ready with advice when one commits a solecism.

"Don't go oncet when you can go twicet," Whitey will then say. "Going oncet is a dirty habit. It leaves you open for a left hook." To me he oncet explained, "Why should I tell him when he done good? It will give him a swelled head."

Like Whitey, I don't want to give the newspapers a swelled head.

I am philosophical, like a lobster eater who knows that the total number of lobsters in the world is on the decline, but is sure they will last him out. Even in this role I infrequently grow melancholy, remembering that I myself as Sinbad am an inhabitant of this diminishing-lobster world; it makes me feel like an Athenian after Syracuse, or my father after Johnson licked Jeffries. I feel as naked as a critic without a fellowship, or a professor of communications without a grant.

Yet who, noting the press's reaction to a given situation, can fail to be cheered by seeing how nearly it matches up with how the press reacted when a similar situation last occurred? Thus, with the word "labor," the association is "stubborn." With government, "wasteful." With the poor, "pampered"—or malingering or undeserving.

The "taxpayer" is always "overburdened," but it occurs to me as I write that he is always represented in editorial cartoons as a small, shabby man in underclothes and a barrel (the kind of fellow who if he had a wife, two children, and no imagination, would be caught for an income tax of about $8) and never as an unmistakably rich man, like, say, the proprietor of a large newspaper. The man in the barrel is always warned that a frivolous project like medical care for his aged parents is likely to double his already crushing tax burden. The implication is that the newspaper owner is above worrying about *his* parents, and of course he is, because his old man left him the paper.

Obits: 1945

THE AUTHORS of newspaper obituaries, or obits, are a frustrated and usually anonymous tribe. The biographical notices of public characters which they prepare in advance of their subjects' departures are filed away in the papers' libraries marked, for example, "Hold until wanted —bring up to date 1947," and can be released only by the deaths of the protagonists. This is naturally a source of anxiety to the obit writer who has embalmed a subject with phrases in which he feels he can take some pride. Sometimes the obituarist conceives a deep grudge against an elder notable who, by stubbornly refusing to expire, delays public recognition of a superior rewrite job. The late John D. Rockefeller, Sr., outwore the patience and contributed to the alcoholism of three newspaper generations. Much of the decline in editorial esteem of the late David Lloyd George, and perhaps also of George Bernard Shaw, may be ascribed to irritation of a like origin.

Theodore Dreiser, who died on December 28 in his seventy-fifth year, probably suffered somewhat from this professional reaction. By contrast, Gen. George S. Patton, Jr., who predeceased Dreiser by a week, was sixty years old and at the very peak of his obituary value. Patton had been in the news more prominently since 1942 than ever before in his life, and since there was always a possibility during the war that even a very superior officer might decease abruptly, his obits had been kept up to date by highly rated members of the New York newspaper rewrite batteries. It is probable, also, that during the strike last summer of the newspaper delivery men, high-priority obits in all offices received a good refurbishing. Dreiser's, to judge from internal evidence, had on most papers been confided to young reporters who had returned early from dinner assignments where the guest of honor failed to show up.

There was therefore a piquant discrepancy between the newspaper treatments of the two decedents. Only *PM* (a day or two late, as usual) gave Dreiser a more considerable sendoff than Patton. Max Lerner, of that paper, wrote a full-page editorial on the novelist, while Ralph Ingersoll polished the General off in five paragraphs and a line.

A member of the *Daily News* staff named Kermit Jaediker set the tone for the Patton pieces when he retrospectively chronicled the General's birth as the most prodigious since that of Pantagruel. "This laconic young man with the pink complexion, the sandy hair, the steel-blue eyes, and the stuff of legend woven into his six feet of bone and muscle, was born Nov. 11, 1885, on his father's ranch in San Gabriel, California," Jaediker wrote. Born six feet high and with all his hair, Patton never stopped growing in the minds of rewrite men and their editors, and after his death one or another of the New York papers gave him credit for every achievement of Allied arms in the European Theater of Operations except the Battle of Stalingrad. This is a convention of the Only Free Press in the World, like a preacher's eulogy at a funeral. When you write a man's obituary, you become his advocate.

It is probably this tradition which explains why the *Sun* said, "The troops under him, revivified by his leadership, swept up Gafsa on the long drive to El Guettar, Mateur, Bizerte, and triumph in North Africa." The "long drive" south from Gafsa to El Guettar is perhaps nine miles, and that is as far as the troops got under Patton. Mateur and Bizerte are in the opposite direction, about a hundred and fifty miles to the north. The Americans won their great North African victory there—under the command of Gen. Omar N. Bradley. The *Times* leaned even farther from the perpendicular when it related that at El Guettar Patton won "the first major American victory over Nazi arms." Maj. Gen. Terry Allen commanded the 1st Division when, without assistance from Corps, it won the wholly unpremeditated battle of El Guettar, repulsing a surprise attack by the German 10th Armored Division. The First was technically under Patton's command, of course, just as he was under the British General Alexander's and Alexander was under General Eisenhower's. But Allen won the battle.

Mr. Jaediker pursued the motif with the not unpicturesque statement "The legend burgeoned in the African campaign when the rasping, swearing tankman, two pearl-handled six-shooters dangling on his hips, led our forces in the conquest of Tunisia." If Patton rasped for Jaediker, he went "swashbuckling his way across the sands of North Africa" for a writer named George Adams, of the rival *Mirror*. "Swashbuckling," I take it, is a sort of third gait, between a walk and a run. The *Herald*

Tribune said he had more flair than any other general since Custer, though what poor Custer had a flair for I wouldn't know—certainly not Indians. There are limits, however, even to the convention of the funeral whoop-it-up-and-holler, and I thought that Donald Mackenzie, another *Daily News* writer, transcended them when he wrote of "the brilliant breakthrough by his [Patton's] Third U. S. Army at St. Lô and Avranches." The Third Army was not activated until after the breakthrough near St. Lô, which was managed by four infantry and two armored divisions of the First Army, under the command, for the operation, of Gen. J. Lawton Collins, of the VII Corps. St. Lô itself had been taken several days earlier, by the 29th Division, also of the First Army. Avranches was not reached until after the breakthrough, and as a consequence of it, on July 28. Patton's army began its existence on August 1.

Future Plutarchs, if they use the files, will have the same difficulty in selecting anecdotes to season their narratives as they will in determining General Patton's share in operations. There were plenty of stories, and the obituarists told them differently. The *Herald Tribune*, for example, said that Patton waded across the Sure River on a submerged footbridge, while the *Daily News* said that he swam across it twice (with the corroborative detail that it was flooded "in the depth of winter"). The *Times*, probably referring to the same river, called it the Sauer and said that he had denied swimming in it.

Then there is the matter of narrow escapes. Several of the papers were in accord that he had had three during the European campaign. One was when a large dud shell hit eight feet from his motor vehicle, which is close. Another occurred when a shell hit his headquarters while he wasn't there, which seems to me a rather commonplace type of escape, like that of the people who don't take trains for Miami that get wrecked. On the third escape, however, there was disagreement. The *Herald Tribune* said it happened when flak hit his private plane. The *Times* said it was when a German fighter dived at the plane and Patton's pilot had to touch down quickly. The *Herald Tribune* didn't mention the fighter. The *Times* didn't mention the flak. Could there have been two separate episodes, or did the flak hit the fighter? Mackenzie, the *Daily News* man, added to the standard three/four escapes one that nobody else recorded. He said he had seen a bridge at Chartres blow up "right in Patton's face," covering him with mortar dust but not causing him to turn a hair. Mackenzie could not have been sure of that if the General was wearing a hat. The Plutarchs will learn from practically all the obits that when Patton was a young lieutenant, posted to a new regiment, he asked his commanding officer if there was stabling for his mounts and, when assured that there was, appeared with a whole string of polo ponies. But whereas the *Herald Tribune* said there were a dozen ponies, the *Sun* said twenty-six. And one of the papers even said that only one of his sidearms was a pearl-handled six-shooter. The other, it stated, was a .45 automatic, which he never completely trusted.

The General's temperamental difficulties were conscientiously minimized. The *Mirror's* Mr. Adams said, "Frequently criticized at home, his impetuousness won nothing but admiration from the embattled English and the liberated French." Adams added that Patton got quick results: "When his Third Army slowed at the approaches to the formidable fortress of Metz for lack of gasoline, he acted without hesitation. Officers were sent to the rear with authority to halt all supply vehicles, dump their loads, and send them back for gas. . . . Patton got his fuel." The fact is that in real life Patton got nothing, and his army was stalled for want of gas—though it was not his fault—for two months. "The thing that we [Third Army correspondents] loved him most for," Mackenzie said, "was that he never took one cent of his pay. He sent it all back to soldiers' charities. Patton was a millionaire and didn't have to fight for money." Even a Third Army correspondent, it seems to me, should have understood that being a millionaire made it easier for Patton to give his pay away. What interested me was the implication that all soldiers not millionaires did fight for money.

The most important thing that any of the obit authors set down about Patton, I think, was buried in the body of a story by Robert Richards of the United Press which I read in the *Mirror*. "Despite his reckless reputation in battle, he seldom wasted lives," Richards wrote. "He took big chances only when the stakes were worth it." As Ingersoll said the next day, "He saved many lives. . . . He won battles with thousands of men that might have taken other generals tens of thousands to win."

Patton labored under continual anxiety. Cautious, hardworking, and terribly ambitious, he was the kind of competitor who, in the old Greek phrase, always smelled of the oil of the gymnasium rubbing room. At West Point he never missed football practice but could never make the team. At polo he developed slowly, by dint of enormous concentration and heavy expenditure for mounts. His highest handicap, 4, was attained in 1932, when he was forty-seven years old. He built up his professional skills in the same way, by internal sweat, but he had them ready by the time of the war. The clownish, swashbuckling façade was as spontaneous as the lobby display at Radio City Music Hall.

I can think of several officers other than Patton who might have commanded the Third Army, but nobody but Theodore Dreiser could have

written *Sister Carrie*. Only the *Times* and the *Journal-American*, however, thought Dreiser's death worthy of a place on Page 1. He made
Page 8 in the *Sun*, 11 in the *World-Telegram*, and 12 in the *Herald
Tribune*, which in 1944 devoted a two-column spread on the front page
to the end of William Allen White. The hands that performed the latest
revisions of the Dreiser obituaries evidently belonged to men for whom
he was already a figure of the past.

Literary historians will have as many conflicts to resolve if they take
the Dreiser obits seriously as the military boys will be up against reading
the Patton pieces. The *Times* and the *World-Telegram*, for example,
said flatly that Dreiser, when he died, was a member of the Communist
party, but the *Sun* said, "He was never accepted as a member of the
party," and the *Herald Tribune* said only, "On his sixty-fourth birthday
he told interviewers he was through with Communism."

The *Journal-American* obit writer said of *Sister Carrie*, "That novel,
which, by today's standards, is comparatively harmless, deals simply
with the sorrowful life of a village maiden in a big city." The *Herald
Tribune* said, more accurately, that the great protest against *Carrie* in
1900, when the book appeared, was based on the circumstances that the
heroine was not a maiden and that the story nevertheless had a reasonably happy ending. The *Journal-American* also said that "Dreiser's struggle against the school of Dean [sic] Howells and Louisa May Alcott,
his fight against the prettyfying of the basic facts of living, opened the
door to an era that gave the world such writers as Sinclair Lewis and
William Faulkner." These pairings seemed to me a bit mysterious, but
at least the sentiment was right.

The *World-Telegram* held Dreiser down to six paragraphs, including
the statement about his party affiliation; the *Post* said pontifically that
he was "oversentimental from his earliest days in Terre Haute, Ind.,"
and the *Sun* was sober and factual (except about the party matter).
But the *Herald Tribune*'s story, I thought, was the daisy of the lot.
Nastily patronizing, it began with the premise that Dreiser did not know
how to write. "In 1921 the New York *Tribune* wrote of him," the *Herald Tribune* said in 1945, " 'he is probably the worst writer who ever
wrote a good novel in the history of all literature.' " Since the measure of
writing is its total aesthetic effect, this makes as little sense as a reference
to a bad cook who produces excellent food. Some good books are better
written than others, some bad books are worse written than others. *Herald Tribune* '45 contained no hint of who the *Tribune* '21 critic was,
or what he has written since, or whom among his contemporaries he
considered "good writers."

Having put old Dreiser in his place, the *Tribune* obit man must have reached for another batch of envelopes, which turned out to be full of clippings about the time, in 1931, the deceased had slapped Sinclair Lewis's face. The *Herald Tribune* treated this significant episode at considerably greater length than the story of how Patton slapped the soldier. Mr. Lewis, the obit noted, had (before the slapping, of course) told reporters that if the 1930 Nobel prize had not gone to him, it should have gone to Dreiser. The obit writer seemed to feel that Dreiser should have been grateful.

The obit went on to quote "one critic" who said of Mr. Dreiser that "he was himself an American Tragedy," and to recite his participation in "various liberal movements that caught his fancy," as a result of which "he raised his voice again and again" as his "liberalism gained momentum." It also talked a lot about a dispute Dreiser had with Paramount Pictures and three times referred to his novel *Jennie Gerhardt* as *Jennie Gebhardt*. There was nothing in it to indicate that Dreisers outrank four-star generals.

The Colonel Looks on Marathon

MARCH 25, 1950

PERIODICALLY, Col. Robert Rutherford McCormick, publisher of the World's Greatest Newspaper, quits his atomic-bomb-proof eyrie in his Symphony in Stone, the Tribune Tower, in Chicago, to soar off into the Wild Blue Yonder on a mission of aerial reportage. These missions are flown in a converted Flying Fortress named, in honor of the World's Greatest Newspaper, the "Chicago Tribune." The Colonel bought the flying Chicago Tribune—as distinguished from the printed one, which he inherited—out of government surplus, in 1948. There had been overproduction of Fortresses during the war, he told *Tribune* readers at the time, and he had got it for less than the price of a small new plane. From the points where he alights, the Colonel tells *Tribune* readers what the world outside looks like to him (pretty dismal, except for a few bright spots, such as General MacArthur's Japan and General Franco's Spain). The proprietor of Dick Tracy, Moon Mullins, and John O'Donnell does not permit the syndication of his own contributions. By reserving them for the *Tribune,* he may feel that he is protecting the publication's position *as* the World's Greatest Newspaper. Whatever his reasons, as I have discovered while making Chicago my temporary headquarters, he is unjust to readers in less favored regions. For the Colonel is a travel writer in the great tradition, like de Tocqueville, Lemuel Gulliver, and George Borrow, and he brings back memories of Tom Swift and his balloon. The countries he visits merely provide background.

The Colonel is currently abroad on the fifth reconnaissance of importance he has made since the recent war. His entourage includes his wife, her daughter by a former marriage, a woman secretary, and a lady's maid, in addition to five crewmen. On the Christmas card that the Colonel and his lady sent to *Tribune* employees last December was a photograph showing the couple standing beside the flying Chicago Tribune with their luggage. In the upper right-hand corner of the card was the line, "To the ends of the earth we go, go, go—Kipling." Although he was British, and an Empire man at that, Kipling is one of the Colonel's favorite poets.

A map and timetable of the Colonel's itinerary are published in the *Tribune* before each departure. On the present journey, which has been called by WGN, the McCormick radio station, "a three-continent fact-finding flight," the Colonel was scheduled to inspect Bermuda, the Azores, Spain, Greece, Egypt, Saudi Arabia, Pakistan, India, Burma, Thailand, Iran, Turkey, Italy, France, Denmark, and Iceland, in that order. On March 4, however, at which time the Colonel had reached Karachi, it was announced that he would skip Burma, because of "discouraging reports," and the *Tribune* of March 11 let it be known that he would also omit Iran. The latter news was carried in a modest Reuters dispatch, datelined Teheran, that read: "Col. Robert R. McCormick, editor and publisher of the Chicago *Tribune,* has notified the American embassy here that he has canceled his visit to Iran scheduled for March 14. He had already had 'satisfactory talks' with Shah Mohammed Riza Pahlevi in Pakistan, where he attended a dinner in the Shah's honer, he said."

The same day's *Tribune* carried the following Associated Press item from Bangkok: "Col. Robert R. McCormick, editor and publisher of the Chicago *Tribune,* left today in his private plane for New Delhi, India. Col. McCormick, who during his two-day visit here had talked with Premier Pibul Songgram, said he believed the premier is conscious of the Communist threat to his country. He added that Thailand appears relatively prosperous."

These are not outstanding examples of the Colonel's knack of reaching and communicating conclusions rapidly. In an interview granted to Percy Wood, a *Tribune* correspondent, and some Egyptian newspapermen, in Cairo on March 2, the Colonel engineered a scoop of sorts by reporting on the condition of France, which he was not scheduled to visit until March 24. "France is atheist and anarchic," he said. "Her greatest hero, Pétain, is held in prison by his political opposition."

There is, though, evidently some limit to the Colonel's power of reporting by anticipation—a journalistic innovation, incidentally, almost as important as the method of judging newspapers by their gross weight, which the *Tribune* revealed in 1946.* He can report on a country three weeks before he goes to it, but not a full year before. "Asked to comment on the British election results," Mr. Wood wrote, "the publisher said, 'Ask me a year from now. I'm going there next year.' He said that a Truman-Stalin conference would be useless, because 'no statesman ever keeps his word.' The publisher added, however," Wood continued, "that 'we can lick everyone, including Russia.' Declaring that individuals bring on war, Col. McCormick said, 'The last one was caused by Hitler and Roosevelt; maybe the next one will be brought about by Truman and Stalin.' " (Colonel McCormick then went in for one of those historical digressions that are his specialty. "Empires, except the Roman, don't last," he told Mr. Wood and the Egyptians, whose land was once the seat of a fairly durable empire itself. "The Turkish empire didn't last, nor did that of Louis XIV, nor Hitler's. The British Empire didn't last, and the Russian empire won't." This marked a slight switch in the Colonel's historical line. On February 20, he had told the Associated Press in Newark, "There has never been a successful empire since Charlemagne's." By March 2, he had apparently decided that Charlemagne was a bust.)

In Madrid, on February 23 (I'm making no effort here to keep Colonel McCormick's observations in chronological order), the publisher told Spanish reporters and the Associated Press that he believed the dangers of atomic warfare to be overrated (despite his preparations for protecting Tribune Tower workers against atomic radiation). "It would be hard on little, concentrated countries like England," he said. "In the United States we have lots of space."

* This story, besides recording an epoch-making discovery in journalometry, is an outstanding example of the *Tribune*'s depth reporting. Their foreign correspondent, like his patron and pattern, is historically minded.

On March 6, in Karachi, Reuters reported, and the *Tribune* duly noted, Colonel McCormick invited Liaquat Ali Khan, the Pakistani Prime Minister, to have lunch with him at Cantigny Farm, the publisher's estate near Wheaton, Illinois, sometime this spring. After lunch on the forthcoming occasion, according to the dispatch, "a number of Pakistani women in the Prime Minister's party will go shopping in Chicago with Mrs. McCormick." The Colonel was reported to have "commended the self-reliance, energy, and high purpose of Pakistan's statesmen." (It was Liaquat Ali Khan who arranged the dinner with the Shah, a providential visitor in Karachi, and thus made the Colonel's trip to Iran unnecesary.) The Egyptian statesmen didn't come off so well. Once he had left Cairo, the Colonel, a Reuters man wrote, "denounced the new Egyptian constitution as a complete phony." In Bombay, the Colonel, as filtered through Reuters, "denounced President Truman's civil-rights program as a new form of slavery." He said, "I believe every employee must have freedom to choose his employer and every employer freedom to choose his employee." (He did not say, as far as I could make out, what happens when the choice is not reciprocal.) The *Tribune* headline on this story read

COL. MCCORMICK

HITS AT TRUMAN

ON CIVIL RIGHTS

and must have made many of that newspaper's readers think the Colonel was already back home.

All these third-person dispatches, even though most of them include quotes, are dilute stuff for straight-McCormick addicts, however. We prefer the species of first-person journalism that he sends along under his own by-lines—"By Col. R. R. McCormick," to fit in a single column, and "By Col. Robert R. McCormick" when he has a double. This, for us, is the Real McCormick.

The Colonel, as a travel writer, points for one big Sunday piece each week, which is also read over WGN at nine o'clock, Central Standard Time, on Saturday evening, as part of a radio program called "Chicago Theater of the Air," which he has sponsored since 1940. The reading is sandwiched in between halves of a cut-down version of some operetta or musical comedy, the director accelerating the tempo of the performance if there is an unusually large amount of McCormick to be squeezed into the middle. When in residence, the Colonel appears at the studio, and generally reads an address on some historical incident in British-

American relations—the Battle of New Orleans, for example. When he is on the wing, he carries on by recorded voice or by deputy. Collections of the Colonel's addresses, well printed on heavy paper, are to be had free of charge at the Tribune Tower, but a request for them there, I have found by personal experiment, elicits a certain amount of astonishment.

Colonel McCormick's weekend piece does not always absorb all his creative energy while traveling, and he sometimes can't wait to jack up the standards of the World's Greatest Newspaper. The first McCormick by-liner of the present *tournée,* under the head COL. MCCORMICK TELLS ABOUT HIS BERMUDA FLIGHT, appeared on Wednesday, February 22. It was briefer than many, but it set the mood for a trip through space with the man who has admitted introducing the machine gun to the Army, light opera to the American public, and aspirin to atomic warfare. It read, in part: "After a tiresome delay which one experiences only from New York customs officers and posing for a few pictures in the cold wind [a *Tribune* photographer, Al Madsen, is also a member of his party], we took off yesterday for Bermuda at 4:30 P.M. . . . followed by a 55-mile an hour wind, we lost sight of land in 15 minutes more. . . . Over the ocean, of course, there are no landmarks, but we passed four checkpoints where the navigator pinpoints his position by triangulation. From above the clouds we could see no ships. After dark, the northern lights came out. I have not asked whether they are used as navigational aids. . . . The lights of Bermuda appeared at 8 P.M., New York time, and I said what I had not mentioned before—that, with a 55-mile per hour wind, our survival equipment would not be any better than a 5 cent cigar."

The Colonel is intrepid, but he knows *Tribune* readers worry about him. In 1948, when he bought the winged Chicago Tribune, he sought to reassure his public by devoting most of a "Chicago Theater of the Air" address to a review of the safety factors involved. "Hot and cold food and coffee will be taken on at the different stops, as we do not propose to risk the additional hazard of a stove," he said then. "Neither will there be any smoking on board, and matches taken along for emergency will be in hermetically sealed metal boxes. . . . Calculations indicate that in a four-engine plane two engines will fail together once in 250,000 flights. The same odds are that one could make a million flights before three of four engines would fail simultaneously. . . . If one or two of my engines go out I can make port on the others. Stationed in the North Atlantic Ocean are seven weather-rescue ships on a full-time basis and another on a half-time basis. . . . All these ships have experienced crews aboard . . . constantly standing by for rescue, should their assistance be required. . . . If it were conceivable that both of the pilots should become incapacitated, any one of the other crew members [radio operator, engineer, and navigator] can make a safe landing on an airfield. . . . If all of the crew should become incapacitated, I can hold the plane on an even keel and hit Europe somewhere, in which event the passengers and crews will have to bail out." Happily, the assistance of the rescue ships was not needed. Since then, *Tribune* readers have grown accustomed to the Colonel's flights, and now, when he takes to the air, they are able to bear the strain.

The Colonel followed his dispatch from Bermuda with a by-liner, twenty-four hours later, headed COL. MCCORMICK REACHES MADRID. The piece ran about two columns. The Colonel did not miss the chance for another shot at Gomorrah. "After New York City . . . it was pleasant to get here where there is plenty of water and you don't feel you are depriving someone else when you take a bath," he wrote. "The first stop on our aerial tour was Bermuda," he continued, by way of recapitulation. "Everybody knows that Bermuda is a first-class winter resort." After a short disquisition on the geology of the islands, the Colonel noted, with perhaps a wistful thought for Chicago: "There is segregation of races in the schools and a rather small minority of white people keep control of the legislature by a heavy property qualification. All of the police are white. On the other hand, the colored people are contented and extremely well off."

"We had a little turbulence as we left the island," the report from Madrid also noted. "Then it became extremely cold. . . . From this, and from habit, I was up several times in the night. Of course, legally, I was only a passenger and all five [members of the crew] were vastly superior to me in air knowledge, but the years of responsibility could not be shaken off." The Colonel got the plane safely to the mainland, after a stopover in the Azores, with which he was not greatly taken, finding the peasants poor. "Our soldiers make the best ambassadors we have, with their polite manners, their high education, and high standard of living," he wrote. "The Portuguese, however, are suspicious of their intentions, due partly to the fact that when the English came to Portugal to fight Napoleon they shipped all of the Portuguese industries to England and kept them there, and also because they learned of Roosevelt's plan to occupy the Azores in times of peace."

The Colonel said nothing about Madrid in that dispatch (aside from announcing that he had arrived there), probably because he wanted to save his best stuff for the Sunday paper. But an Associated Press interviewer at the airport there quoted him as saying his present tour would be the end of his travels. "I have been everywhere else," the Colonel declared. "This will be my last big trip." I was sorry to hear it, and glad to read a week later that he had apparently reconsidered and would be going to Britain in a year. The AP story from Madrid also recorded for *Tribune* readers the embarrassing mistake about the Spanish Republican flag that had been painted on the Colonel's plane instead of the Franco flag. The Colonel had evidently forgotten to read copy on his fuselage.

In Colonel McCormick's first Sunday piece from Madrid, he wrote that he had had an interview with General Franco, whom he called "the originator of war as we have known it for the last fifteen years." Franco, according to the Colonel, "originated the maneuver of moving troops by air." (This innovation, by the way, has also been credited by the Colonel to Ulysses S. Grant. At the time he gave Grant the laurels, he explained that the Civil War General had moved troops by train but pointed out that the principle was the same.) The Colonel also wrote that Franco had invented dive-bombing. (Colonel McCormick never cites authority, being it.)

Elsewhere in his report after interviewing Franco, the Colonel executed two journalistic maneuvers that were as innovational, in their way, as the martial ones he attributed to his subject. For one thing, he began his story, "I have just come from an interview with Gen. Franco," and then didn't tell anything the General had said. And he displayed even more originality in facing a problem that has long baffled many other reporters—how to present a colorful introduction without pushing the main part of the story down to the bottom of the page. The Colonel accomplished this by simply leaving out the introductory material and running it a week after what it was supposed to lead up to. His first piece, the main part of the story, consisted of an account of the Spanish Civil War as the flying publisher sees it in retrospect. The American government, he said, sent "a Communist brigade, outrageously named Lincoln, to fight with the Spanish Communists. These men fought well, but did as much harm to their cause by their cruelty to civilians." Despite the presence of this expeditionary force, the Colonel continued, Franco, with some German and Italian assistance, "originated the original blitzkrieg, broke through the defense, and rushed on without stopping to the capture of Barcelona. This practically ended the resistance. Franco granted amnesty to all nationalist soldiers who were not convicted of atrocities. Perhaps his trial of those guilty of atrocities furnished the example for allied trials of war criminals after the World War, but not for Justice Jackson's legalized murder of German political leaders. Franco's strategy was in the best tradition. His tactics were original. Whether Guderian or Patton improved upon them is open to question, but no one denies that they imitated him. [No one except the Colonel, so far as I know, has even suggested it.] So Franco remains the greatest general to appear on the European scene. MacArthur's great strategy of the Pacific was of a different nature. . . . Whatever we think of [Franco's] political principles, no one can question his idealism or his patriotism. In addition to being a great general, he may turn out to be a great statesman."

The second weekend piece from Madrid, in which Colonel McCormick presented the introductory material about his visit there, was entitled "Spain and Greece" and shared the WGN bill with *No, No, Nanette,* after which it went a double-and-a-single on the editorial page. With it, I thought, the Colonel really hit his stride. "The time of the last broadcast did not permit me to give my full impression of Madrid," he started off. "The approach to Generalissimo Franco's home presented the most dramatic peacetime picture I have ever seen. He lives in a former royal hunting lodge, I should say about the size of the late Potter Palmer mansion. [The reference is to a large and hideous Chicago residence that has just been torn down.] Following a straight avenue, we [I assume he means himself and Mrs. McCormick] first perceived two horsemen who, on closer approach, were seen to be two Moorish cavalrymen on Arab horses. On their heads were octagonal steel spiked helmets. Their robes covered the lower part of their faces. Reins and accoutrements looked like the middle ages. Two flags were at the end of the lances which they dipped in salute as we passed by." After describing three more sets of guards and some tapestries, the Colonel reported that he had been "introduced into the presence of the Generalissimo, who, in his capacity of chief of state, was in civilian clothes." He then continued: "Last week, I told of the interview. [He had apparently forgotten that he hadn't.] As we departed, the guard of honor was dismissed. . . . How different it was some years ago when I called on King Alfonso at his massive palace in Madrid." Alfonso had been guarded by "pikesmen in shabby clothes who clashed their halberds on the floor as they had done in the time of Henry V," the Colonel reminisced, and this had given him the tipoff on Alfonso, "an energetic, clever man who, however, could not resist the changing times."

"Taking off for a night flight, we passed first over Barcelona and then over Rome—the grandeur that was Rome," the second Sunday report continued. "The ghosts of the Caesars are grinding their ghostly teeth that their capital has become a checkpoint for airplane flights." En route to Athens, the Colonel learned that his pilots had received some faulty weather information from the Azores. "When we come back across the North Atlantic, I hope the same joker will not be on duty," he said, and then, "Returning to Athens after 30 years, I recognized only the old palace, much like a New England summer hotel, the Stadium, and, of course, the Acropolis. The Acropolis, obviously, has not changed. Except for when it was blown up by the Venetians in the 17th century, I do not suppose it has changed since Pericles built it with money from the subject states that should have been used for self-defense and caused the fall of Athens. . . . The ECA (Economic Cooperation Administration), anxious to brief me on its efforts, pointed out the roads it had built, so superior to those of Illinois, and the railroad it had rebuilt with money taxed from American railroads. . . . My informants appeared intelligent and were clearly sincere. Like others, they have taken the best jobs they could find and were performing them to the best of their ability. It is at home that the 5 percenters are doing the collecting. Our [nation's] presence in Greece was the work of the English wing of the State Department. . . . The Hitler plan to get control of the Suez Canal route to India was being adopted by the Russians. . . . The State Department plan to use the American Army to protect this British pipeline was, of course, backed by the beneficiaries of ECA expense. . . . How futile it has all been is perceived when we see Egypt, India, Ceylon, and Thailand all free and the Suez Canal of no further use to a vanishing empire."

Some good may yet result, though, the Colonel decided. The Greeks, he observed, are learning from the Americans "a way of life they could not have learned otherwise."

"The [American] Army has shown them the power of the Republic," the Colonel said. "The navy, also in the Mediterranean to protect the lifeline to India, points out to the nations along its shores that Columbia rules the waves. . . . The elaborate plans under a clever deception, to return our Republic to European control, are defeating themselves. The Republic is pushing forward in Europe.

"And so, as I take off across the ancient battlefields, I recall the words of Byron:

> *The mountains look on Marathon*
> *And Marathon looks on the sea;*

And musing there an hour alone,
I dreamed that Greece might still be free."

Maybe Colonel McCormick is going to become a convert to the Truman Plan, after all.

My Name in Big Letters

IN SEPTEMBER, 1930, when I left the *Journal,* it was apparent that Mr. Hoover had laid his egg. But I had a plan to get a job. I had thought of it so often that I didn't see how it could fail. . . .

As soon as we got to New York, I looked in the classified telephone directory for a sign painter. I found one with a shop fairly near the Grand Central Station and ordered a sign to be carried by a sandwich man. The sign was to say, front and rear, "Hire Joe Liebling." The sign painter, a Hungarian who liked to use bright colors, advised an orange job with blue lettering. It cost eleven dollars, fully rigged. I gave him a five-dollar deposit. He promised he would have it ready next day.

I then went down to Battery Park, where there always were sandwich men advertising passport photographers. The passport bureau was at the Custom House then; there was none at Radio City because Radio City hadn't been built. I addressed myself to a man who was carrying a sign that said 6 PHOTOS FOR 75 CENTS, and asked him if he knew any sandwich men at liberty who would consider an engagement for a couple of days. He said sure, there were lots of colleagues laying off, because the volume of display advertising had fallen off drastically. He lived in a rooming house on Greenwich Street, under the elevated railway, that was largely patronized by sandwich men. He promised to find a good reliable practitioner for me. The regular tariff, he said, was two dollars a day. I said I would want the man only from early noon to sundown. Jim Barrett, the city editor of the *World,* was the man I wanted to see the sign, and Barrett wasn't at the office mornings. I guess I wasn't interested in a job on the *Evening World.* I gave my sandwich man friend the sign painter's address and told him to have his candidate meet me there at noon next day.

The man who reported to me on the morrow was a superannuated Norwegian seaman named, with startling originality, Larsen. He wore a full beard. I considered this an extra attention-getter which made him a bargain at the two-dollar rate. I gave him his sign and his instructions. He was to walk up and down Park Row in front of the entrance to the Pulitzer Building, and not talk to anybody unless they asked him what the sign meant. If that happened he was to say he didn't know. But he would report to me at six each evening in front of a cafeteria on the west side of City Hall Park, to describe the people who had asked him questions. We then rode downtown together on the subway and I told him to go to work.

I watched him for a while from a bench in City Hall Park. Seeing my name on the sign made me feel self-conscious and furtive, as if the people around me knew who I was. Larsen was a good, experienced sandwich man. I could tell from the way he slid his feet over the sidewalk. It must be extremely difficult to walk that slow without standing still. After a time I got tired of seeing my name in big letters and went away for a walk of my own without getting paid for it.

At six I kept my rendezvous with Larsen and bought him a dinner at the cafeteria. As we ate I asked him about his day. Nobody had spoken to him whose description at all resembled Barrett's. It had been my hope, of course, that Barrett would see him. It would hit Barrett right on the funny bone and he would see what a resourceful young fellow I was. When I walked in, perfectly deadpan, and sent in my name to him, he would start laughing again and ask me to come in and choose a job. I arranged with the boss of the cafeteria to leave the sign in his basement overnight so Larsen could get it next afternoon.

Again I went to the park to watch him, and again I met him at the cafeteria at six. People by now had accepted his presence, it seemed, and weren't asking questions. Maybe they thought Joe Liebling was another passport photographer. After the third day I figured Barrett must have at least heard of the gag, so I paid Larsen off for the last time and stowed the sign away in a friend's apartment, where for all I know it still is.

On the fourth afternoon I went to see Barrett. He greeted me cordially but without any unusual emotion. "I hadn't any idea you were in town," he said. "Thought you were still up in Providence."

I didn't know whether or not he was kidding me, but I weakened. "Haven't you seen my sign?" I asked pitifully.

He said no, he hadn't. When I told him about it, he said that he always used the rear entrance to the building, on William Street, so that it was no wonder that he hadn't seen a sandwich man walking on Park Row. He thought it was a funny story, but it hadn't proved to him that I was very resourceful. I should have either learned Barrett's route in advance or made the old sailorman circumnavigate the building instead of just working one door. Barrett said the *World* wasn't hiring—nobody was. The panic was on.

I eventually recovered the capital I had invested in the sandwich-man deal.

I sold the story of the misadventure to the Sunday *World* metropolitan section, at space rates, for twelve-fifty, late that year, and in January sold it again to *Editor & Publisher,* the newspaper trade magazine, for seven-fifty. As I had paid out only eleven dollars for the sign and six dollars in wages, this left me with a net profit of three dollars, if you don't count my time or the meals I bought for Larsen.

Synonyms

❧ ❧

ONCE THE TEXT has been cleared, the sports copyreader has a chance for his nearest approach to creative effort: the composition of a headline. This is a form of art, like the Japanese hokku or writing on the head of a pin, which must be exercised within extremely exiguous limits. One form of head I remember called for two lines of 16½ spaces maximum (16 was preferable) with a dozen words falling away under them in an inverted pyramid called a bank. A space is a unit used in headline writing, roughly equivalent to the space a letter takes up. However, M and W count 1½ spaces, and I counts only ½. The interval between two words is counted a ½-space. So a fellow can write GIANTS BEAT (or DEFEAT, STOP, TOPPLE, BATTER) REDS, but just GIANTS TRIP PIRATES, because PIRATES is 2½ spaces longer than REDS. GIANTS TRIP PIRATES would not look quite so crowded. In the second line you can elaborate: 2-1 AS OTT HOMERS, perhaps. Of course not many ballplayers have names as easy to fit into a headline as Ott. You'd be surprised how quickly an evening passes amid big intellectual problems like that.

To top is probably the most useful headline synonym for to beat, defeat. It occupies only *three* spaces. The trouble with it is that sometimes all the copyreaders on a desk start to use it simultaneously and every baseball headline has somebody topping somebody else. Then the man in the slot gets stuffy and accuses his subordinates, the men on the rim, of a certain lack of originality.

I once did one long, hard job of rewrite. There was a big fire in Fall River, Massachusetts. We had an office there, but the two or three men who staffed it were not nearly enough to cover the story. So most of the night staff of the *Journal* was sent down to the fire, and I remained in the office to write the running story as they telephoned it in. I did at least five thousand words that night. It taught me how few synonyms there are for fire—just blaze, flames, and conflagration, and conflagration is lousy. I must have used each about four hundred times. Some fellows that age would have weakened and used "holocaust," but I didn't, and it is one of the few things in my journalistic career of which I am justly proud.

Interviewers

BEFORE INTERVIEWING Gamelin, I knew that I would have to document myself on his views, his past, and enough of his technical background and jargon to make him feel that I knew what he was talking about. The preparation is the same whether you are going to interview a diplomat, a jockey, or an ichthyologist. From the man's past you learn what questions are likely to stimulate a response; after he gets going, you say just enough to let him know you appreciate what he is saying and to make him want to talk more. Everybody with any sense talks a kind of shorthand; if you make a man stop to explain everything, he will soon quit on you, like a horse that you alternately spur and curb. It is all in one of Sam Langford's principles of prizefighting: "Make him lead." Only instead of countering to your subject's chin, you keep him leading. Once I asked Sam what he did when the other man wouldn't lead, and he said, "I run him out of the ring." This is a recourse not open to the interviewer.

In the summer of 1940 I went up to the Hotel Carlton in Washington to talk to Gen. John J. Pershing about the subject of a profile I was then working on. I did everything I could to get the old man to loosen up, including pretty obvious flattery.

"When they started to cut down the Army after the Armistice in 1918, General," I said, "you were against it, weren't you, because you foresaw this new European crisis?"

The old boy looked at me in an angry, disgusted manner and said, "Who the hell could have foreseen this?"

The worst thing an interviewer can do is talk a lot himself. Just listening to reporters in a barroom, you can tell the ones who go out and impress their powerful personalities on their subject and then come back and make up what they think he would have said if he had had a chance to say anything.

One of the best preps I ever did was for a profile of Eddie Arcaro, the jockey. When I interviewed him the first question I asked was "How many holes longer do you keep your left stirrup than your right?" Most jockeys on American tracks ride longer on their left side.

That started him talking easily, and after an hour, during which I had put in about twelve words, he said, "I can see you've been around riders a lot."

I had, but only during the week before I was to meet him.

There is almost no circumstance under which an American doesn't like to be interviewed, an observation which I have had a chance to verify in cracks in the Tunisian rocks, under mortar fire. We are an articulate people, pleased by attention, covetous of being singled out.

Experts

Now AND THEN I enunciate a truth with such clarity that I hate to boggle with the wording afterward—it is suitable for framing. Thus:

There are three kinds of writers of news in our generation. In inverse order of worldly consideration, they are:

1. The reporter, who writes what he sees.
2. The interpretive reporter, who writes what he sees and what he construes to be its meaning.
3. The expert, who writes what he construes to be the meaning of what he hasn't seen.

To combat an old human prejudice in favor of eyewitness testimony, which is losing ground even in our courts of law, the expert must intimate that he has access to some occult source or science not available to either reporter or reader. He is the Priest of Eleusis, the man with the big picture. Once his position is conceded, the expert can put on a better show than the reporter. All is manifest to him, since his conclusions are not limited by his powers of observation. Logistics, to borrow a word from the military species of the genus, favor him, since it is possible to not see many things at the same time. For example, a correspondent cannot cover a front and the Pentagon simultaneously. An expert can, and from an office in New York, at that.

Foreign News

THE LAZY MIND, faced by recurrent but changing problems, takes refuge in a formula. This may be a religion, a pill, or a system for playing the horses. When dullness is compounded with avarice, it is even surer to happen. The farmer who won't see a doctor takes Carter's Little Liver Pills for every ailment. The bettor who has neither the imagination to see nor the intelligence to treat every race as a new problem, buys for five dollars a "system," based on progression in wagering, or track condition, or astrology.

Nothing so infuriates the dullard as the failure of his formula, which always occurs. Nothing so delights me as the spectacle, if I am safely clear of the wreckage. I find no ballad more exhilarating than the one about the railroad train that blew, she blew, with its delightfully detailed description of the individual consequences: the flagman, for example, who rolled on the grass, and where his flagpole lodged. When one is a passenger on the train, though, it is less amusing, and we are all dependent on this rambling wreck of an industry for our sense of direction.

The formulas most newspapers have fallen back on for foreign news are few. One is "Man go to church, good man, no lie. Man not go to church, bad, lie." ERGO: "Franco, Salazar, Adenauer, Christian Democrats, good, truthful. Communists, bad, whatever they say lie." In handling any story outside the United States, then, it is necessarily true, and you have solved your problem in reporting without trouble or expense.

Thus, as an example of formula thinking, if Sicilians riot because living conditions are ghastly, and a Communist leader says, later, "Look at Sicily, living conditions are ghastly," then *living conditions cease to be ghastly*. By agreeing with *any* charge, the Communist takes the truth out of it, first, because he is trying to turn it to his own advantage—which, to revert for a moment to nonformula sanity, has not one thing to do with whether it is true or not—second, because even if it were not true it would be to his advantage, so he would invent it. It is therefore a lie, because (*a*) Communists are liars, they do not go to church; (*b*) they invented it. And the Sicilians themselves are liars, because they allowed the Communists to agree with them, thus putting themselves in the position of people who agree with liars. How can you agree truthfully on what is necessarily a lie?

The thing to do, for anybody a Communist agrees with, is to retract his original statement. Else he becomes a fellow traveler. You are on a train and a Communist gets on. That makes you a fellow traveler just as much as if the Communist were on the train first and *you* got on.

A second formula is that *all* trouble is the fault of Communists. Trouble means anything like Cubans getting mad because American sailors make water on a statue; they wouldn't have been so particular if Communists hadn't put them up to it. It was Communistic not to like Clark Gable. No surer test, except maybe hot dogs and hamburgers and miyulk. Anybody that would rather drink wine than miyulk is a Red, sure as the Chicago *Tribune* is the World's Greatest Newspaper.

These and a couple of allied formulas eliminate the trouble of finding out what the hell is going on, which a number of troublemakers used to say was part of the function of a newspaper. They save money, too. Or perhaps, to preserve the order of importance of these points to newspaper owners, I should switch the two preceding sentences around.

Smörgåsbord

NEWS-MAGAZINE coverage is of course supplementary. *Time* and the David Lawrence thing perform the service of the waiter-captain who meets you in front of the *smörgåsbord* table and says, "Let me help you make a selection." He then fills your plate with all the items the management particularly wants to get rid of. They specialize in réchauffés of newspaper dispatches, livened with sauces prepared on the premises. (At Time Inc., you are likely to get a bit of Chiang Kai-shek straight out of the deepfreeze with every meal.)

In *Time*'s beginnings this was all its foreign service consisted of, and since its proprietor made a great deal of money that way, he cannot see any use for reporters of his own. He has a considerable number now, including, for limited spans now and then, some good ones. But he has never been able to bring himself to believe them unless they tell him what he already thinks.

❦ ❦

Newspaper photographs of Earl Long were usually taken without warning when he was scratching his pants, or when a reporter acting as the photographer's picador had provoked him into a scream of rage.

One-Ownerships

❦ ❦

THERE ARE one-ownership newspaper cities like Providence, as I have acknowledged, where the readers, like subjects of a benevolent despot, are a bit better off for news than those of other cities, like Boston, where a low-grade competition persists. There are also cities, like New Orleans, where the over-power in silly hands has led to large-scale disaster. There the *Times-Picayune* company, which owned the only morning paper and the *States*, one of the two evenings, bought the *Item*, the other evening paper, "forcing to the wall" the competing publisher by pressing 3.5 million dollars against his navel.

Further note: Mr. S. I. Newhouse has now bought the *Times-Picayune* company, with the *Item* in its belly, for 42 million dollars, proving that the newspaper industry is in financial straits.

❦ ❦

My point here is not only that there are evil, or potty, or capricious, as well as benevolent, despots, but that it is evil that men anywhere be forced to depend, for the information on which they must govern their lives, on the caprice of anybody at all. There should be a great, free, living stream of information, and equal access to it for all. Our present news situation, in the United States, is breaking down to something like the system of water distribution in a Casbah, where peddlers wander about with goatskins of water on small donkeys, and the inhabitants send down an oil tin and a couple of pennies when they feel thirst.

Vox Pop

NEWSPAPERS WRITE about other newspapers with circumspection. The two surviving press associations, whose customers are newspapers, write about newspapers with deference. Newspapers write about themselves with awe, and only after mature reflection. They know and revere their awful power; like a prizefighter in a bar full of non-prizefighters, they are loath to loose it. That is why they wait until late in a Presidential campaign to let the public know which man they support. The public is not supposed to be able to guess.

The newspaper of even moderate self-esteem thinks that if it stated at the beginning of a campaign which candidate it favored, the other fellow might cancel his speaking engagements and quit. To avert this contretemps, the newspaper holds its right cocked as long as possible, or until the unsuspecting fellow it is going to hit has got so far along with his campaign that he will be ashamed to pull out. The newspaper bites its editorial lip—or, more accurately, the publisher bites the editor's lip. On 80 per cent of American newspapers, he makes the editor restrain himself until he can see the whites of the Democrats' eyes. On a dwindling 20 per cent, he makes him wait for the whites of the Republicans' eyes. (Headline over a story in the *World-Telegram* on October 18: U.S. DAILY NEWSPAPERS SUPPORT NIXON 4 TO 1, SURVEY SHOWS.) According to legend, though, the decision is unpremeditated.

The editorialist, impartial, observes the conflict until, revolted by the gross idiocy of one party or the other, he can contain his wrath no longer. Indignation mounts within his breast, and the bursting point is reached. This happens on all papers at about the same stage of the campaign. They begin to pop all over, and the press associations carry the pops, gravely and without comment. The preponderance of pops is supposed to show the general trend of reasonable thought throughout the country—vox pop, as it were.

Behind the News

THE ARREST of Lavrenti P. Beria, which broke in the newspapers here on the morning of Friday, July 10, offered a great opportunity for the dissemination of the journalistic commodity known as the news behind the news, or on-the-one-hand-this-and-on-the-other-hand-that. In this respect, it resembled the story of the death of Josef Stalin, which produced some of the finest news-behind-the-news-behind-the-news writing in the history of creative art.

Within a week after Stalin's announced demise, the American public knew that he had died of natural causes or been murdered subtly, either on the date named by *Pravda* or several weeks earlier; that the people of Moscow had demonstrated grief but (a *Journal-American* scoop) the demonstration had been a carefully organized fake; that his death portended either a hardening or a softening of policy toward the West, which, in turn, would lessen or increase the chances of open war; and that his death would either precipitate an immediate struggle for power among the surviving leaders or impel them to stand together until they got things running smoothly. It was freely predicted that in the event there was a struggle, Malenkov would destroy his associates or his associates would destroy him. The subject permitted a rare blend of invective and speculation—both Hearst papers, as I recall, ran cartoons of Stalin being rebuffed at the gates of Heaven, where Hearst has no correspondents—and I have seldom enjoyed a week of newspaper reading more.

The Colonel

The Colonel

Balmy Clime

WHEN WE HAD medicated ourselves against the hyperborean blasts—for the rule of the Great Transition allows exceptions for therapeutic purposes*—the Colonel said, "Joe, if I were holding, I would be at this moment in Florida, the land of lime pie and short-priced favorites. But the spirit of adventure deteriorates, and I will not venture forth unheeled, as I did in prewar days."

"Pre-what war?" I inquired undiplomatically.

"Pre-World War II," he said. "Release from responsibility brings to the Long Rider a second blooming, and I may say that I never felt younger in my life than in what must have been about 1935, when I checked in at a small but pleasant hotel at Miami with just seven dollars in my right breech. I discovered from perusal of the local press that a political contest of sorts was in progress, and by attaching myself to the headquarters of one of the aspirants I quickly assured my sustainance while I enjoyed myself. I ghostwrote radio campaign talks for this Huey Long in little, and he attained a summit of eloquence which much puzzled those intimately acquainted with his illiteracy. The climate was delightful."

"I adapted myself so well to my environment that I became at one point manager of the hotel," he said, "as well as senior resident. My tenure was transitionary but notable. Managements succeeded one another in that hotel with the rapidity of Roman emperors immediately after Nero. It was in a perpetual furor of reorganization, like the French government.

"From the beginning I learned to love the life there. Upon awaking

---

* The Hour of the Great Transition is noon, when the Colonel abandons Golden Gin Fizzes for beer, to which he adheres, theoretically, until he goes to bed the following morning.

in the morning, I would lie abed in my room on the second floor, and through the wide-open window would come the song of the mockingbird and the voices of Flo and Jack, a couple on the fourth floor, by inclination disputatious. The colloquy, to say the least, was startling.

"This Flo was a Miss America emerita, but of not too old a vintage, tall and still lissome and a natural blonde. Her boyfriend made book on the dog races at night, and that, naturally, left them the afternoons free to play the horses, a frequent cause of their recriminations.

"Her voice would assume a plaintive, irritating timbre, and his would become denunciatory, even menacing. But just as I would begin to apprehend the sounds of open violence, a member of the hotel personnel would shove the *Daily Racing Form* under their chamber door, and the exchange of strictures would lose audibility while they read it in bed. They got only one copy, and naturally that would bring them together, and they would become reconciliated.

"By the time they reached the lobby, ready to drive out to the track, her demeanor would be imperturbable and her attire modish, and no one could imagine her vocabularial arsenal, or the asperity of which she was capable. Similarly her consort was the personification of affability, punctiliously allowing her to precede him and never permitting her to light her own cigarette.

"She had quite a wardrobe, including the tastefully renovated vestiges of the raiment bestowed upon her when she was a beauty-contest winner, and presented what Mayfair would term a smashing exterior. Sometimes of a morning I would hear Jack complain that she had so many suitcases and hatboxes in their room that he had no place except the bed for sedentation.

"We all became well acquainted, like travelers Chaucerian at some wayside inn, and in the evenings, while Jack was at the dogs, Flo and I would sometimes sit together playing gin or cribbage. Dogs had slight attraction for her; she said the greyhounds had faces that reminded her of a snoopy little old schoolteacher she disliked in her native Alabama. Her distrust was justified. Jack became afflicted by a couple of bettors who always seemed to know which dog would win. They took him good, and from the matutinal dialogues I learned that my friends' circumstances were stringent. This naturally placed a further strain upon their relations. Adversity sometimes brings people closer together, but not when they are of different sexes."

The Colonel and I had somehow found our way to a small table midway between the telephone and the head of the stairs that led to the men's room, and the medication was having a restorative effect, so we repeated the dosage, the Colonel this time enjoining the waiter to tell the bartender to leave off all the fruit except lemon and to omit sugar.

"While their star was declining," the Colonel said, "mine was in the ascendant. The hotel had fallen into the hands of a couple of young fellows from New York who had managed to extract a profit from it, but they became enamored of change. One got married and bought himself a couple of two-year-olds. They were not good enough to win at Hialeah, so he acquired a horse trailer which he hitched to his white De Soto convertible and headed for Oaklawn Park, Hot Springs, Arkansas, with his bride. His partner had a girl too, but he omitted to marry her, possibly because the union would have been of a bigamous nature. They too began a journey, but to New York. In departing, the two hoteliers appointed me locum tenens, or manager in their absentia.

"I had had time to study the problems of the Florida hotel business, which I had found largely psychological. Tenants who missed out on one week's room rent would become diffident about approaching the cashier with a payment next week lest they be demanded to shell out the bustle beyond their capacity to pay. With each successive rent day their recalcitrance would increase, and the hotel manager merged with the jungle tracker, ever pursuing and never catching up.

"On the day I assumed office, I placed an imposing carnation in my buttonhole. I put on an expression of stern grandeur and assumed an early station behind the desk, from which I could see the various delinquents descend the stairs. I called them all over one by one and accosted the moratorium. 'Beginning today we tear everything off and start afresh,' I said, 'but from now on you will have to get it up.' The new policy was universally acclaimed; I felt I had been destined for the hotel business and had mistaken my vocation.

"In midafternoon I walked across the street to the House of Usher, a bar proprieted by a couple of ushers from Madison Square Garden who in the course of long service had hustled the price of a saloon. We started celebrating my accession to power, and all would have been well save for an accident unforeseeable. Mine host who had started north with his girl had incurred a certain amount of enmity in Miami. Some troublemaker had put the finger on him and he had been halted just after crossing the border between Florida and Georgia and arrested for intent to violate the Mann Act. After a night in a disagreeable jail, he and his girl, bail furnished, had returned to Miami in a state of disgruntlement, and he had entered his own hotel demanding to be assigned to a room. The bellboy had signified to him my whereabouts, and members of the lobby gab circle had apprised him that I had torn up the tabs.

"With none of these preliminaries was I, of course, acquainted, when, hearing my name thunderously invoked, I looked up from a table in the House of Usher to see this man glaring from the doorway. On his face he wore a demoniacal expression. I had barely time to brush a buxom stranger from my knee when he was upon me. 'You are fired!' he detonated, like Professor Hatfield's Gatling gun. So I reverted to my status as a guest.

"Meanwhile," the Colonel said, "Jack has gotten what seems to be a break. The big booking syndicate which has the monopoly in the leading Miami Beach hotels is continually in search of new business. A representative, unaware that Jack is in dire straits, asks him why he doesn't give the syndicate book a bet. Jack is unable to believe his ears. He bets five hundred on a horse at eleven to five. It comes in, and he and Flo are in love and business again. He has his check next day and bets five hundred on another horse. This too wins, at eight to five, and all is well. Then he has three losers, and pays each time. He bets again, loses, and omits to pay off, hoping he can recoup at the dogs.

"A couple nights later I am sitting in the lobby with Flo, playing klabiash, when there irrupt two credit men for the syndicate. I can feel the vibration. They ask Jack's whereabouts, and Flo says he will not return until late. 'All right,' say the credit men, 'we will be around to see him in the morning. It is nothing of consequence, just a small tab he has neglected to discharge.' When Jack walked in half an hour later, Flo told him what had happened and he kept right on walking, up to the room to pocket his shaving kit and then out into the night until he cools off.

"It leaves Flo in a position of difficulty, but she is resourceful, and I am there, an experienced Galahad. I get her a job with this political organization, running the women's committee for Yulch, my candidate for Governor, and this takes care of her feed bill amply. Her one insoluble problem is the arrearage in room rent. Jack has enjoyed the confidence of the management. An old guest of several seasons' standing, he has frequently run long tabs and squared them. But now he has vanished into the empyrean. The boys demand payment instantly, or it will be the plug in the door, and confiscation of Flo's extensive wardrobe. They have repudiated my moratorium, accusing me of conspiracy with my fellow beneficiaries.

"I will revert to the transitional, lest I lose the thread of my narration," Colonel Stingo said, calling for a bottle of Black Wolf ale. The waiter asked if he meant Black Horse, and the Colonel, with grave mien, said, "Black Wolf is much superior. It is brewed in the Yellowknife country, two hundred miles within the Arctic Circle, the home of the world's richest unexploited gold deposits. I have frequently seen a bottle sold for one ounce of gold dust. But Black Horse will be all right.

"I got up one week's room rent in advance for Flo," he said, "gaining for her a brief respite from the hoteliers' fury. I urged on them consideration of the possibility Jack would raise some scratch in the interim and communicate with her, in which case she could discharge all. But the rent itself, fifty dollars a week, as I remember, was excessive for her current increment, particularly as the season was now virtually at a close, and you could get a room and bath for a dollar a day at many nearly empty hotels in other parts of town. I engaged one for Flo at a distance of several miles.

"We devised a pardonable stratagem," the Colonel said. "My room and hers fronted on a lot where hotel guests parked their cars. Rosebushes and other floral ornaments were trained against the side of the hotel. Flo would pack a suitcase or hatbox with her finery, choosing consignments in order of cherishedness, and bring them down from her room to mine, without the necessity of passing laden through the lobby, which would have entailed interception. Then she would continue on down and walk around back of the hotel to the parking lot. I would drop the luggage into the bushes and she would retrieve it and convey it to her car, a battered but rakish vehicle.

"She would drive to her new lodgment and leave the stuff, then return. We got out all her feminine frippery in this manner, but there remained two problems—her wardrobe trunk and her parrot. The ponderous trunk, of mighty dimensions, was insoluble. She could not carry it down the stairs in the first place, and in the second, if I had dropped it from the window, the impact would have caused a detonation like that of a clap of thunder, the harbinger of a new hurricane. She therefore reconciled herself to its loss.

"But the parrot, Pat, was her companion of longest tenure, antedating Jack and a number of other human predecessors. His hawking and rawking in the mornings, similar to those of a middle-aged man with catarrh, had roiled and moiled me on occasion, conflicting as they did with the songs of the mockingbirds. But when I remonstrated with Flo, she had said they were a perfect reproduction of Mr. Westmacott, a banker with whom she had been associated subsequent to her elevation to beauty queen. 'Pat is in a sense my diary,' she said, 'and besides,

Cunnel, honey, those are not little old mockingbirds you hear in the morning. Mockingbirds sing at night. What you hear is just little old Pat imitating mockingbirds.'

"I had been well aware of the nocturnal habits of the generality of mockingbirds," the Colonel said, "but I had assumed this was a special strain imported from Las Vegas, Nevada, which is a twenty-four-hour town.

"At any rate she could not induce herself to relinquish Pat to his fate, possible reappearance on two blue plates as halves of a broiled spring chicken. So it was decided she would tie a pillowcase around the cage, with Pat inside, and I would drop it as gently as possible into the roses, where she would be as usual standing by."

The waiter had by this time delivered the Black Horse, and the Colonel sent him back for a garniture of bourbon. "It is a moment that I cannot recount without extraordinary stimulus," he said. "I find myself overcome by retroactive emotion."

When reinforcements had arrived and he had incorporated them he said, "As I received the parcel from her hands, I could hear poor Pat muttering imprecations, but I disregarded them, reminiscent as they were of many of the departed Jack's matutinal remarks. When Flo had had time to reach her appointed post, I looked out to see if the coast was clear. Sure enough, all was propitious. She was alone in the lot, and I leaned as far out the window as I could, dangled the muffled cage at arm's length, and let go. It plummeted down, landed in the rosebush, a perfect hit, right on the target. But the pillowcase was torn off, and I must assume that a number of brambles had penetrated between the bars. Also the cage came to rest upside down.

"Flo rushed, motherlike, to the retrieval, scratching her sun-lacquered arms as she dived into the shrubbery to rescue darling Pat. When she had placed the cage right side up, the bird of retentive memory spoke, in a voice of thunder: 'You sonofabitch, you do this to me?' "

We paid our check, and passed out into the night.

The Life Spiritual

✵❦ ❦✵

WHEN I FIRST worked upon Colonel Stingo to set down his memoirs, he said, "You don't know what you're getting into, Joe. I am not the fine man you take me to be."

My effort to set him right on that score resulted in an estrangement, but we became friends again.

At another time he appeared to believe I was giving him too much of the worst of it, for he said, "It is only a boob that conducts an enterprise in such a manner that it leads to embroilment with the law. I myself have never collided with it head on. But I have had many associates less wise or fortunate. One was Dr. Orlando Edgar Miller, a Doctor of Philosophy of the University of the Everglades, Rushton, Florida. Dr. Miller, when I first met him, was of appearance pre-eminent. Sixty years old, straight as an arrow, with snow-white hair and black eyelashes. He affected a Panama hat, Palm Beach suit and white buckskin shoes even in the dead of a New York winter. He presented an undeviating outward semblance of sanctity, but he was a deviator, a dear old fellow. Having drawn the multitude toward him, first thing you know he had his hands in all their pockets.

"During the course of the revivals he conducted, frequently lasting for weeks if the supply of boobs held out, he professed a diet of one orange a day, but he was a practiced voluptuary. He did not like oranges, but he ingested plenty other comestibles. 'We eat too much, and no mentality can be alert when the body is overfed,' he used to proclaim in Carnegie Hall, where he lectured to throngs, and then he would take a taxi to a speakeasy called the Pennwick and eat a steak with a coverture of mushrooms like the blanket of roses they put on the winner of the Kentucky Derby.

"After that he would plunge his fine features in eight or nine seidels of needled beer, about forty-proof, a beverage worthy of revival, for it combined the pleasant Gambrinian taste with an alcoholic inducement to continue beyond the point of assuagement. Or he would decimate a black bottle of Sandy MacDonald Scotch, landed at Rockaway Point and conveyed fresh to the table by courtesy of Big Bill Dwyer. Scotch, like the lobster, tastes best when fresh from the ocean, a truth which we have forgotten since repeal.

"But let him, in the lobby of Carnegie Hall after one of his meetings, be introduced to a man with upwards of fifty thousand dollars and he would ostentatiously gnaw an orange peel. It was my duty to keep him informed of the financial status of the potentially regenerate, a task for which I was well qualified by my experience as credit man for Tex Rickard's old Northern gambling house at Goldfield, Nevada, and in a similar capacity for Canary Cottage at Del Monte, California, and the late Col. Edward Riley Bradley at his Casino, Palm Beach, Florida. Many a man rife with money makes no outward flaunt. His habiliments, even, may be poor. But, Joe, when it comes to rich men, I am equipped with a kind of radar. The houses I worked for collected on ninety-five per cent of markers, an unchallenged record.

" 'Not the mythical bacilli but improper breathing causes tuberculosis,' this old Dr. Miller would hold forth in public. 'Among the ancient races who understood proper breathing there was no such disease.' The cure he espoused was by the laying on of hands, calisthenics, and giving the right heart, and the women flocked to be laid hands on, even the most buxom averring a fear of dormant maladies. In his pulpit appearances he stressed spiritual values—Biblical exegesis, personality, and love. He advised women to pull their husbands' hair to prevent baldness. He was a regular cure-all.

"He was accompanied on his forays by the Countess Bonizello, a lady born in Davenport, Iowa, but who had married, she recounted, an impoverished member of the Italian nobility, since deceased. She had at any rate been long enough on the Continent to acquire that little froufrou, and spoke a certain patois—French and English. She gave evidence of having been in early life a beauty, and she was full of guile and could handle men and was a real good fellow. When they hit a town, she would take a suite at the best hotel and he would assume a simple lodging in accord with his ascetic pose. She would play the role of a wealthy devotee who had followed him from Europe, platonically, of course, and she would organize the social side of the revival.

"She had in fact met him in England, so they said. There, in 1914 just before the First World War, he had conducted revivals in the Albert Hall. He induced the Duke of Manchester to put the O.K. on a line of credit for him, and was going to build a sanatorium for the cure of tuberculosis by his methods when unfortunately a woman died under his ministrations, and the British Medical Association—'captious without a point of criticism,' the old doctor used to say—had him haled before a court. 'As if other practitioners never lost patients,' he said. 'Why, an Austrian Prince named Hohenlohe paid me a thousand quid, when the pound was worth four dollars and eighty-six cents and several mils, because he was so pleased with the way I treated him. That was what inflamed Harley Street against me.' The court let him off with a reprimand, but the publicity queered his act in England, and he came home. Here he emphasized the spiritual shots in his bag, preaching that right living is the road to health, but the American Medical Association suspected he was laying hands in private, and he had to put up with persecution which seldom affected his monetary success."

A look of reminiscent admiration suffused the old Colonel's countenance.

"Of my adventures with Dr. Miller I could speak endlessly," he said, "but my purpose is only to illustrate the fine line between *fas* and *nefas*. There was no need for him to transgress that line. He was a man of great animal magnetism, reminding me of the appellation by Max Lerner of Gen. Dwight D. Eisenhower—'the charismatic leader'—which Mr. Lerner says means one you follow because he seems to have a kind of halo around him. Dr. Miller once said he was good for two hundred and fifty thousand a year on a purely spiritual plane. He drew tease from the repentant like soda through a straw.

"But eventually the day came when the old doctor overweened himself. Some Hollywood sharks sold him the idea of becoming a movie star. The old ham could fancy himself and the Countess bedazzling unseen multitudes. There seemed to him nothing ludicrous in the proposition. Essentially he was a boob too. The idea was to form an independent producing company and sell stock to people who came to his revivals. The way of separating the sheep from the goats—to wit, the holding from the nonholding—at these meetings was to distribute envelopes among the multitude, specifying that only contributions of a dollar or more were to be enclosed, and the donors were to write their addresses on the envelopes if they wished free literature.

"The doctor was not interested in the addresses of people with less than a buck. Such were requested to drop their coins in the velvet-lined collection box, where they wouldn't jingle. The jingle has a bad effect on suggestible people who might otherwise give folding money.

"We had a follow-up system on the names. Paid workers followed up each prospect. If, as occasionally occurred, they encountered a scoffer who had invested a buck just to see what would happen, the name was scratched from the mailing list. Incidentally they were pretty good estimators of a chump's net wealth. I went to one of a series of meetings an

exegizer held at Carnegie Hall this winter, and the old operating procedure is still standard. We left no room for improvement.

"When we swapped towns with another big preacher—like Dr. Hall,
the hundred-dollar-Bible man—we sometimes swapped mailing lists. But
we would always keep out a few selected prospects, and so, I suspect,
would the other prophet. The ready-made list helped in the beginning,
but the one you could trust was the one you made yourself. The purpose of this labyrinthian digression is to indicate that after ten years of
list making, old Dr. Miller had a mighty lever to place in the hands
of a stock salesman.

"I was assigned to write the scenario and it was unique, indisputably.
It was the only one I had ever written. It was called the *Bowery Bishop*
and was based on what I remembered reading about Jerry McCauley's
Bowery Mission. Dr. Miller, of course, was to play the saintly missionary,
and there were two young lovers. It had been intended that the Countess
should play half the love interest, though her bloom was no longer of
the first blush pristine, but at the last minute she backed out. She said
there were reasons why she did not want her photograph too widely
distributed. This was of good augury for the enterprise, the promoters
said, as the film would be surer to click if the doctor had the support
of some well-known movie names.

"We engaged two great stars of the silent films to play the young
lovers. With a scenario, stars, and a sucker list, the promoters were all
set to go. The stock salesmen were getting twenty-five per cent commission. The nature of the promotion literature was such, however, that
I felt sure trouble impended. Purchasers were not only assured of a
large profit, but guaranteed against loss. I declined office in the company. I went out to Honolulu to arrange a great Miller revival there,
which was to begin simultaneously with the release of the picture, and
when I returned to California, the inevitable had ensued.

"Stock had been sold to the amount of three hundred and twenty
thousand dollars, of which two hundred and forty thousand had been
turned in to the treasury. With part of the two hundred and forty a
picture had been made. But only a handful of theaters were available to
show the film, which was, as one might expect, a turkey. The old doctor,
seized by foreboding, had hit the booze and played away the rest of the
money on horses and the stock market, deluding himself that he might
thus recoup solvency. I advised him to lam before the inauguration of
the uproar, and he sought sanctuary in Australia, where I commended
him to the good offices of some friends I had in the fight game there.

The Countess Bonizello left by the same boat. I had one or two letters from him after he got out to Sydney saying he was making plenty tease. The revival business in the Antipodes had been in a crude stage before he arrived, he wrote. The surpliced choir with which he embellished his performances and the social éclat imparted by the Countess had remedied all that.

"But such peripheral triumphs did not content him. In 1926 or so I had a letter from him dated Calgary, Alberta, and so I knew he had ventured back to the outskirts of the battlefield, and he was contemplating a new campaign. The next tidings were bad. He was under arrest, and California authorities were trying to extradite him. They did, and he got six.

"We disappeared from the surfaces of each other's conscious lives, like two submarines, interrupted in a mission of destruction, which submerge without the formalities of parting.

"Now," Colonel Stingo said, "we do a fade-out and pick up the thread of our narrative again in the winter of 1936. The place is New York, and my condition is distinctly nonholding. I am inhabiting a rendezvous of the discomfited known ironically as the Little Ritz, on West Forty-seventh Street, in New York, and in the period subsequent to Dr. Miller's misfortune I have known many ups and downs, but now I am for the nonce down. I have the price of a meal, though not in a restaurant such as the Voisin, the Colony or Gilhuly's, and I am heading for the Automat. But before eating I decide to take a walk to increase my appetite, for I may not be able to raise the price of another repast that day. Chicken today, feathers tomorrow, and dear old Dr. Miller is far from my mind.

"It is snowing, and I cannot help regretting the climate of California, and perhaps conceding the foolhardiness of my renewed challenge to the metropolis. But as I pass the Union Church on West Forty-eighth Street, I see a message of hope: the Rev. Orlando Edgar Miller is conducting a service there. I enter and there he is in the pulpit, as straight as ever. The ten years, including six with time off for good conduct, have touched him but lightly. I tried to make my advent unobtrusive, secreting myself in a side pew, but the dear old rascal made me immediately.

" 'I see among us a dear good friend, Mr. James Macdonald of California,' he said. 'I am sure he has a message for us. Will you come forward, Jim?' So I walked down the center aisle."

"Were you abashed?" I asked the Colonel. "Or were you prepared to speak after such a long spiritual layoff?"

"I have an invaluable precept for public speech," the Colonel said. "It is to think of five topics, one for each finger of the hand. On this occasion, I remember, I thought of the Christmas season, which it was, the miracle of the loaves and fishes, the Poor Little Match Girl, Oliver Twist, and Tiny Tim. I began by saying that as I gazed upon the countenance of my reverend friend, Dr. Miller, the Ark of the Covenant of the Lord had fallen upon me, and that I was moved beyond expression to find here, at this Christmas season, when so many were in want, a living reminder of the miracle of the loaves and fishes, whereby the Lord had provided for many although the supply of comestibles looked limited. My prospects for spiritual nourishment had looked bleak as I wandered down the cold street, I said, and then I saw the name of Orlando Edgar Miller and knew my hunger would be satisfied. These were the times when multitudes, like the Poor Little Match Girl, were expiring of hunger—spiritual hunger—and cold, not knowing that just around the corner was a man who might warm them and stoke them to Divine Grace. He was not angry when, like Oliver Twist in the story, they turned to him again and asked for More, evermore—and like Tiny Tim—

"'We shall have to let Tiny Tim go until some other time,' that dear old rascal doctor said, 'for we have so many other beautiful features of our services to complete before six o'clock, when we must vacate the premises according to the terms of our lease. This church is not ours alone, though I would willingly remain far into the night to hear the conclusion of Brother Macdonald's beautiful train of thought.'

"I could tell from his dear old face that he had a hard time restraining hilarity, knowing full well the purport of my parablism.

"He motioned me to a seat on the front bench until the end of the service. The collection, I was glad to see, was of comfortable proportions, including many envelopes. When he came down from the platform, I went up and shook hands with him and he gave me the address in the West Seventies where he was living and told me to go on ahead up there and he would come along as soon as he had finished his routine of benevolent adieux. 'I must clinch my sales for God,' he said.

"I went on along up to the address, which was an old brownstone house that he had taken over *in toto*. The Countess was not in evidence, but three hatchet-faced old secretaries, well past the mid-century, were. It was a ménage most circumspect, and I could sense that the field of the old scalawag's deviations had narrowed with the infirmities of age. The Florabels regarded me with some suspicion, as of an outwardly un-sanctified appearance, but when the old boy arrived, he led me directly into his study.* There, having locked the door, he went to an old-fashioned wall safe and drew out of it a black bottle of unclerical demeanor and we went to it and had a fine time.

"We rode upon the flying carpet of reminiscence: for example, how we had prevailed upon one of the leading oyster growers of the Pacific Coast, a Scandinavian gentleman, to endow a two-week revival featuring hymns with special lyrics composed in his honor, as: 'Thank you, Mr. Snorensen,' to the tune of 'Onward Christian Soldiers.' The lyrics were thrown upon a screen, as those of popular songs were in movie theaters of that era. I had first used this device to publicize a fight between Burns and an Australian heavyweight named Bill Squires, at Colma, California, in 1906. After the revival proper, Mr. Snorensen treated all the executives of his company and their wives to an esoteric course with graduation ceremonies in white robes and white mortarboard hats and presented them all with fountain pens. We beat that squarehead for forty grand, and he had starved hundreds of oyster shuckers to death.

" 'Those were wonderful days, wonderful,' the dear old doctor said. 'And by the way, Jim, we parted so hastily that I never did pay you the last week's salary you had earned.' This was a bow to convention, simply the old man's way of offering aid without embarrassment to me, for he knew full well that I had held out an ample share of the Hawaiian contributions to the revival he had never held there. So he slipped me a hundred, which in those depression days was riches.

"When we had fortified ourselves enough to face those Gorgonic old spinsters, we sallied forth and took them all out to a vegetarian restaurant where they stuffed themselves with nuttose and date pudding, and then the old doctor put them in a taxi and said he and I would walk home together, since he had not completed his daily pedestrian exercise of fifteen miles. We went to Al Muller's bar north of Madison Square Garden and got stiff as boards, and finally the Ark of the Covenant of the Lord fell upon the old doctor, and he spake.

" 'Jim, there is just one thing I have never been able to understand,' he said. 'Why did they leave you outside when they put me in?' "

---

* A Florabel, in the Colonel's idiom, is the antithesis of a Lissome, his highest term of aesthetic praise for a female. It had its origin in his reaction to the newspaper photograph of a woman so named.

Pointy Shoes

WE GOT A TAXI and made our way to the Museum. It was still mid-afternoon. When we arrived, we had to fight our way in through a vast circular agglutination of schoolchildren in the rotunda, forming a human aspic around a miniature whale *sous cloche*. This was labeled OSCAR, THE BABY WHALE, and a card under the glass explained that Oscar's mother when killed had been sixty-eight feet long and that Oscar, if he had survived the ordinary period of gestation, would have been born twenty feet overall. Oscar and the children packed the rotunda. The Colonel made a way through the juvenile plankton, making effective though surreptitious use of his pointy shoes, for a few small shrieks of pain mingled with the gabble in his wake. I fancied that, following him, I stepped on one or two small prostrate bodies. However, these may have been knocked down by their playmates and trampled to death hours before our arrival.

Beer

ON THIS particular noon, Colonel Stingo was in good form, attributable, he informed me, to his not having met with a villain on his excursion of the previous night. A villain is anybody who induces him to switch from beer to hard liquor when he is out late. Beer seems to preserve my friend like a beetle in amber.

Maturity

❧ ❧

HE WAS THEN, by his own count, seventy-two. "I have three rules for keeping in condition," he said. "I will not let guileful women move in on me, I decline all responsibility, and above all, I avoid all heckling work. Also, I shun exactious luxuries, lest I become their slave."

Algeria: 1956

The Orange Trees

❧ ❧

Now THAT "they" sally from the dark for more serious depredations, it is as if this course of events, divined and feared for so many years, had been expected. The Algérois, strolling along the Rue Michelet after their late dinners to kill time until the midnight curfew, have the agitated air of the crowds in Camus's novel *The Plague*, when the visitation is first rumored. Patrols of soldiers, tommy guns at the ready, weave their way among the tables of the sidewalk cafés, where the bright fluorescent lighting is designed to improve their aim. The Algérois, looking drawn, settle in sticky groups around the sticky tables and consume *animenthe,* a mixture of anisette and crème de menthe, or Verigoud, a brand of bottled fruit juice; it has been a long, hot, humid summer— a season that in these parts lasts from May to late September, by which time even the Algérois who were born here complain about the weather. The Moslem waiters and taxi drivers look at them as if they were stones or dead trees. Some of the Moslems are fairer and speak a more grammatical French than their customers; these are not Arabs, of course, but Berbers, only a few of whom can speak Arabic. Even here in the city, there are not enough Europeans to do all the work, and outside it, in the vineyards, the fields, and the phosphate mines, "they" are indispensable. Extermination is not economically feasible. Café business has slowed down some since a bomb exploded in one of the Rue Michelet cafés the other evening, just before the fluorescent lights went on, and another blew up a café on the nearby Rue d'Isly. There were forty-four injuries altogether but no immediate deaths, although seventeen pedestrians and café patrons are reported to be on the critical list. Even so, I imagine business will soon pick up again. The nights are still warm, and one must do something with one's evenings.

I was not present when the bombs went off, but I had an instructive look at another phase of "their" campaign a couple of days later, through the courtesy and misfortune of a French friend who lives in Algiers and owns a small farm twenty miles out of town. He bought the farm a couple of years ago, primarily as a summer-weekend place, because his job keeps him here the year round. It seemed a safe investment at the time, with some eight hundred orange trees in full production and a nice bit of well-irrigated farming land. The farm lies in a valley folded in among mountains—green ones, not the savage, naked kind you find in the interior—providing a setting that suggests Alsace or northern Italy, rather than Africa. About five miles from my friend's place is the end of the main runway of the Maison Blanche Airport—the fourth-busiest in "the Occident," according to the *Guide Bleu,* being outranked only by London, Paris, and Brussels. Almost the same distance from the farm are the dam and reservoir of El Hamiz, which keep a hundred square miles of farmland green.

Early in September, when I first visited my friend on my present trip to North Africa, he told me that he and his wife hadn't spent any week-ends on the farm during the past summer, because "they" took over the countryside after nightfall. He employed three Berbers—a farmer and two boys—to look after his place, he said, except for one field that a Berber neighbor was working on a sharecropping basis. The European farmers around him were continuing to work, but at the end of each day they withdrew with their families to the protection of the nearest town, Fondouk, leaving their buildings and cattle in the care of their Moslem foremen. Usually, when they returned in the morning, build-ings and cattle were still there, but sometimes they weren't; a house or barn had been burned or some animals had been driven away, or both. When these sad events occurred, there were never any witnesses.

"Only a couple of nights ago, the *fellagha* drove off thirty-five bul-locks belonging to a European neighbor of mine," my friend said. "It must have taken quite a bit of doing to drive all those beasts off into the mountains, but the gendarmes can't turn up a soul who saw a hair of their hides."

I asked if only the farms of Europeans were raided.

My friend said no—that Moslem farmers suffered as often—and added, "But among the Moslems they seem to pick their victims on a political basis, selecting those whom they consider excessively friendly toward us or who have refused to contribute to their cause, while their choice of which European farms to attack appears to be entirely capri-cious."

He told me that not many Europeans in the valley had been killed, but enough to make the rest cautious. Only a few days earlier, for example, *fellagha* had seized four European workmen in a road-construction gang and had killed two of them and released the other two. At about the same time, they had stopped a bus on a regular evening run between Algiers and Maréchal Foch, a town a couple of miles beyond Fondouk, and, after soaking it with gasoline, had burned it. The one passenger, a European, had escaped by first hiding under a seat and then bolting off into the dark. They had spared the driver and the conductor, both Moslems, but had confiscated the day's receipts.

It was hard for me to believe that the rebels had such a free hand in a district so near Algiers, and I asked my friend if there were troops stationed nearby. He said that Fondouk and Maréchal Foch were both jam-packed with soldiers but that their presence didn't affect the situation in the surrounding countryside after dark. It did ensure the farmers and their families a safe place to sleep, though, because there was no question of rebels' attacking a town held by a battalion of infantry. (At hardly any time during the present uprising have the French encountered more than a hundred and fifty *fellagha* in a group, and even a hundred constitute what the communiqués call "an important concentration.") My friend said that thus far his own place hadn't been molested. Twice a week, he drove out from Algiers to make sure that it was still there and to get a supply of fresh melons and tomatoes for his dining table. His three employees kept grubbing in the ground as if nothing untoward were happening, and the wholesalers' lorries made their rounds, as always, picking up cases of garden produce harvested on the farm and crediting them to his account. The oranges from his grove would be ready to pick in January.

At the time of this conversation, I was about to start for the Sahara, a peaceful part of the world, but I told my friend that when I returned I would like to go along with him on one of his trips to the farm. He said he would be glad of the company. So when I got back, a week later —I traveled by plane, not dromedary—I called him up, and we made a date to visit his place on the following Tuesday morning. Then, on Monday evening, he telephoned me at my hotel, the Saint-George, to say that he was afraid our plans for the excursion would have to be modified. His farmhouse had been burned and his orange trees cut down two nights before, and he was going out there the next morning to file a claim for damages at the mayor's office in Maréchal Foch. He hoped I still wanted to accompany him. I said I certainly did want to, and, although I was sure I knew what the answers would be, went on to ask whether the *fellagha* had hurt his farmer, and, if not, whether the farmer could identify them. He replied that the farmer maintained he hadn't been around when the raid took place. "He was in such a state of excitement and fright that he couldn't make sense yesterday," he said. "So the gendarmes in Fondouk locked him up overnight to calm him down. They notified me by telephone and I asked them to release him so that he could start cleaning up the place, but I gather he still isn't making much sense."

I asked my friend if he had any insurance, and he told me that he had the usual policies—fire, theft, and so on—but that they were no comfort, because the company writing them wouldn't pay off on damage by terrorists; no company would. "I've got to have an appraisal of the damage made by a licensed agricultural expert, and then put in a claim for government compensation, just as if it were for war damage," he said. "I'm going to put in for all the traffic will bear, but nothing can repay me for the orange trees—eight hundred of them, ten years old and all heavy with fruit. It takes seven or eight years to grow an orange tree to the point where it's in full production. I don't mind losing the house so much, since we weren't using it anyway. And they didn't burn the barn, or harm my two oxen. They are simply unaccountable."

I offered my sympathy, but he said it was an occurrence he had discounted long in advance; it was only the trees he didn't like to think about. As a matter of fact, he continued, he had figured his investment in the farm was lost, for all practical purposes, as soon as "they" took over the region. "I bought it for seven and a half million francs [$21,-000], and, of course, no one would buy it now at any price," he said.

When I awoke the next morning in my room at the Saint-George, the content of my friend's telephone message seemed implausible in retrospect. All the anguish of the times comes to seem implausible at the Saint-George, which is one of the hotel's chief attractions for its present clientele. It stands on a hill high above Algiers—a dollar taxi ride from the center of town—amid gardens that might be mistaken for a fair-sized botanical park. Even while serving as Allied Headquarters during the North African campaign, the Saint-George was an ivory tower, in which no commander with less imagination than Eisenhower could have visualized conditions as they existed in the field, five hundred miles away. Still, the presence of white-helmeted MPs all over the place and, out back, of a parking area full of jeeps gave a hint that fighting might be in progress somewhere on the same continent. Now, however, there is no suggestion whatever that all is not well with the world, and the Saint-George is again the excellent hotel it was before 1939, except that the majority of its guests, instead of being wealthy English couples in search of the sun, are French executives, who have either left their families in France or daringly brought them—their wives, at any rate —to this hilltop, where they leave them when they descend to their offices in the city every morning. If a chap takes his lunch and a swim at the Yacht Club, which is in the military port, well protected by trenches and sentries, and then comes straight back to the hill after work, he is in a good position to assert that reports of the *dissidence* are greatly exaggerated.

The white-coated staff of the Saint-George, which includes a sprinkling of Moslems, is apolitically polite, except for a couple of the waiter captains—old Bemelmans types—who are apolitically discourteous. The food is of an international pallor; the diner who closes his eyes may imagine himself in Switzerland. There are tea roses *en espalier* on the terrace of my room, No. 18, which is a cubbyhole no more than thirty by twenty-five feet (not counting the hall and bathroom), and which stands me about eight dollars a day. A brass plaque on its door bears an inscription, in English, that reads: "In this room, from December, 1942, to July, 1944, many conferences were held by General Dwight D. Eisenhower, Commander-in-Chief in the Mediterranean Theater, and by General Sir Henry Maitland Wilson, Supreme Allied Commander, Mediterranean Theater, at which decisions vital to the strategy of the war in the Mediterranean were reached."

While I was waiting for my friend to call for me, I went out on my terrace and sat down to look over the morning newspapers. They contained nothing of much interest, except for an account of a French second lieutenant stationed here who, already condemned to death for treason, had now been convicted again, this time of desertion, and sentenced to deportation from Algeria for life. "The sentences will run concurrently," the story added provocatively. The rest was run-of-the-mill —terrorists had hauled an old gentleman, who happened to be the uncle of the vicar of the cathedral, off a bus and shot him; two military postmen had been killed by a sniper on a street in Algiers; and in the suburbs a farmhouse had been burned, a jeep driver shot from ambush, and two or three Moslems killed. On the credit side of the ledger, the papers—French, of course—reported a total bag of nineteen rebels killed in eastern Algeria, where the forces of order had suffered only a few casualties, and those just slight wounds. Twenty shotguns had been confiscated and two rebels killed in Kabylie, also at a trifling cost in slight wounds. (A possible reason for the high incidence of only slight wounds among the forces of order is that the rebels are armed for the most part with nothing more powerful than shotguns.) And so it went.

In all, incidents of violence were reported from twenty-seven localities, which indicated that the *œuvre de pacification* was proceeding briskly.

I had just about completed my survey of these lugubrious score sheets when the telephone rang, announcing my friend's arrival. His appearance in the lobby of the Saint-George did not jar with the hotel's atmosphere of calm conservatism. He is one of those Frenchmen who have grown so accustomed to the Algerian climate that they wear collars, ties, jackets, and full-length trousers even when the temperature hovers around a hundred. He led me out to his smart convertible, and we set off as if for a pleasure drive, the way we might have three years ago. After threading our way through city traffic, we got onto the Route Moutonnière, or Sheep Road, which is the main highway leading east from Algiers and is called that because long before it was paved, Berber shepherds used to drive their animals over it to market them in the city. The road—smoother now but hardly wider, and crowded with vehicles —cuts through a region of warehouses, factories, and slaughterhouses that much resembles the *faubourgs* of a European city.

In the stream of traffic were French Army jeeps and lorries with soldiers lolling in them, displaying rear-area boredom. Most of them were young Frenchmen who had not yet lost their European paleness. The conscripts and the *rappelés*—fellows called back to the colors—are too soft at first to hunt the *fellagha* in the mountains of the interior. They are fed into safe areas to leg them up. Their presence is supposed to reassure urban dwellers and keep terrorists at a distance. The Légionnaires, parachutists, and other rugged types perform the *actions d'éclat,* the *coups de main,* the *coups durs,* and the *offensives foudroyantes* that produce the results the Algerian press acclaims as "fruitful" whenever the troops kill more than one rebel at a time. The vocabulary of French military journalism, preserved almost intact from the First World War, is a pretty incandescent medium for the description of this kind of fighting, but the journalists have no other. The enemy, however, who is conventionally described as *lâche,* or cowardly, does not always consent to confine his attentions to the *corps d'élite* assigned to seek him out but occasionally bushwhacks a section of conscripts on a training march. This adds an element of apprehension to the distaste most of the boys feel for the present interruption of their civilian lives.

The traffic thinned out as we reached junctions with roads leading to a number of important suburbs. We passed the entrance to the Maison Blanche Airport, drove parallel to the airfield for about a mile and a half, then turned off on the road to Fondouk. On either side of us lay neat, geometrical, carefully tended vineyards and orchards, a checkerboard that I had admired from the sky on my return from the south a few days earlier. Algerian vineyards, which have been laid out more or less scientifically within the last fifty years, cover areas that would seem like Texas ranches to the grape growers of Burgundy or the Bordelais, whose ancient little patches of land straggle at odd angles up and down slopes. Even if he has the help of a large family, the proprietor of an Algerian vineyard must call in hired labor to work his land properly.

Gangs of Moslem laborers—men and women—were at work among the vines of the places we passed. The men wore blue denims and big straw hats, like Mexican laborers; the women had bandannas around their heads. The only evidence of trouble I saw was a series of miradors —watchtowers on stilts—flanking the buildings of one of the big *domaines*. Guards are posted in them every night, with rifles and searchlights, to defend the vintage. It is a solution usually open only to a big proprietor, who can afford to hire guards or has enough European employees to organize watches. "In the commune of Saint-Pierre-et-Paul, east of here," my friend said, "almost every small farm has been attacked, at one time or another, except that of a retired army officer who has a large progeny. He and his wife and the children take turns standing guard from dark to dawn, ready to shoot, and everybody for miles around knows it. It's a good argument for big families."

Fondouk is a fair-sized town but a definitely rural one; on reaching it, I felt that we were at last out of the suburbs. The farms around it, which have a more modest aspect than those we had passed earlier, grow wine grapes, garden truck, wheat, and tobacco. Fondouk was full of soldiers of a regiment recently arrived from France, and the cafés were doing a whacking business. It was the hour of the noon *apéritif*, and the atmosphere was cheerful. My friend stopped at the police station, ostensibly to ask if the authorities had any clue to who had burned his house; actually, he told me, he just wanted to pass the time of day and hear the local gossip. He enjoyed his visits to the town, he said; it was such a friendly place. When he came out, he said that the gendarmes had asked him to bring in the two boys he had working on the farm, as well as his sharecropping neighbor; the law wanted to ask them some questions. He went on to explain that while Fondouk was the town where he had his *relations* and did his marketing for the farm, his property lay just over the boundary line, in the commune of Maréchal Foch. He would therefore have to go to the town of Maréchal Foch to file his claim for compensation.

Beyond Fondouk, the road was a pretty one, climbing between gentle hills; the mountains looked kind and attractive, but there was no other traffic to be seen and I think we both felt a trifle lonely. As we approached a charred patch in the middle of the road, my friend said, "That's where they burned the bus." I remarked that all those soldiers back in Fondouk might be doing something more useful than imbibing Ricards and playing billiards for the next round. It was the kind of observation that always occurs to people who get out of sight of troops during a war. To be sure, this wasn't a war officially, but still, I reflected, the passenger in the bus hadn't had any opportunity to raise the quibble. The *fellagha* had considered him a belligerent.

"There's my house, or what's left of it," my friend said, pointing to a slope rising from the road perhaps a mile ahead of us. On it I saw the typical white walls of an Algerian farmhouse but not the customary red roof.

Turning up a tributary road leading in the direction of the farm, my friend said, "It's like a lost valley here. That used to be its charm for us." Soon we came to an extensive and orderly orange grove bordering one side of the road. "My neighbor's," he told me. "His grove adjoins mine, and not one tree in it has been touched. He's in France." My friend did not have to tell me when we reached his property, for beyond a certain point, although the land was still given over to orange trees, every one of them had been toppled; each trunk had been sawed part way through and then snapped, sending the foliage sprawling to the ground.

"Eight hundred and three trees," said their proprietor. He is a graduate of the École Polytechnique and likes figures. "Let's say arbitrarily that it would take a man five minutes to demolish a tree in that fashion. That's four thousand minutes, or about sixty-six man-hours. Assuming they started down from the mountains just after dark, arrived here at around midnight, and left before dawn, they would have had a total of, at most, five hours in which to do the job. So I figure there must have been at least a dozen men—maybe a score."

Rather surprisingly, in that isolated region, a small roadside restaurant came into sight ahead of us. It was closed, of course. "Last year, this was very handy for me and my wife on Sunday nights, when she didn't want to have to cook and then clean up the kitchen before going back to town," my friend said. "The *patronne*, a woman from Fondouk, served an excellent supper. She used to have a good Sunday automobile trade, because it's cool out here, compared to Algiers. She's back in Fondouk now, helping her husband run a bar. Well, here we are." He swung the car off onto a driveway that brought us still farther up the slope, to his barnyard, where we got out. The two Berber boys, both in their middle teens, were working together on an onion bed, weeding it with short-handled hoes. They kept right on working. A man in levis and a fez came hurrying toward us from the desecrated orange grove. He was the farmer—Abdelkader, by name. Short and bowlegged, with stooped shoulders, long arms, and a long nose, he looked like a Berber Eddie Arcaro. When he reached us, he shook hands with his employer and me, and then assumed what he evidently considered a proper attitude of dejection, staring at his toes and shaking his head slowly.

"What time did it happen?" the boss asked, and Abdelkader swung his arms high over his head, palms forward, disavowing all knowledge.

"Did anybody you know recognize any of them?" the boss persisted. At this, Abdelkader brought his hands down over his eyes, as if scooping tears from them, then thrust his arms straight out sidewise, his fingers spread wide. He went through a whole series of similar calisthenics of negation in response to further questions, and finally my friend gave up. "Let's go look at the house," he said to me, and we walked a few steps farther up the hillside, to where the white walls stood. As we approached them, I became aware of a strong smell, like that of roasted coffee, and when I stepped in through the gaping doorway, I saw a great heap of barley in a corner, toasted dark brown by the heat. The farmer had stored it there, intending to use it as poultry feed, my friend said, and now the heat of the fire had turned it into one of the commonest wartime substitutes for coffee.

The house, which had consisted of three rooms—two bedrooms and a kitchen—was a mere shell, and its tile floors were deep in ashes. It was the only building that the marauders had touched; the barn, the tool shed, and the chicken run were undamaged, and the livestock had also been spared: the chickens in the run and two small, well-muscled cream-colored oxen that the farmer used for plowing and that were just then grazing on the side of a hill above the orange grove. I wondered if "they" had intentionally overlooked these buildings and animals, so that Abdelkader could continue to work the farm, on which he and his family were dependent for a living. The house and the orange trees contributed nothing directly to the family's nutrition, whereas the livestock did, and "they," it seemed to me, might have realized how unlikely it was that if the oxen, at least, were killed or stolen, my friend would invest in replacements. It occurred to me, too, that in leaving the chickens and oxen behind, the rebels must have been conscious of no protein deficiency in their current diet.

"Did you bring the basket?" Abdelkader, who had followed us up to the ruined house, asked his employer. "I have some beautiful tomatoes for madame." But my friend, distrait, had not thought of the family larder this time. Abdelkader then silently produced a receipt showing that he had sent two cases of melons and one of tomatoes to market. His boss pocketed the slip of paper and told him, "Keep working. We've got to drive over to Maréchal Foch now, but we'll be right back. Tell the boys and Ali I want them to be ready to go to Fondouk with me when I return." Ali was the sharecropper.

We got in the car again and set out for Maréchal Foch. On the way, my friend said the gendarmes had reason to believe that no more than five or six armed *fellagha* from up in the mountains were involved in raids like the one on his place—that they often recruited a score or more of men from the locality to do the hard work, such as cutting down trees. "In that case, it would be strange if Abdelkader did not know at least some members of the local contingent," he remarked. "But if he should give them away, he would be in danger of having his throat cut. On the other hand, he may have put them up to it. How is one to know?"

Maréchal Foch is a smaller and scrubbier place than Fondouk. So many soldiers and military vehicles were gathered there that I wondered if they were expecting an attack by a panzer division. The *mairie* was a two-story building, and the *maire* occupied the upper floor with his wife and family. My friend had brought with him a list of his losses, typewritten on the proper form, but the *maire*, who received us in his living quarters, said no, no, that was not enough. The supplicant would have to get the list typed in triplicate, and, moreover, append to the three copies an *attestation de non-warrant*—a bit of legal French that stumped me completely. My friend mumbled that he would have to go all the way back to Algiers for these emendations and then make another trip out to file his claim. "That's right," the *maire* said impassively. "But there's no hurry. You have three months in which to file."

Back downstairs, I asked my friend what an *attestation de non-warrant* was, and he said he didn't know, either, but hadn't wanted to admit his ignorance to such a bumpkin of a *maire*. (We found out later in Algiers that it is an affidavit stating that there is no mortgage on the property involved in the claim.)

On the return trip to the farm, my friend grumbled a good deal about the treatment he had received from the *maire*. "These monkeyshines of civilian red tape have empoisoned everybody," he said. "When the gendarmes telephoned me in Algiers to tell me my house had been burned, they wanted me to come out immediately. And do you know why? To file a proper *plainte* against, as they put it, 'persons unknown for trespass, breaking, entering, malicious damage, and arson.' The whole region is contaminated."

We stopped shortly before we reached the driveway to the farm, to pick up the sharecropper the police wanted to question; he was a Berber with a brick-red complexion, blue eyes, and a reddish-blond mustache. The two boys were ready and waiting for us—a pair of pie-faced louts who under ordinary circumstances would have been tickled to ride in the sleek convertible. But now they weren't. Their faces were self-righteously blank. *"Maktoub,"* they seemed to say. "Fate. What will be will be." *Maktoub* gets to be a bore in North Africa. When we arrived in Fondouk with Ali and the boys, the gendarmes told my friend that they would not need them until the next day, if then. So we drove the trio to a general store, where they bought bottles of green pop, and there we left them.

The Earl

"Nothing But a Little Pissant"

✦❦ ❦✦

WE HAD LEFT New Orleans at four, and Earl was slated to speak at
eight. The owner of the old station wagon had said he could make it
to Alick in four hours easy. It began to look not at all that easy.

I tried to estimate the station wagon's speed by clocking it between
signposts. From BUNKIE, 27 MI. to BUNKIE, 20 MI., I caught it in a con-
soling seven minutes, but the next post, a good bit farther on, said
BUNKIE, 23 MI. Bunkie is the leading *bourgade* between Baton Rouge
and Alick—it has a population of 4,666—but there were other one-
street-of-storefronts towns that the road ran through. By now it was dusk
and the stores were lighted, so that, coming out of the dark, we galloped
episodically between plywood maple-finished bedroom suites in the windows on one side of the street and mannequins with $7.98 dresses on
the other, scaring from our course gaunt hounds that looked like Kabyle
dogs.

The entrance to Alick was little more impressive than these others,
except for two electric signs. One was a straw-hatted spook flapping
great wings over the Hocus-Pocus Liquor Store and the other a symbolic
giraffe and dachshund over a used-car lot. They disappeared at every
other flash in favor of a legend: "High Quality, Low Prices."

Hurrying through otherwise undistinguished streets, we passed between cars parked thick along the approaches to the courthouse square
and heard the loudspeaker blaring long before we got there. Somebody
was on the platform in front of the courthouse steps, standing too close
to the microphone and blasting. The crowd, massed immediately around
the speaker's stand, thinned out toward the sidewalks.

My companion let me out and drove on to find a parking space, and
I ran onto the lawn for my first look at the Imam in the flesh. As I
crossed over to the forum, a boy handed me a pink throwaway, which

I examined when I got within range of the light diffused from the flood-lamps over the platform:

GOVERNOR LONG SPEAKS
Governor Long Opens Campaign for Re-Election

Come Out and Bring All your friends to hear the truth. Come out and see Governor Long in person. Nothing will be said to offend or hurt anyone.

The Governor, on the platform, was saying to somebody I could not see over in the other wing of the audience, "If you don't shut up your claptrap, I'm going to have you forcibly removed. You just nothing but a common hoodlum and a heckler."

"Amen," an old man in front of me yelled. "Give it to him, Earl."

Whoever it was that Earl was talking to in the crowd had no microphone, so we couldn't hear him, but he must have answered in tones audible to the Governor, because the latter shouted into the mike, "I knew your daddy, Camille Gravel, and he was a fine man. But you trying to make yourself a big man, and you nothing but a little pissant."

"Amen, Earl," the old man yelled. "Give it to him."

The fellow in the crowd, now identified for me as a lawyer from Alick who was the Democratic National Committee man from Louisiana, must have spoken again, for the Governor thundered, "Mr. Gravel, I got nothing against you personally. Now you keep quiet and I won't mention your name. If you don't I'll have you removed as a common damn nuisance." He paused for the answer we couldn't hear and then bellowed, "If *you* so popular, why don't *you* run for Governor?"

It sounded like a dialogue between a man with the horrors and his hallucinations. But the National Committeeman, Earl's interlocutor, was there in the flesh. He had brought his ten children, and they were all mad at the Governor.

The night was like a heavy blanket pressed down on the lawn. Men stood in their sleeveless, collarless shirts, and sweat caked the talcum powder on the backs of the women's necks. Anti-Long newspapers the next day conceded the crowd was between three and four thousand, so there may well have been more. Plenty of Negroes, always in little groups, were scattered among the whites—an example, I suppose, of Harry Golden's "vertical integration," because in public gatherings where there are seats, the two colors are always separated into blocs.

"That's the way I like to see it," the Governor said, from the stand. "Not all our colored friends in one spot and white friends in another. I'm the best friend the poor white man, and the middle-class white man, and the rich white man—so long as he behave himself—and the poor colored man, ever had in the State of Loosiana. And if the N.A.A.C.P. and that little pea-headed nut Willie Rainach will just leave us alone, then *sen*sible people, not cranks, can get along in a *rea*sonable way. That Rainach wants to fight the Civil War all over again."

There were two colored couples, middle-aged, in front of me, next to the old white man who didn't like Gravel, and now one of the colored men shouted, "Amen!" The old white man gave him a reproving look, but he couldn't bawl him out for agreeing with a Long. Nobody can object to *rea*sonable and *sen*sible, but Long hadn't said what he thought *rea*sonable and *sen*sible were, and it occurred to me that he probably never would.

I had been looking at him with an amateur clinical eye since I got there, and his physical condition seemed to me to have improved several hundred per cent since his stump appearance with Joe Sims on the Fourth of July. Late hours and a diet of salted watermelon, buttermilk, and Vienna sausages cut up in chicken broth had put a dozen pounds back on his bones. Walking between grandstands and paddocks had legged him up, and he pranced under the floodlights that must have raised the temperature to 110 or so. I remembered when I had seen first the referee, Ruby Goldstein, and then the great Sugar Ray Robinson himself collapse under the heat of similar lights in a ring on a less oppressive night in New York.

Uncle Earl wore a jacket, shirt and tie, a pattern of statesmanlike conventionality, on a night when everybody off the platform was coatless and tieless. The tie itself was a quiet pattern of inkblots against an olive-and-pearl background, perhaps a souvenir Rorschach test from Galveston. The suit, a black job that dated from the days when he was fat and sassy, hung loosely about him as once it had upon a peg in the supermarket where the Governor liked to buy his clothes.

He left the dude role to Morrison. And in fact, before the evening was over, he said, "I see Dellasoups has been elected one of the ten best-dressed men in America. He has fifty-dollar neckties and four-hundred-dollar suits. A four-hundred-dollar suit on old Uncle Earl would look like socks on a rooster."

It is difficult to report a speech by Uncle Earl chronologically, listing the thoughts in order of appearance. They chased one another on and off the stage like characters in a Shakespearean battle scene, full of alarums and sorties. But Morrison, good roads, and old-age pensions popped in quite often.

Of Dodd, the state auditor, a quondam ally and now a declared rival for the Governorship, he said, "I hear Big Bad Bill Dodd has been talking about the inefficiency and waste in this administration. Ohyeah. Ohyeah. Well, let me tell you, Big Bad Bill has at least six streamlined deadheads on his payroll that couldn't even find Bill's office if they had to. But they can find that *post office* every month to get their salary check—Ohyeah."

It was after the "*rea*sonable and *sen*sible" bit that he went into his general declaration of tolerance. "I'm not against anybody for reasons of race, creed, or any ism he might believe in except nuttism, skingameism or communism," he said.

"I'm glad to see so many of my fine Catholic friends here—they been so kind to me I sometimes say I consider myself forty per cent Catholic and sixty per cent Baptist." (This is a fairly accurate reflection of the composition of the electorate.) "But I'm in favor of *every* religion with the possible exception of snake-chunking. Anybody that so presumes on how he stands with providence that he will let a snake bite him, I say he deserves what he's got coming to him." The snake-chunkers, a small, fanatic cult, do not believe in voting.

"Amen, Earl," the old man said.

The expressions on the Governor's face changed with the poetry of his thought, now benign, now mischievous, now indignant. Only the moist hazel eyes remained the same, fixed on a spot above and to the rear of the audience as if expecting momentarily the arrival of a posse.

"I don't *need* this job," he said. "I don't *need* money." He stopped and winked. "I don't miss it except when I run out."

There were shouts of laughter, the effect he courted.

"Amen, Earl. You tell 'em, Earl."

His face turned serious, as if he had not expected to be so cruelly misunderstood.

"I'm serious about that," he said. "You know I'm no goody-goody. But if I have ever misappropriated one cent, by abuse of my office, and anyone can prove it, I'll resign.

"I know lots of ways to make a living. I know how to be a lawyer, and a danged good one. I know how to be a traveling salesman. I know how to pick cotton, and have many times, although I've seen the days when to get my hundred pounds I had to put a watermelon in the bag."

There were gales of tolerant laughter now, even from farmers who would shoot any of their own help they found cheating on weight.

"All I ask," he said, with the honesty throbbing in his voice like a musical saw, "is a chance once again to help the fine people of the Great State of Loosiana, and to continue to serve them as their Governor."

Even a group of great louts in T-shirts, perhaps high-school football players, were silent and by now impressed; earlier in the address they had made a few feeble attempts at heckling, like yelling, "Hey, Earl, what's in the glass?" when the Governor paused for a drink of water. These boys might be from well-to-do anti-Long families, but they had the endemic Southern (and Arabic) taste for oratory, and they knew a master when they heard him.

Mr. Gravel, down near the platform, must have again attracted the Governor's attention, but now Uncle Earl, the creature of his own voice, was in a benign mood from offering his own body to the Great State of Loosiana.

"Mr. Gravel," he said, "you got ten beautiful children there, I wish you would lend five of them to me to bring up." It was one of Earl's well-publicized sorrows that he, like the Shah of Iran then, had no legitimate heir, and he handed peppermint candies or small change to all children he saw, even in years when there was no election. "He bought those candies by grosses of dozens," an ex-associate told me.

Mr. Gravel, still inaudible except to Earl, must have declined this overture, because the Governor shouted to the crowd, "He used to be a nice fellow, but now he just a goddamn hoodlum!"

"Leave him alone, Earl, we come to hear *you* talk!" the old man near me shouted back.

"I was in Minneannapolis once, talking to the Governor of Minnesota, a great expert on insanity," Uncle Earl said, "and he told me an astonishing fact—there are ten times as many crazy people in Minnesota as Louisiana. I suppose that is on account of the cold climate. They cannot go around in their shirt-sleeves all year around, go huntin' and fishin' in all seasons, as we do. We got a wonderful climate," he said, and paused to wipe the sweat from his face with a handkerchief soaked in Coca-Cola, which he poured from a bottle out of a bucket of ice handed him by one of the lesser candidates on his ticket. The bugs soaring up at the edge of the lighted area and converging on the floodlights formed a haze as thick as a beaded curtain.

"On account we got so few crazy people, we can afford to let Camille Gravel run around."

"Leave him up, Earl," the old man yelled. "You got him licked."

"Some sapsuckers talk about cutting down taxes," the Governor said, apropos of nothing he had been talking about. "Where are they going to start cutting expenses? On the *spastic* school?" (When any opponent suggests a cut in welfare expenditures, Earl accuses him of wanting to take it out on the spastics. This is the equivalent of charging the fellow would sell his mother for glue.) "They want to cut down on the *spastics?* On the little children, enjoying the school lunches? Or on those fine old people, white-haired against the sunset of life"—and he bowed his own white head for a split second—"who enjoy the most generous state pensions in the United States?

"We got the finest roads, finest schools, finest hospitals in the country—yet there are rich men who complain. They are so tight you can hear 'em squeak when they walk. They wouldn't give a nickel to see a earthquake. They sit there swallowin' hundred-dollar bills like a bullfrog swallows minners—if you chunked them as many as they want, they'd bust."

"Amen, Earl," the old man said. "God have mercy on the poor people."

"Of course, I know many *fine* rich people," the Governor said, perhaps thinking of his campaign contributors. "But the most of them are like a rich old feller I knew down in Plaquemine Parish, who died one night and never done nobody no good in his life, and yet, when the Devil come to get him, he took an appeal to St. Peter.

" 'I done some good things on earth,' he said. 'Once, on a cold day in about 1913, I gave a blind man a nickel.' St. Peter looked all through the records, and at last, on page four hundred and seventy-one, he found the entry. 'That ain't enough to make up for a misspent life,' he said. 'But wait,' the rich man says. 'Now I remember, in 1922 I gave five cents to a poor widow woman that had no carfare.' St. Peter's clerk checked the book again, and on page thirteen hundred and seventy-one, after pages and pages of how this old stump-wormer loan-sharked the poor, he found the record of that nickel.

" 'That ain't neither enough,' St. Peter said. But the mean old thing yelled, '*Don't* sentence me yet. In about 1931 I give a nickel to the Red Cross.' The clerk found that entry, too. So he said to St. Peter, 'Your Honor, what are we going to do with him?' "

The crowd hung on Uncle Earl's lips the way the bugs hovered in the light.

"You know what St. Peter said?" the Governor, the only one in the courthouse square who knew the answer, asked. There was, naturally, no reply.

"He said, 'Give him back his fifteen cents and tell him to go to Hell.' "

He had the crowd with him now, and he dropped it.

"Folks," he said, "I know you didn't come here just to hear me talk. If this big mouth of mine ever shut up, I'd be in a devil of a fix. I want to introduce to you some of the fine *sin*cere candidates that are running with me on my ticket. My ticket and the independent candidates I have endorsed are trained, skilled, and have the wisdom and experience to make you honest, loyal and *sin*cere public servants."

He turned to the triple row of men and women who sat behind him on undertaker's chairs, the men swabbing, the women dabbing, at their faces with handkerchiefs, while the Governor talked like an intrepid trainer who turns his back on his troupe of performing animals.

A reporter who had his watch on the Governor said that his talk had lasted fifty-seven minutes, and he was not even blowing.

"And first," he said, "I want to introduce to you the man I have selected to serve under me as Lieutenant Governor during my next term of office—a fine Frenchmun, a fine Catholic, the father of twenty-three children, Mr. Oscar Guidry."

The number of children was politically significant, since it indicated that Mr. Guidry was a practicing, not a *soi-disant*, Catholic. The candidate for Lieutenant Governor had to be a Frenchman and a Catholic, because Uncle Earl was neither.

Mr. Guidry, a short, stocky man who reminded me of a muscular owl, arose from his chair like a Mr. Bones called to front center by Mr. Interlocutor. He appeared embarrassed, and he whispered rapidly to Uncle Earl.

"Oscar says he has only fourteen children," the Governor announced. "But that's a good beginnin'."

Mr. Guidry whispered again, agitated, and Earl said, "But he is a member of a family of twenty-three brothers and sisters." He turned away, as if washing his hands of the whole affair, and sat down.

Mr. Guidry, throwing back his head and clasping his hands in front of him, as if about to intone the "Marseillaise," began with a rush, sounding all his aitches: "I am *honored* to be associated with the Gret Governeur of the Gret Stet on his tiquette. Those who have conspired against him, fearing to shoot him with a pistol ball . . ." and he was off, but Earl, seated directly behind him, was mugging and catching flies, monopolizing attention like an old vaudeville star cast in a play with a gang of Method actors.

Pulling his chair slightly out of line, he crossed his legs and turned his profile to the audience, first plucking at his sleeves, which came down about as far as his thumbnails, then, when he had disengaged his hands, picking his nose while he looked over at Alick's leading hotel, the Bentley, across the street, described by the *Louisiana State Guide* as "a six-story building of brick and stone, with a columned façade and a richly decorated interior." He stared at it as if it contained some absorbing riddle.

When he had finished with his nose, he began to bathe his face, his temples and the back of his neck with Coca-Cola from the cold bottle, sloshing it on like iced cologne.

"Cool yourself off, Earl," a voice piped up from the crowd, and the Governor shouted back, "I'm a red-hot poppa."

When he had wet himself down sufficiently, he drank the heeltap and set the bottle down. Then he lit a cigarette and smoked, dramatically, with the butt held between his thumb and middle finger and the other fingers raised, in the manner of a ventriloquist. While he smoked right-handed, he pulled out his handkerchief and blotted his wet face with his left.

He sat unheeding of the rumpus raised by his adherents, like a player in a jazz band who has finished his solo, or a flashy halfback who poses on the bench while the defensive team is in. The candidates ranted and bellowed, putting across a few telling although familiar points.

"In the great state of Texas, biggest and richest in the United States, there is an old-age pension of thirty-one dollars a month. Here in Loosiana we got seventy-two."

But the bored crowd stood fast, knowing that a whistle would blow and the star would throw off his blanket and come onto the field again to run rings around the forces of Mammon. Sure enough, after what seemed to me an endless session of subordinate rant, the Governor threw away the last of a chain of cigarettes and shook his head like a man waking up on a park bench and remembering where he is. He got up and walked to the microphone so fast that the man using it had barely time to say, "I thank you" before the Governor took it away from him.

"You shall know the truth, and the truth shall set you free," the Governor said, "but you will never get to know the truth by reading the Alexandria *Town Talk*. You all read in that paper that I am crazy. Ohyeah. Do I look any crazier than I ever did? I been accused of saying the fella that owns that paper is a kept man. Maybe he ain't, but I'd like to be kep' as good as he is. He married a rich woman. That's about the best way I know to save yourself about ninety-eight years' hard work."

"Amen, Earl, it's the truth," the old man in front of me cried, and the Negroes laughed at what was apparently a well-established local joke.

"Maybe some of you are here because you've never seen a man out of a nuthouse before," the Governor said tolerantly. "Maybe you want to see a man who has been stuck thirty-eight times with needles. Oh, the first man stuck me, stuck me right through the britches. He didn't get me in the fat part, either, and oh, how it hurt! Maybe I lost a little weight, but you would have, too. Occasionally I say hell or damn, but if it had happened to you all, you'd say worse than that. Christ on the Cross Himself never suffered worse than poor old Earl!

"Oh, not that I'm fit to walk in Christ's shoes!" he bellowed to preclude any confusion. "I'm not good enough, when a fellow slugs me on one cheek, to turn the other side of my scheming head. I'm going to slug him back."

"Amen, Earl. You tell him, Earl. Who you goin' to hit first, Earl?"

"Down there in that court in Texas in Galveston before that Texas judge, I felt like Christ between the two thieves. He reared back his head and he said, 'Father, forgive them, for they know not what they do!' "

At this point he was interrupted by wild handclapping from a group of elderly ladies wearing print dresses, white gloves, straw hats and spaceman eyeglasses, who had been seated quietly on the platform through the earlier proceedings. They were under the impression that it was an original line.

I next remember the Governor in his seat again, head down, exhausted, having given his all to the electorate, in a pose like Bannister after running the first four-minute mile. It occurred to me that he was like old blind Pete Herman fighting on heart alone, by a trained reflex. Pete is a friend of the Governor's.

As Earl sat there, one of the assisting speakers, a fellow with a strong voice, grabbed the microphone and declaimed the family battle ode, "Invictus."

When the man came to the part where it says:

> *Under the bludgeonings of fate*
> *Ma haid is bloody, but* unbowed

Earl flung up his head like a wild horse and got up like a fighter about to go into a dance to prove he hasn't been hurt. He called for a show of hands by everybody who was going to vote for him, and I waved both of mine.

I left him surrounded by children to whom he was passing out coins, "a quarter to the white kids and a nickel to the niggers."

My companion had rejoined me after parking the car, and we walked together through the breaking crowd.

"How could his wife have done him like she done?" a woman was asking another, and a man was saying, "Got to give da ol' dawg what's coming to him."

My friend saw Gravel, a handsome, tanned man in a white sports shirt and black slacks, standing where the lawn ended at the pavement, and walked over to him. Two or three reporters were already there, asking Gravel what he had said when Earl said what.

The National Committeeman said he had come to hear the speech because two or three men close to Earl had called him up and warned him that Earl was going to blacken his name.

"I wanted to be there to nail the lie," he said. He said Earl started the argument.

Six or eight of the ten Gravel children played hide-and-seek around their father's legs, and as he talked, another boy, about eleven years old, ran up and said to a slightly younger girl, his sister, "The Governor wanted to give me a quarter, but I wouldn't take it."

"Why not?" the girl asked, and I decided she had a bigger political future than her brother.

Gravel said he had to go home because there was a wedding reception there, and the rest of us walked back toward the Bentley, where all the rocking chairs on the porch were already occupied. The row of glowing cigar ends swaying in unison reminded me of the Tiller Girls in a glowworm number.

Blam-Blam-Blam

NEXT DAY, with Uncle Earl expected to appear at the Mansion at four in the afternoon, I called on Theo Cangelosi, his bête noire, in the morning.

The attorney was a long, bony man, with the long, bony face of a Savonarola, a likeness particularly noticeable in the nose and chin. He practiced law in one half of a double white clapboard house on a wide, shady street near the Governor's mansion.

"People suffering from Earl's affliction frequently turn against their nearest and dearest," he said. "Their anger is in proportion to their affection before they took sick. Earl is under the impression that I helped Mrs. Long get a first mortgage on their new house for forty thousand dollars and that she kept the money, but I never even saw the cash. I just sent the papers to the bank. Both Earl and Blanche signed them, and if he didn't get his share it's his own fault." Mr. Cangelosi looked sad and injured. "Now Earl's putting out that Blanche shared the money with me," he said.

"Earl really turned against me when I wouldn't help him try to escape from that hospital in Texas, but I just didn't want him to get into trouble. I went down there to see him when he sent for me, and the first thing he said was 'I'm pretty good at getting around people, and I've been talking to the guards on this floor, and I believe that if I had a thousand dollars in cash I could bribe my way out. You take this note and go back to the City National Bank at Baton Rouge and get me the money, ya hear, and I'll be all right.'"

Mr. Cangelosi took from a desk drawer a slip of ruled yellow paper and showed me the message, in the wobbly script of a man having a lot of trouble: "Treasurer, Louise Gottlieb, Earl Long Campaign Fund Account, City National Bank, Baton Rouge, Please pay over to bearer $1000 in $100 bills.—Earl K. Long."

The Governor was an old friend of Lewis Gottlieb, the bank chairman, but he had spelled Gottlieb's name Louise, indicating considerable residual confusion at that moment. (The thirty-eight shots had not, perhaps, worn off.)

"I heard that somebody did slip him fifteen hundred dollars," I said.

"Yes," said Mr. Cangelosi, "but that was later, at the hearing, and it wasn't me. I was trying to protect him. If one of those guards had taken his money and then shot him trying to escape, I would have blamed myself forever. I have always acted in his best interests."

I thanked Mr. Cangelosi and walked out into the blood heat and down to the bank to confirm the existence of an Earl Long Campaign Fund.

Mr. Gottlieb, looking little like a Louise, said there was such an account, but it wouldn't be ethical to tell me how much there was in it. I surmised that there might suddenly get to be a lot in it if the income-tax people ever disputed the Governor's blanket contention that the money people hand him is intended as campaign contributions. He might then formalize the status of cash in hand by making a large deposit.

"I imagine Earl is up in Winnfield making catfish bait for the special session," Mr. Gottlieb said. "He's probably putting together a program of legislation aimed to give every senator and representative something for himself: a bill to appropriate funds to widen a road in one parish, a bill to raise the salary for a kind of job some senator's cousin has in another. That's the kind of thing Earl's good at—knowing every local politician in the state and remembering where he itches. Then Earl knows where to scratch him."

Lunch in the Capitol House confirmed my theory of culture belts. The Capitol House lies within ninety miles of Galatoire's and Arnaud's in New Orleans, but its fare bears a closer resemblance to Springfield, Illinois, where a distinguished hostess once served me a green salad peppered with marshmallow balls. So Dover, within twenty-three miles of the French coast, eats as un-Frenchly as the farthest side of England.

A statewide convention of high-school football coaches was in session, and there seemed to be hundreds of them—a cross between the plantation overseer and YMCA secretary. In the night they congregated over bottles of bourbon, building character for transfusion to their charges in the fall, and in the day they attended seminars on whipless slave-driving and how to induce adolescents to play on two broken legs.

The Governor's Mansion at Baton Rouge, like the State House, is a monument to the administration of Huey Long. The story goes that the Martyr, when he gave the architect his riding orders, said he wanted a replica of the White House so he would know where the light switches were in the bathrooms when he got to be President. Huey lived in it from 1930 to 1932, and Earl inhabited it briefly for the first time in 1939, when he filled out the term of the unfortunate Mr. Leche. After that he lived in it again as Governor from 1948 to 1952 and began a third tenancy in 1956. When I saw it, Longs had been masters of the house for ten out of the nineteen years of its existence, almost enough to give it status as an elegant old gracious family mansion. Earl and Miz Blanche had built their new house in a newer and more stylish part of Baton Rouge, before the Governor decided against moving.

Tom and I arrived half an hour before the hour appointed for the Governor's press conference. We were in company with Margaret Dixon, editor of the Baton Rouge *Morning Advocate,* one of the few people in Louisiana who could usually get along with Earl. Mrs. Dixon, handsome, stable and strong, has a firm, serene personality. She is the kind of woman motherless drunks turn to instinctively to tell their troubles with their wives.

"Earl is the funniest man in the world," she said over her shoulder as she drove. "Life in the Capitol would be dull without him. Did you hear what he said to Leander Perez, the States'-rights man, the other day? 'What are you going to do now, Leander? Da Feds have got da atom bomb.' And when Blanche went to live in the new house, he said she had 'dis-domiciled' him. He has a style of his own—he's a poet. He said he was so groggy when he got off the plane that took him to Houston that he felt 'like a muley bull coming out of a dipping vat.' I don't know why it should, but the 'muley' makes that line sound a hundred times funnier. It just means without horns."

"It particularizes the image," I suggested. "Bull is a word so general that it blurs: the dumb bulls in Spain, the tight bulls in flytime. 'Muley' makes you see a bull of a peculiarly ineffectual kind."

"You sound more like Huey," Mrs. Dixon said. "Earl says, 'Huey tried that highbrow route and he couldn't carry his home parish. I carry Winn Parish every time.'

"He praises Huey up, but he never misses a chance to mention when he does something better—in 1956, when he won the Governorship on the first primary, without a runoff, the first thing he said was 'Huey never done that.' "

Now we were on the Mansion driveway lined with laurel and packed with press cars.

Inside, the press had taken over, as if the Mansion were the scene of a first-class murder and the cops were still upstairs. Reporters in large groups are ill at ease, and they try to make up for it by acting too easy. Each is preoccupied with his own time situation—his paper's deadlines and the accessibility of telephones. Each, before a public conference, shapes in his mind what would make a good story if the principal said it, and how he can trap him into saying it. If the principal delays his appearance, the reporter begins to wonder whether he will have time to write the story. Then, with further delay, he begins to wonder if he will have time to telephone. Next, he gets angry. He resents his subjection to the whims of his inferiors, and he vents his resentment by a show of elaborate contempt.

We turned left inside the fanlighted door and went down a couple of steps into a great reception room furnished like a suite in a four-star general's house on an army post, where the furniture comes out of the quartermaster's stores. The bleakness of such pieces, all bought on contract sale, increases in proportion to the square of their sum: two hotel sofas are four times as depressing as one; three, nine times. The Governor's drawing room, of good height and proportions, contained at least twenty-six paired pieces, all covered with pink or green brocade chosen for its wearing qualities. The mauve drapes were of the tint and gloss of the kind of spun-sugar candy that is usually filled with rancid peanut paste; the carpets were a flushed beige. There were two wall mirrors reflecting each other, a blackamoor candelabra, three chandeliers, and no pictures. There was not a piece of furniture from before 1930 nor a portrait of a former Governor or his lady. I wondered where the loot from the old Mansion was.

Huey had cleared out the lot, as a link with the hated aristocratic past. As it was, it made a perfect waiting room—a place in which boredom began in the first ten seconds.

At half past four the Governor's press secretary, an intimidated former state senator named Fredericks, appeared at the top of the two steps. He announced that the Governor's party had telephoned from the road: they were still about fifty miles from town, and the Governor had given orders to serve cake and coffee to the reporters and tell them to wait. Negro servants in white jackets served coffee and sponge cake, both good. A couple of the bloods of the press who covered the beat regularly had found their way to some bourbon concealed from the rest of us and came smirking back.

One fellow went about canvassing colleagues to join him in a walkout. He proposed that everybody go off and leave the Governor flat—insult to the press, showing up so late. That would let him see where he stood. His colleagues, knowing where they stood, paid no heed.

An hour passed, and the Governor's party arrived. State troopers shoved us back, and the Governor's party headed straight upstairs, to "wash up and be right back." A minute later, word came down that the Governor was going to shave. The Negroes served more coffee, this time without cake. Nobody talked of leaving now.

A reporter with good connections learned the cause of the long delay from a state cop who had ridden in the convoy. "Governor stopped at a few farms along the way to buy some guinea hens, but he couldn't get the right price on them."

Forty-five minutes more, and the Governor made his entrance. He hadn't shaved but had taken a nap and put in a telephone call to a woman friend in Alick. Fortunately for the press, she had not been at home. Once on the line, he talked for hours.

Mrs. Dixon said that this was his first press conference in the Mansion since deputy sheriffs, whom he called bone crushers, had hustled him down his own steps and into an ambulance on the night of May 30.

He was wearing a black mohair suit even less elegantly adjusted than the one at Alick, and a sober necktie of black with atom-bomb mushrooms of white and magenta. He moved to a seat in the middle of a long sofa with its back to the cold fireplace. There, crossing one leg over the other knee, which exposed his white cotton socks, he faced his familiar persecutors with the air of a country Odysseus home from a rough trip, with no Penelope to greet him.

This Odysseus didn't care if he never set eyes on Penelope again. A woman reporter asked him if he was going to make it up with Mrs. Long, and if he didn't think that would help him get the women's vote in the primary.

He said, "If dat's da price of victory, I'd rather go ahead and be defeated. After all, lots of men have lost elections before."

Somebody asked him if he was set on the special session of the Legislature and he said he was, that the call would go out before five o'clock the next day. That was the latest moment when he could call a session for Monday, August 11. The Governor must include with the call a list of the legislation he means to propose; none other can be voted at the session. He said he was readying his list.

A reporter asked him if he would include any new tax bill, and he said no, if the state won its suit against two oil companies, "we might get by with no taxes at all." But if the money did not come in that way, he would try for some new taxes at the regular session. This was a flat assumption that he would run and be re-elected.

He had already said that, rather than cut state services, he would be in favor of "any kind of a tax but a sales tax, because that falls on the poor devil."

Now he began again to lay into the rich people, who "wanted to cut out the spastic school," but the reporters, who had heard that number in his repertory, managed to get him off on Cangelosi.

"There never has been a man who *mis*used and unduly *ab*used my confidence like Cangelosi," the Governor said. "If he hadn't a done me like he done, and rubbed it in, I might forgive him, but that long-legged sapsucker made more money than any man I ever knew," he said, adding quickly, "of which I have not participated in any of the profits."

The Governor's moist hazel eyes, filled with sweetness, clouded over at the memory of what he had suffered. His voice, low and hoarse at the beginning of the conference, as it well might be after the weekend of stump-speaking, rose indignantly, like a fighter knocked down by a fluke punch.

"They misled me," he said. "The reason I was feeling so poorly at the last Legislature was I had kept on postponing an operation that I was to have at the Oshner Clinic in New Orleans. When my sweet little wife and my dear little nephew got me to go on that plane, they told me a damn lie that I was going to Oshner for my operation.

"Then when they got me to the plane, the bone crushers strapped me to the stretcher and a doctor stuck me through the britches with a needle. My wife and my nephew promised they would come right down to Oshner next day to see me. But the plane flew me to Galveston, and my sweet little wife hasn't showed up yet, neither my little nephew. When the plane landed me at that airport, there, they told me I was going to a rest house, where I was promised a double bed and quiet. The doctors gave me pills to make me sleep. First I took them one by one, then by the paper cupful. Then I got to chunkin' them in there by the wad. While I was in that condition, they got me to sign a thing that I wouldn't sue them for kidnaping. I went contrary to what my lawyers would have wanted." This, I learned long later, was precisely true. His Texas counsel believed he had his transporters cold under the Lindbergh Act.

Uncle Earl looked out at the reporters with bottomless pity in his eyes, as if he were recounting the ills, not of one storm-tossed traveler, but of all our common kind.

"They snatched me out without even enough clothes on me to cover up a red bug," he said, "and a week after I arrived in Texas I was enjoying the same wardrobe. They put me in a room with the door open and crazy people walking in and out all night; one of them thought it was the toilet."

"Pardon me," said a lady of the press, interrupting, "but what was the operation you were expecting?"

"I guess you can guess," the Governor answered, and he pointed down. "On my lower parts."

He was still intent on his sorrows. "Then, this Corner here," he said. "Wasn't he a nice judge to commit me to Mandeville when I come back? We been on opposite sides in politics as long as I remember, but if the position had been reversed, I might have given him a break. And Bankston, the superintendent, a man I appointed myself, could have left me out, but he wouldn't. But I got out, all right. I put *him* out and *got* out."

"Governor," a reporter queried, "what is your personal opinion of who's going to win this election?"

"I am," the seated orator replied without hesitation. "Uncle Earl. It's going to be a case of Katy bar the door. Little old Dellasoups Morrison will be second."

"And third?" pursued the questioner.

"Jimmie Davis, if he stays in the race," the man who picked himself said. "And little Willie Rainach and Big Bad Bill Dodd a dogfall for fourth." In country wrestling, a dogfall means that the men lose their footing simultaneously and both go down, which makes that fall a draw.

"We going to have a party here tomorrow, a homecoming party for the press," he said, "and you are all invited. Going to have something for everybody—religious music over here on one side of the room and honky-tonk on the other. But no Bedbug Blues—that's Jimmie Davis' tune."

There was a good deal of the discourse that I have not recorded. Carried away by the stream of idiom like a drunk on a subway train, I missed a lot of stations.

Somebody asked the Governor what he thought of the Luce publications' having asked for a change of venue to a Federal court in his libel suit for 6 million dollars. He said he didn't care what kind of court the case came up in.

"They going to find themselves lighter and wiser when it's over," he said. "The Luce people been going on too long picking on people too poor to sue them, and now they're going to get it in the neck. Mr. Luce is like a man that owns a shoestore and buys all the shoes to fit himself. Then he expects other people to buy them."

This was the best thing said about publishers, I felt, since I myself wrote thirteen years ago, "To the foundation of a school for publishers, without which no school of journalism can have meaning."

I put all my admiration in my glance and edged my chair up to the end of the Governor's sofa. When I try, I can exude sincerity as far as a llama can spit, and the Governor's gaze, swinging about the room, stopped when it lit on me. My eyes clamped it in an iron grip of approval.

I inched forwarder, trying not to startle him into putting a cop on me, and said, "Governor, I am not a newspaperman. I am with you all the way about publishers. Nor am I primarily interested in politics. I came all the way down here to find out your system for beating the horses."

An expression of modest disclaimer dropped like a curtain in front of the cocky old face.

"I got no particular system," he said. "I think I'm doing good to break even. I think horse betting should be dissected—into them that can afford it and them that can't. I think if you can afford it, it's a good thing to take your mind off your troubles and keep you out in the air."

"Do you play speed ratings?" I asked. The Governor, in his eagerness to talk simultaneously about all phases of handicapping, choked up—it was the bronchiectasis—and began to cough.

Quickly, I offered him a lemon drop and he accepted it. Once it was in his mouth, I knew, from my experience among the Arabs in the opposite end of the interrupted sea, that I had won. He had accepted my salt; now he would reciprocate. The bronchiectasis struggled with the lemon drop for a moment and then yielded.

The Governor's throat cleared, and he said, "Yo'all stay'n' eat."

"Y'all stay, too," the Governor said to Miss Dixon and Tom and a couple of other press people. "There's aplenty." I imagined he must have a great surplus of supermarket bargains in the larder. "Just set here and wait. We got a lot to talk about."

The reporters and television men who had deadlines were already clearing out. Earl shouted after them, "Y'all come back and I'll say this—" But they, who had waited for him so long, had had enough.

There had been so many people in the room, and for so long, that they had taken the snap out of the air conditioning. The men staying on for dinner—about fifteen of us—took off their coats and laid them down on chairs and sofas.

One of the women guests, a Northerner, inadvertently sat on a jacket a political gent had laid aside. It was a silvery Dacron-Acrilan-nylon-airpox miracle-weave nubbled in Danish-blue asterisks. She made one whoop and rose vertically, like a helicopter. She had sat on his gun, an article of apparel that in Louisiana is considered as essential as a zipper. Eyebrows rose about as rapidly as she did, and by the time she came down, she decided that comment would be considered an affectation.

A colored man brought a glass wrapped in a napkin to the Governor —"Something for my throat," the latter explained—and the members of his inner council gathered at his flanks and knees for the powwow on catfish bait. One of the bills Earl had in mind would give individual members of the Legislature scholarship funds to allot personally to young people in their districts. Another would raise the salaries of assistant attorney generals, whose friends in the Legislature might be expected to respond. There were various local baits, funds for construction. The compounders kept their voices low and mysterious, as if saying "One-half pint of fish oil, one ounce of tincture of asafetida, one ounce of oil of rhodium—that will fetch them," or "Mix equal parts of soft Limburger cheese and wallpaper cleaner—never fails." Sometimes a conspirator would be unable to suppress a laugh.

A Mr. Siegelin, a political catfisherman arriving late, brought with him two children, a girl of about ten and a boy of five.

"Give them Cokes," the Governor said, and while a state cop hurried off to fill the order, he said to the little girl, "I hope you ain't going steady yet."

The little girl shook her head, and Uncle Earl said, "That's right. I went with more than a hundred before I made up *my* mind."

Made it up too soon at that, he probably thought, as he wondered about Miz Blanche and the mortgage money.

The children took their Cokes and settled down on facing identical love seats to drink them, while their father, a fair man in shirt-sleeves, sat down to join in the bait suggestions, with his equivalent of "Cut smoked herring into bits. Soak in condensed milk several days." The group was still in the midst of bait-mixing when a plug-ugly, either a state trooper or a bodyguard from civilian life, came to the top of the steps leading to the dining room and shouted, "It's ready!" By his tone I judged him ravenously hungry.

The catfishermen remained engrossed in their concoctive delibera-tions, and the plug-ugly shouted at Mrs. Dixon, whom he judged less engaged, "C'mawn, *Maggie!*"

Mrs. Dixon rose, and the catfishermen, Southern gentlemen after all, perforce rose too and rushed toward the dining room in her wake, the Governor dragging the two children.

The ballroom smacked of Bachelors' Hall, lacking the touch of a woman's fastidious hand, but the dining end of the Mansion, I was happy to see, was well kept up. The long table under the great chan-delier was covered with a mountain range of napkins folded into dunce caps, with streams of table silver in the valleys between them, and the iced tea, Sargassified with mint and topped with cherry, was pretty near *Ladies' Home Journal* color-ad perfection. Negro waiters and waitresses swarmed about, smiling to welcome Odysseus home. None of them, either, seemed to miss Penelope. The wanderer, his heart expanding in this happy atmosphere, propelled me to a seat at the head of the table.

He took his place at my left, with the Northern lady across the table from him. Around the long board crouched plug-uglies in sports shirts, alternating with the guests: Tom, Mrs. Dixon, Senator Fredericks, Siege-lin, the two Siegelin children clutching Coca-Cola bottles, and half a dozen politicians I hadn't met. The colossal figure of Mr. Joe Arthur Sims, the Governor's personal counsel, dominated the other end of the table. Mr. Sims had his right arm in a plaster cast that kept his hand above his head, as if perpetually voting Aye. He had sustained an odd sort of fracture on July 4, he explained. It had followed hard on his stump speech for the Governor, a great oratorical effort, but he denied that he had thrown the arm out of joint. He said he was in an auto crash.

The Governor said, "We don't serve hard liquor here. Da church people wouldn't like it. But I'll get you some beer. Bob," he called to one of the somber seneschals, "get da man some beer." Quickly, the waiter fetched a can, two holes newly punched in the top, ready for drinking, and set it down on the table.

The beer bore an unfamiliar label, and the Governor said, "Dat looks like some of dat ten-cent beer from Schwegmann's." (He had probably bought it himself, on one of his raids for bargains.) "Dat looks like some of da stuff dat when da brewers got an overstock, dey sell it to da supermarkets. Get da man some *good* beer. And bring a glass—hear?"

He looked so healthy now that I ventured a compliment. "You fooled those doctors, all right," I said. "You're like that Swede Johansson—you have your own way of training."

"You see dat fight?" the Governor asked, suspending his attack on the salad, which he was tossing between his dentures with the steady motion of a hay forker. I said I had.

"I didn't see it, but I would have if I thought da fellow had a chance to lick Patterson," the Governor said. "Patterson's pretty good." (If he looked at the return fight, he was let down again.)

"I hear they've got a law here in Louisiana that a white boy can't even box on the same card with colored boys," I said.

"Yeah," said the Governor, "but dat kind of stuff is foolish. If dere's enough money in it, dey're bound to get together."

I recognized the theory of an economic resolution of the race conflict.

He sat there like a feudal lord, and his *maisnie*, the men of his household, leaned toward him like Indians around a fire. The trenchers went around, great platters of country ham and fried steak, in the hands of the black servingmen, and sable damsels toted the grits and gravy. There was no court musician, possibly because he would have reminded the Earl of Jimmie Davis, but there was a court jester, and now the master called for a jape.

"Laura, Laura," he called out to one of the waitresses, "set your tray down—dere, hand it to Bob. Tell us what your husband does for a living."

"Prizefighter, sir," the girl said.

"Show us how he does when he goes in da ring," the Governor ordered.

The girl, long, thin and whippy, was instantly a-grin. This was evidently a standard turn, and she loved the spotlight. She got rid of the tray and showed how her husband climbed through the ropes, lifting her right knee high to get over the imaginary strand, and holding the hem of her short skirt against the knee as a boxer sometimes holds his robe to keep it from getting in his way. Once inside, she danced about the ring, waving her clasped hands at friends in the imaginary crowd. Then she retired to a corner and crouched on an imaginary stool until the Governor hit the rim of a glass with a gravy spoon.

The girl came out, sparring fast, dancing around the ring and mugging for friends at ringside, with an occasional wink. The opposition didn't amount to much, I could see. Laura's husband, impersonated by Laura, was jabbing him silly. Then her expression changed; the other man was beginning to hit her husband where he didn't like it. Her head waggled. She began to stagger. Even the bodyguards, who must have seen the act often, were howling.

"Show us how your husband does when he gets tagged," the Governor ordered, and Laura fell forward, her arms hanging over the invisible ropes, her head outside the ring, her eyes bulged and senseless.

The feudal faces were red with mirth. I applauded as hard as I could. Laura stood up and curtsied.

"You gonna let him keep on fightin'?" the Governor asked.

"I don't want him to," Laura said, "don't want him get hurt. But I don't know if he'll quit."

"Is he easier to live with when he loses?" a State Senator asked.

"Yes, sir, he is," the jester said, and took her tray back from the colleague who had been holding it.

The meal went on.

"Dat's da way some a dese stump-wormers going to be when dis primary is over," Uncle Earl said. "Hanging on da ropes. If it's a pretty day for the primary, I'll win it all. I'll denude dem all, da *Times-Picayune* included."

Outside the air-conditioned keep, the enemy might howl, but inside, the old vavasor held his court without worrying.

"Da voting machines won't hold me up," he said. "If I have da raight commissioners, I can make dem machines play 'Home Sweet Home.'" He laughed confidingly. "Da goody-goodies brought in dose machines to put a crimp in da Longs," he said. "Da first time dey was used, in 1956,

I won on da first primary. Not even my brother Huey ever did dat.

"Da machines is less important dan who's allowed to vote," he said. "I appointed a man State Custodian of Voting Machines here dat run up a bill of a hundred and sixty-three thousand dollars for airplane hire in one year, just flying around da state, inspecting da machines. Good man, Southern gentleman—da *Times-Picayune* recommended him and I thought I'd satisfy dem for once. Den he got an appropriation from da Legislature to keep da machines in repair, but it said in da contract with da voting-machine company dat da company had to keep dem in repair for one year for free. So he split da money wit da company—dey sent him six thousand dollars, and den another six thousand, but I grabbed half of da second six thousand for my campaign fund. Should have took it all."

The cellarer he had sent for the name-brand beer returned with a report that none except the supermarket kind was cold.

"Dey keeping da good beer for demself," the Governor said indulgently. "You drink dis." It tasted fine.

The Northern woman, who had listened with awe to the career of the voting-machine man, asked, "What happened to him?"

"I denuded him," the Governor said. "It's an electoral office now."

"And where is he now?" the woman asked, expecting, perhaps, to hear that he was confined in a *cachot* beneath the Mansion.

"He's hypnotizing people and telling fortunes and locating oil wells," the Governor said, "and he got himself a fine blonde and built her a big house and quit home."

Outside of the *Lives of the Troubadours*, which was compiled in the thirteenth century, I had never known a better-compressed biography. I felt that I knew the denuded hypnotist well. I remembered the comparable beauty of the Governor's account of the last day of a beloved uncle in Winnfield: "He got drunk and pulled a man out of bed and got into bed with the man's wife, and the man got mad and shot my poor uncle, and he died."

I asked him what he thought of Governor Faubus of north-neighboring Arkansas, who had won a third term by closing the schools, and he said Faubus was a fine man, but nobody had told him about the Civil War.

"Fellas like Faubus and Rainach and Leander Perez and da rest of da White Citizens and Southern Gentlemen in dis state want to go back behind Lincoln," he said. "And between us, gentlemen, as we sit here among ourselves," he said, arresting a chunk of fried steak in midair and leaning forward to give his statement more impetus, "we got to admit dat Lincoln was a fine man and dat he was right."

Then, as he turned back to the steak, skewering it against a piece of ham before swallowing both, he caught my look of astonishment and cried, too late, "But don't quote me on dat!"

Since he has won his last primary, I disregard his instructions. It was a brave thing for a Governor of Louisiana to say and would have made a lethal headline in his enemies' hands: LONG ENDORSES LINCOLN; HINTS WAR BETWEEN STATES ENDED.

We had up another can of beer, and the Governor and I shared it with a sense of double complicity.

"Laura, Laura," the Governor called to his jester, "get rid of dat tray."

"Yes, sir, Mr. Governor," and the star turn passed the grits to a co-worker.

"Now, Laura," the Governor said, "can you make a speech like Mr. McLemore?" (McLemore had been the White Citizens' candidate in '56.)

This was plainly another well-used bit of repertory. The Prizefighter and Mr. McLemore may be Laura's *Cavalleria* and *Pagliacci*, always done as a double bill. But I'd love to hear her sing Jimmie Davis.

She took a stance, feet wide apart and body stick-straight, looking as foolish as she could.

"Ladies and gentlemen," she said, "do not vote for Mr. Earl Long, because he has permitted da Supreme Court of da United States to make a decision by which, by which, Little White Johnny will have to attend da same school with Little Black Mary. If you wish to prevent dis, vote for, vote for—" and she hesitated, like a man fumbling in his mind for his own name. Then, running her hands over her body, she located, after some trouble, a white card in her breast pocket. The card, a planted prop, showed she had expected to perform. She took the card, peered at it, turned it around and finally read, "McLemore. Dat's it. Vote for Mc-Lemore."

The Earl howled, and so did all his guests and men-at-arms. I do not imagine that Penelope would have found it all that funny. She probably cramped his style.

The meal ended with a great volume of ice cream. The Governor, in high humor and perhaps still thinking of the frustrated voting machines, said to the lady across from him, "Would you mind if I told you a semi-bad story?"

She said she would not mind, and the Governor began: "There was an important man once who had a portable mechanical-brain thinking machine that he carried everywhere with him. Da machine was about as big as a small model of one of dose fruit machines dey have in a

Elks clubhouse. When he wanted a answer—How many square feet in a room by so and so much? or, Has dat blonde a husband and is he home?—he submitted his question and da machine answered it correctly. He would write out da question on a piece of paper and put it in a slot, da machine would read it, and pretty soon it would go blam, blam, blam —blam, blam, blam—dat was da brain working, and it would give him a printed slip with da correct answer. Well, finally da man got jealous of dis machine, it was such a Jim-cracker, and he thought he take it down a little for its own good.

"So he wrote out a message: 'Where is my dear father at this minute, and what is he doing?' He put it in da slot, and da machine says, 'Blam, blam, blam,' very calm, like he had asked it something easy, and it write out da answer: 'Your dear father is in a pool hall in Philadelphia, *Penn*-sylvania, at dis moment, shooting a game of one hundred points against a man named Phil Brown. Your dear father is setting down watching, and Phil Brown has da cue stick and is about to break.'"

"Philadelphia, *Pennsylvania*" had the romantic sound in the Governor's mouth of Coromandel in Sinbad's.

The Governor's manner changed, and his voice became indignant. " 'Why,' da man says, 'dat's da most unmitigated libelous slander I ever heard of. My dear father is sleeping in da Baptist cemetery on da side of da hill in *Pittsburgh*, Pennsylvania, and has been for da last five years. I am sure of da dates because my dear mother who is still living reminded me of da anniversary of his death and I telegraphed ten dollars worth of flowers to place on his grave. I demand a *re*investigation and an *apology*.'

"And he writes it out and puts it in da slot. 'Dis time I got you,' he says. 'You ain't nothing but a machine anyway.'

"Da machine reads da message and gets all excited. It says, 'Blam, *Blam*' and 'Blam, *blam*,' like it was scratching its head, and den 'Blam, blam, blam, blam . . . blam, blam, blam, blam,' like it was running its thoughts through again, and den 'BLAM!' like it was mad, and out comes da message."

All eyes were on the Governor now, as if the ladies and men-at-arms half expected him to materialize the ticker tape.

"Da message said 'REPEAT,'" the Governor said, "It said 'REPEAT' and den, 'RE-REPEAT. Your dear father is in a pool hall at Philadelphia, *Pennsylvania*, playing a game with a man named Phil Brown. YOUR MOTHER'S LEGALLY WEDDED HUSBAND is in the Baptist cemetery on the side of the hill in *Pittsburgh*, *Pennsylvania*, and has been there these last five years, you BASTARD. The only change in the situation is that

Phil Brown has run fourteen and missed, and your old man now has the cue stick. I predict he will win by a few points.' "

It broke everybody up, and soon the Governor said to the outsiders politely, "Y'all go home. We got a lot to do tonight." But he said he might be able to see me at nine next morning.

I arose at that hour and got over there, but there were already so many cars on the driveway that if it hadn't been morning I would have guessed there was a cockfight in the basement. Inside the Mansion, the nearly bookless library on the right of the door that serves as a waiting room was full of politicians, all wearing nubbly suits and buckskin shoes, and each sporting the regulation enlargement of the left breast beneath the handkerchief pocket. (This group included no left-handed pistol shot.) The length of the queue demonstrated that the public reaction to the speeches had been favorable, and that the sheiks who had raided the herds in Earl's absence were there to restore the stolen camels.

A Negro in a white jacket came in and asked the ritual "Y'all have coffee?" Since I had no deal to offer, I just had coffee and went.

Odysseus ruled in Ithaca again.

Note on His Honor

꙳ ꙳

THERE WAS a picture of Mayor Morrison in a colonel's uniform at the Eiffel Tower after he liberated it in 1944, and snaps of him laying cornerstones and greeting a delegation of Uruguayan schoolchildren. In all of them he was smiling and fighting politely for the center of the picture, even at the risk of being trampled by a horse.

Sports

From Sarah Bernhardt to
Yukon Eric

❦ ❦

In the prelude to one of the Arabian Nights stories, the Caliph Haroun-al-Rashid feels blue and asks the Grand Vizier for remedies. The Vizier suggests looking in a glass, visiting the baths, and listening to sweet music; if all these fail, the Caliph will just have to find another woman.

I, when the cares of the real world press hard upon me, sometimes visit the office of *Wrestling World*, a publication that has its being in Room 418 of the Longacre Building, a well-worn office structure on the northeast corner of 42nd Street and Broadway. The editors, cultured fellows in their eighth decades, are Ned Brown and Al Mayer.

Mr. Mayer, who has a white mane, a black mustache, and a hypnotic eye, came to the United States from France forty-five years ago, as stage manager for Sarah Bernhardt on one of her transcontinental tours. Much later, when he was New York correspondent for *La Nación,* of Buenos Aires, that newspaper sent him an Argentine heavyweight prizefighter on consignment. The editors of *La Nación* were not interested in a share of the fighter's earnings; all they wanted was an exclusive ghostwritten first-person daily story of his adventures. The fighter was Luis Angel Firpo. Mayer took him on and made a quarter of a million dollars, which he no longer has. He also ghostwrote the daily story.

Mr. Brown, as a young medical student turned newspaper reporter, determined from the wrinkled skin on the severed hand of a widely distributed corpse—the head never did turn up—that the defunct's last employment had been as a rubber in a Turkish bath. In the early part of the twentieth century, Turkish baths specialized in curing hangovers,

227

and Mr. Brown, like Haroun-al-Rashid, knew them all. Checking these establishments in midtown, he soon found one where a man had not reported back for work after his day off. The management thought he must be on a bender and had decided to fire him. Brown traced the man to his neighborhood saloon, where the bartender also reported him missing of late, and thence to his lodgings, where he spotted the murderer and murderess. They were subsequently convicted and executed. This coup might have been expected to lead to a career of crime detection, but it didn't; Mr. Brown became a boxing writer, and a good one, on the old *World*. Since that paper's demise, in 1931, he has been what he describes as a protean publicist. His appearance, like Mr. Mayer's, is distinguished, but in the sterling Anglo-Saxon rather than the Continental manner, with wintry blue eyes and white hair.

What with Mr. Brown's talent for detection and Mr. Mayer's backstage approach to histrionics, it might be assumed that they would take a cynical view of a sport that has been frequently charged with insincerity, but they don't. The November number of *Wrestling World*, for example, carries on its front cover a striking portrait study of a gentleman named Hard-Boiled Haggerty, who, the caption states, is "Hot on Trail of Lou Thesz for Championship Match." Mr. Haggerty's head rises between his shoulders like the Sphinx between two pyramids; his face is dabbled with what I at first took to be grains of Puffed Rice but now believe to be drops of sweat, for his expression makes it evident that he has just emerged from triumphant combat. His neck is slightly wider than his face, and only his ears break the sweeping line from collarbone to top of cranium. Without them, he would have the silhouette of a 155-mm. shellcase. The rear cover carries a likeness of June Byers, "New Undisputed Women's World Wrestling Champion," and a pleasing contrast to Mr. Haggerty. Miss Byers is wearing what looks like a Spanish shawl over a bikini; she is on high heels and appears to be tapping her right foot impatiently, an ill omen for somebody. Interposed between Mr. Haggerty and Miss Byers are thirty-four pages of text and pictures. The latter include shots of Yukon Eric, a hero type who wrestles in blue jeans, in action against Wladek Kowalski, a villainous character whom the sourdough has lifted to his shoulder with one arm. There are also views of Ray Thunder Stern, another hero, high in the air before landing kerplunk on the convex frontal elevation of a villain named Bibber McCoy, who lies flat on the canvas to receive him; of a masked marvel called El Diablo; of a German-style villain known as Ach Du Lieber Kurt von Poppenheim, who is accoutered with a beard, a monocle, and a homburg; of Oyama Kato, a Japanese-style villain, coldly sneering;

and of Eric the Great Pedersen, a Scandinavian Body Beautiful.

What *Time* would call the cover story is headed HAGGERTY HUNGERS FOR TITLE. "Generally Haggerty's battles turn out to be 'audience participation' affairs," the story says, in part. "For Hard-Boiled uses the archvillain style of wrestling, in which everything goes—including the temper of the crowd. And so the stormy petrel of the mat has had some rough encounters with the crowds that flock to see him get licked. When he doesn't, they resent it and try to take matters into their own hands as he wends his way toward the dressing room after a battle." The accompanying art shows Hard-Boiled laughing evilly as he squeezes an agonized opponent's chin—the fellow's face is covered with ketchup or blood—and frowning in villainous perplexity as he tries to identify his own legs, which are interlaced with those of a wily challenger.

The last quarter of the magazine is devoted to the affairs of the Wrestling Fan Clubs Association of America, a form of literary audience participation devised by Mr. Brown. The clubs are dedicated to individual wrestlers, or to small groups of wrestlers who are linked by nationality or genre. There are about a hundred and twenty clubs listed in the magazine, with the names and addresses of their corresponding secretaries, and all of them get out bulletins and hold conventions and write letters to *Wrestling World*. Brown's daughter Eleanor conducts a department called "Cousin El's Mailbox," in which she publishes and answers the club members' letters.

On my visits to Room 418, Mr. Brown and Mr. Mayer and I usually discuss great figures of the past, like Mme. Bernhardt; Firpo; Gyp the Blood, a gunman after whom Mr. Brown once named a cocktail; and Charles E. Chapin, the city editor of the *World* who murdered his wife. Our conversation touches only incidentally on the industry with which Mr. Brown and Mr. Mayer are now associated, and in which my interest has long been so mild that it verges on distaste. During my acquaintance with the wrestling business, I have seen it down, up, down, and pretty far up again, like one of Yukon Eric's opponents lifted high above the mat. When I began to read sports pages, wrestling was in a state of profound depression, owing to the earnest efforts of a number of wrestlers to defeat each other. Conducted honestly, wrestling is the dullest of sports to watch, but wrestlers with an honest background can lend a fake verisimilitude to their work that non-wrestlers find it hard to duplicate.

In the thirties, when every other business in the country was on the rocks, wrestling hit a peak of prosperity, under the aegis of a large, disarming man named Jack Curley, who was a walking embodiment of the popular conception of a promoter. Curley had a large corps of hungry genuine wrestlers at his disposition. His ore-extraction process was always the same. The world's championship was held by a veteran wrestler named Jim Londos, who had a dramatic spark lacking in most of his colleagues. (Whether Londos was the best wrestler of his time is dubious, but he was certainly the best spectacular wrestler.) A Foreign Menace, in most cases a real wrestler, would be imported. He would meet all the challengers for the title whom Londos had defeated in any city larger than New Haven, and beat them. After that, he and Londos would wrestle for the world's championship in Madison Square Garden. The Foreign Menace would oppress Londos unmercifully for about forty minutes, and then Londos would pick him up for the airplane spin, which is like the climatic movement of an adagio dance or a hammer throw. Skeptics have pointed out that this movement requires cooperation from the adagio projectile, even if it is a ninety-pound girl. (The hammer weighs sixteen pounds.) Curley never admitted that the airplane spin wasn't on the level, but he never claimed that it was. He just used to grin. Londos would whirl the current Menace around his head and dash him to the mat three times, no more and no less, and the match would end in time for suburbanites to get the trains they caught on theater nights. After the bout, the Menace would either return to Europe or remain here to become part of the buildup for the next Menace.

In the season of 1931-1932, ten such Garden bouts drew an average of $24,000, which, when you consider what you could buy with it then, was a whale of a lot of money. It was a David Belasco period in the production of wrestling; there was a heavy literalism about the whole performance. But it drew the customers. Londos spoiled it all, according to his detractors in the industry, by demanding a genuine champion's share of the gate receipts. He was unfrocked, and within a year the country swarmed with champions. By 1939, I happen to remember, there were fifteen. The first thing a promoter did on going into business was to name a champion; then he signed a lease on an office. The business needed new, streamlined attractions, for the surviving real wrestlers were so old, fat, and homely that they had no gate appeal. Some of them had been professionally active for forty years. Yet, like the Janizaries of the Ottoman decadence, they represented a perpetual threat to their employers, since they could cross them up at any time by throwing the young, attractive champions, who couldn't really wrestle. A wrestling show held in the Garden in 1938 drew less than $5,000, and that was the last one there for a long time.

Professional wrestling took refuge in small clubs in foreign-language neighborhoods, where it became an intimate art form with a European frame of reference, like the antics of the Fratellini clowns in the Cirque Médrano. Wrestlers billed as Italians and Ethiopians one season became Germans and Czechs the next. A wrestler showing as a German Apollo in the Ridgewood section of Queens, where there was a large German-American population, might perform as a Polish Hercules in the Bronx. Grimaces and dialogue registered in the small halls; the kinetic aspect of the art form was subordinated to the mimetic. All the activity that was manifested took the form of a spurious and largely symbolic violence. It was a period of re-evaluation; wrestling was being eliminated from wrestling. An old acquaintance of mine named Jack Pfefer was, as the boys on the literary quarterlies would say, a seminal innovator of this transition. Pfefer, a frail, corvine man who came into wrestling after unsuccessful impresarial efforts in Russian opera and ballet, had no hampering ties to a past in which wrestlers had wrestled; he presented not imitation wrestling matches but pure fantasy.

"I tell them who should win," he would say. "I treat them like a father—like a mother who beats up her baby."

The difference between Pfefer's productions and Curley's was like that between avowed fiction and a Hearst news story. Pfefer's productions were weak in acrobatics but rich in humorous characterization, and so were his players, like King Kong the Fiopian (Pfeferese for Ethiopian) Gorilla Man, a chap of superhuman strength except for his Achilles' heel, which was in his whiskers. King Kong's opponent, on the point of simulated strangulation, had but to touch these and the Gorilla Man released his grip. A gentle pull and King Kong gibbered. A determined tug and he became an abject thing, cowering in terror, while the delighted audience chorused, "Pull 'em again!"

The last of Pfefer's shows I saw was at the Ridgewood Grove Arena in 1939. It drew only $600, but half of that was profit. The performers got sixty-five dollars a week for five shows. They also paid their own subway fares going and coming. Mr. Mayer worked for Pfefer that season as a publicity man, carrying large framed posters from club to club for lobby display. He traveled on the subway, too. At the end of 1944, when I returned from Europe, I learned that Pfefer had taken his comedic gifts to Toledo, Ohio. Wrestling in New York was as dead as prohibition. It came back with television, which tapped new reservoirs of credulity. On the night of Washington's Birthday, 1949, a man named Bill Johnston promoted the first wrestling exhibition in the Garden in eleven years, featuring a grotesque named Gorgeous George. (The New York State Athletic Commission, refusing to recognize wrestling as a competitive activity, insists that all pairings be billed as exhibitions rather than matches.) Newspapers covered Gorgeous George's debut with their drama, moving-picture, and television critics, as well as with their sportswriters. It got tremendous publicity, all bad, but the journalists tried so hard to be funny that they made the subject itself seem amusing. That show lost $1,500, but within a year or two the wrestling productions at the Garden were drawing money again. Last season, six presentations averaged a bit more than $30,000—better than Curley's old mark, though rather less impressive, considering the higher incidence of money.

When I visited the *Wrestling World* office a couple of weeks ago, Mr. Mayer, who knows my views on the branch of drama with which he is currently associated, surprised me by suggesting that I attend the first *soirée* of the current Garden season.

"Psychologically, it would entrance you," he said. "Nationalism is dead. That was neighborhood stuff. On television, it would mean nothing, because you wouldn't know which nationality to make the villain. What the new wrestling public is interested in is villainy as villainy, virtue as virtue. It is very ethical."

To prove the point, Mr. Brown showed me a letter from a woman who said that she was eighty-one and lived in an old ladies' home, and that wrestling, which she saw on television, was all that kept her alive. She knew that if she just kept on watching long enough, the villains would get what they deserved, and this was very comforting. Mr. Mayer said that the Garden show would not be televised, so all the television fans who had the price of admission could be counted on to attend, in order to see their heroes in the flesh. The principals in the main exhibition were Antonino Rocca, a bounding, swaggering, smiling type who specializes in kicks and leaps, and Hans Schmidt, a horrid Nazi villain, libelously averred by a number of his competitors to be a French Canadian.

"In the beginning of his career Schmidt attracted attention by giving the Nazi salute, turning his back on the American flag, and sitting down during 'The Star-Spangled Banner,'" Mr. Mayer said. "Recently he has cut that stuff, because it no longer provokes sufficient animosity. There has been a change in the international climate."

The event that would interest me most, Mr. Brown predicted, was the tag-team match, between two teams of two wrestlers each, with the partners spelling each other as the spirit moved them. "It introduces the team spirit into wrestling," Mr. Brown said. "Self-sacrifice, help the other fellow, all that. It's the coming thing." In the tag-team match, Art Neilson and Reggie Lisowski, both of Chicago, were to oppose Pat O'Connor, of Ireland, and Yukon Eric. These four wrestlers, plus Rocca and Schmidt, constituted the all-star portion of the card, Brown said; all of them had heavy bookings throughout the country, and they would probably be flown into New York for the Garden show and then flown out to their next engagements. The preliminaries would be made up of local talent.

Because I hadn't been to a wrestling show since the new trend began, I decided to see the whole thing, and on the evening of October 26, the date of the exhibition, I went over to the Garden at about six o'clock in order to be sure of a good seat. The box offices in the lobby were already doing a fairly brisk business, at a scale of three dollars, four dollars, and five dollars, but I needn't have been anxious. It was not the frenzy of the old Londos days. I got a seat in the first raised ringside row, and went off to dinner. When I returned, a few minutes before eight-thirty, the lobby was filled with what twenty years ago I would have taken for a convention of the Townsend Club, the national organization that campaigned for liberal old-age pensions. The Townsendites used to contend that their plan would end the depression of those days, because old people would put the money right back into circulation— a short life and a merry one. The crowd at the Garden appeared to support their theory. With shining faces, the Darbys and Joans filed past the bronze statue of Joe Gans, the old colored pugilist, in the lobby, converging on the raffishly ethical entertainment from Jackson Heights and Flatbush and London Terrace and the Grand Concourse. All, or almost all, were in their seats before the first bout started; the evening's excursion had been carefully planned, probably weeks in advance. The audience looked more like a prewar Sunday-night crowd at Lüchow's than like the mob at any other kind of sporting event.

I felt myself absurdly young, although I voted for Al Smith, and heard myself saying as I worked my way in toward my seat, unavoidably stepping on a few toes, "Pardon me, sir," "Excuse me, Ma'am," "Sorry to be so late," although, of course, I wasn't late. "It's all right, son," an old gentleman with a prominent vein in his forehead said as I stumbled past him. I hoped that excitement was not bad for him and that he had consulted his physician before coming. A woman behind me, whom I regarded as I struggled to get my coat off, had the look of Germanic well-to-do-ness that I have always associated with small holders of stock in large breweries. She reminded me of a woman my mother used to call Mrs. Immaculate; she was wearing two pearl earrings that precisely matched her two eyes—large round pearls, small round eyes, small round face. It was a study in juxtaposed circles. Her lips were thin, tight, and straight, and the semicircle of frizzled gray hair visible under her hat was precisely matched by the collar of frizzled gray fur at her throat. She sat between two elderly men, and I could tell that one was not with her, because he was smiling. "I hope he don't stand there until the commencement, Poppa," she said to the man on her other side, and he pretended not to notice.

The participants in the first exhibition of the evening were introduced as Buddy Lee, of Hollywood, and Hal Kanner, of Brooklyn, both around 220 pounds. Lee had platinum-blond hair, which he wore in a kind of Dutch cut, like Prince Valiant's in the comic strip, and he sported a white silk shirt and a red-white-and-blue doublet over his wrestling trunks. To my inexpert eye, this was the costume of a hero, but I quickly perceived from the crowd's attitude that I was wrong. Vanity was the deadly sin incarnated by the nature boy; in the new frame of reference, all wrestlers with this kind of haircut and personality are known as nature boys. Some are more famous than others, but all are considered obnoxious, except by bobby-soxers, who form their fan clubs. The nature boys are given to posing, petulance, and treachery. Kanner, a rugged, honest fellow, was more of a Horatio Alger type—pleasant, but a demon when aroused. While the referee was delivering his homily, Lee made a sweeping upward gesture of both arms, as if asking the referee what would happen if he simply tossed Kanner out of the ring. The crowd booed, and the woman behind me said, "Boy, will he get what he deserves—he's so mean."

The referee waved the contestants to their corners. Lee removed his showy upper garments and flexed all his muscles, as if posing for a barbell advertisement. Kanner advanced, extending a hand in sportsmanlike bonhomie. Lee brushed it aside, and the crowd booed again. Appearing to repent, Lee then extended his hand, but when the Brooklynite approached to take it, the nature boy snatched it away and grabbed Kanner's hair with his left hand.

"Why don't you pull *hiss* hair?" the woman behind me yelled, but it was too late, or else Kanner didn't hear her.

Lee, exerting the leverage of only a handful of hair, threw him into a triple cartwheel, followed by a series of what acrobats call spotted tinsikas and a back flip. Then, as Kanner lay prostrate, the nature boy kicked him in the face. Kanner rose, rubbing his eyes; obviously, the kick had paralyzed an optic nerve. Dr. Vincent Nardiello, the official boxing physician, would have stopped the bout right there, but wrestlers are of sterner stuff. Kanner shook his head, and his optic nerve unparalyzed itself. He descried the faithless Lee and rushed at him, and Lee, made a coward by conscience, shrank away, shaking his blond locks in disavowal of evil intent. It did him no good. Kanner struck him a terrific blow under the chin—about three inches under it and traveling toward his right shoulder, it seemed to me—but the wind it kicked up capsized Lee, who now refused to rise, and held out placating hands and shook his hair some more.

"All those tough guys, they're so yellow," the lady behind me said with contempt.

But by some treacherous turn I do not now recall, the nature boy re-established the equilibrium of the battle. I think it was by a lethal maneuver known in 1939 as the boomps-a-daisy—thrusting his posterior into Kanner's rapidly advancing diaphragm. This, of course, knocked every cubic inch of breath out of Kanner, although he held, at a rough estimate, as much as a barrage balloon. He fell, and Lee kneaded his arms like an osteopath—a tactic that sent a sympathetic shudder through the entire audience. It is a frightful thing when eleven thousand people shudder simultaneously, especially if you are wedged between two of them.

"Disqualify him!" the man with the prominent vein said hoarsely. "Disqualify him!" The man's eyes were glassy, his forehead humid. "Disqualify him!" he croaked. If he collapsed in the midst of that shuddering mass, I knew, the ushers would have to get him out in a breeches buoy.

But Kanner was up. His arms were still on. How he had dislodged the nature boy I am not certain, but I think it was by reaching up one foot behind the sadist's right ear and distracting his attention; then, when Lee turned, Kanner probably got away without being noticed. Various competitors were doing things like that all night, and my memories melt together like a bag of chocolates inadvertently left in a hip pocket. Anyway, Kanner ran at Lee again, and Lee turned away, preparing to give him the awful boomps-a-daisy.

The crowd quavered, in unison, "Look out!," but Kanner needed no warning. Rising on his left toe, he punted Lee through the ropes.

Mrs. Immaculate loosed a peal of joy. "Ha-ha, you poor thing!" she yelled.

Then Lee got out of control altogether. Bounding back into the ring, he began jumping on Kanner's feet. The referee remonstrated. Lee applied another foul stratagem—trying, as I recall, to get Kanner's head under the top rope and saw it off.

"Disqualify him!" the old man near me burbled. "Disqualify him!" His voice sounded like air escaping from an inner tube, but the referee, fifty yards away, must have heard him. He tore Lee from his prey and waved him to his corner. The nature boy protested, hair whipping about wildly, like paper streamers on an electric fan.

The announcer stepped to the microphone. "Lee refuses to listen to the referee," he said. "He is disqualified."

The decent instincts of the crowd were vindicated. "The meanness is in them," the woman behind me explained to her husband, who had not yet said a word, "and they just can't help it, no matter how many times they try."

There were three more preliminary matches, and in each of them the moral issue was as clearly drawn. One match, between two fellows with Italian names—an illustration of what Mayer had said about the abandonment of the national motif—ended, like the chariot race in a circus, with the hero chasing the craven villain three laps around the ring in time that would be creditable at Sportsman's Park, a race track near Chicago with similar turns. In only one exhibition did the embodiment of virtue fail, and then the outcome was written in the stars, for when the men entered the ring, one, introduced as Hans Herman, of Germany, 291 pounds, towered far above his opponent from Yonkers, a pygmy of 228.

Yonkers scuttled between Herman's widely straddled legs a couple of times, and virtue's cheerleader back of me caroled, "Ha-ha, he makes a fool of him!," but the man with the prominent vein, who was by now olive-green with emotion, refused to kid himself.

"What chance has he with a wild animal like that?" he asked all of us. "He's crazy."

Sure enough, Germany threw Yonkers, but the crowd was remarkably cheerful. It anticipated, correctly, that Herr Herman was being fattened for a future sacrifice on the altar of the good and beautiful. Then came a ten-minute break, to permit the audience to recompose its feelings and buy hot dogs.

At the end of the break, the announcer informed us all that the main bout, between Rocca and Schmidt, to a finish, would go on immediately, to be followed by the team match.

"That means Rocca will throw him quick because there's a curfew at eleven, and he'll have to leave time for the tag-team match," a knowing man at my right hand said. While his cynicism surprised me, it also convinced me, because I couldn't imagine a promoter flying four tag-team wrestlers here from Chicago and then not using them. They could have been making money in some place like Wheeling.

"But suppose Schmidt throws Rocca?" I asked, just to make conversation. The man looked at me incredulously and clammed up. It was evident that he considered Schmidt a long shot.

It was then ten o'clock, and Rocca won in twenty minutes, by bounding atop Schmidt's shoulders, wrapping his legs around the reformed Nazi's throat, and then imparting to him a spinning motion, like a top. Having spun tops myself as a boy, I could appreciate the practicality of the idea, and I wondered why no wrestler had ever thought of it before. Rocca, respecting the tradition of the number three, spun Schmidt three times and then flattened his shoulders to the mat while he was still dizzy. In this case, the kinetic element in the art had pushed the mimetic into limbo. The two men's personalities barely emerged through the choreography, but they were a pair of remarkably fine tumblers. Rocca, bounding about in bare feet, gave the whole performance a spot too much chypre for the old Curley days, but the world must advance, I suppose. One awfully cute touch came when he lay on his back and played pat-a-cake on Schmidt's tum with his bare feet.

I had employed the interval in reading the program note on Neilson and Lisowski. "To look at Art Neilson and Reggie Lisowski," it said, "you'd get a first impression they were just clean, overgrown boys. . . . They are recognized as the world's champions, but never has the wrestling game produced a combine that the public has hated so intensely. Several times in recent months, they've had to escape with their lives from irate citizens after messing up local favorites. . . . Evidently, Lisowski and Neilson can only find friendship in one another during their long wrestling treks. 'Who cares?' they say in unison."

I could see that this was an attitude that would not be appreciated by most of my neighbors, and I wondered how Neilson and Lisowski would contrive to remain champions without defeating the heroes. When I saw them enter the ring, I recognized them for what they were; both had long blond haircuts, both wore the Prince Valiant getup, and as they stood elbow to elbow, arms akimbo, pointing their chins at the ceiling, they made an irritating contrast to their opponents, stalwart he-men both. Yukon Eric, who weighed 274 pounds, came into the ring wearing lumberman's boots, as well as jeans, but he took the boots off before the wrestling started. He left the jeans on. Mr. O'Connor looked clean and determined—just the kind of straight man a kindly old sourdough of gigantic strength would befriend. When the insolent nature boys took off their fancy jerkins, however, it could be seen that they, too, were men of gigantic strength. The program said that Lisowski weighed 248 pounds and Neilson 235. I was never sure which was which.

In a tag match, each team operates from a corner, as in boxing. A six-foot length of rope is tied to the top strand of the ring in each corner. The temporarily disengaged member of the team is supposed to hold the end of this rope and move only within its orbit until he can touch, or be touched by, his partner. The fellows doing the wrestling wrestle, but the man getting the worst of it tries to wriggle toward his own corner, so that his presumably fresh partner can relieve him. If either partner is thrown, it counts a throw against the team.

O'Connor began for the good partners, but the lead-off nature boy got the better of him by unfair means—sticking his fingers in his eyes, I think. O'Connor, blinded, staggered back—luckily, back was in the direction of his own corner—and just as the nature boy, with a horrid squeal, was about to hurl himself on the sightless man, Yukon Eric, straining at his leash, touched O'Connor. Striding out into the ring, he pushed his partner aside, hitched up his jeans, and faced the nature boy, who, with a conceited smile, squeezed Eric's huge torso in a grip of steel. Do you know how Eric broke the grip? He just inhaled. His chest expansion flung the foeman's arms apart. They fell helpless, and Eric smiled grimly. Try it again, he seemed to say, and Lisowski—or maybe it was Neilson—did. Eric breathed in again, and the same thing happened. Neilson, or Lisowski, knew what he was up against then, but it was too late, or almost. Eric picked him up in his arms like a baby and threw him up in the air. Unfortunately, he landed within reach of his partner, who came scrambling forward with feigned alacrity, but this didn't fool Mrs. Immaculate. "Ha-ha, you know what you going to get!" she cried, in a pleased tone. The creature—Lisowski it was, or maybe Neilson—had courage, though, and I had to give him credit. He tried to hit Eric, but the titanic miner seized his wrist and flung him into an imitation of a carrousel. Lisowski or Neilson, whoever it was, became so dizzy that he walked toward the *wrong* corner. That brought him within O'Connor's reach, and you know how *he* must have felt after having his eyes gouged out, but he could see all right now. O'Connor grabbed Neilson or Lisowski by the hair and threw him upside down. Having wreaked this bit of vengeance, O'Connor went back to his corner, and Yukon Eric took over again. He picked up Lisowski (unless it was Neilson) and threw him through the air the way he had thrown Neilson before (unless it was Lisowski). By bad luck, he also threw this one too far, landing him at his partner's feet, in their corner. Then mighty Eric walked forward to finish him, as one would finish a gambler whom one had just recognized in a Yukon house of ill fame as the despoiler of one's sister. There were surely some people in the five-dollar seats who could have screamed a warning, but they sat mute with horror as Eric, forgetting all in his rage, advanced into the nature boys' corner, where they *both* could get at him. The nature boys were breaking the rules, but what does that kind care about rules? As Eric stooped to administer the *coup de grâce,* the non-wrestling nature boy slipped the six-foot rope under his throat and strangled him. Then the prostrate devil leaped up and joined in the attack, whacking Eric on the back of the neck with iron fists. O'Connor strained at his legal leash in the far corner, helpless to aid. A Lisowski or a Neilson would have flouted the rule, but a he-man can't.

"Disqualify them! Disqualify them!" a familiar voice screamed.

But the referee was deaf, and justice is blind by definition. The cads did mighty Eric in. It came as a special blow to everybody, because Eric was the strong member of our team; everybody felt safe while he was doing the wrestling.

"That's the only way they always win, with their foul tactics!" Mrs. Immaculate cried behind me. "Without the rope they couldn't a done it."

It was only then that I glanced at my program and saw that the match was two falls out of three. Lisowski and Neilson were back on their feet, and were holding their right fists aloft as if they had done something wonderful in ganging up on poor old Eric. But they had a surprise coming to them. As soon as the second fall started, Pat O'Connor came out and nearly murdered Lisowski or Neilson, whichever. He was determined to avenge Eric. The nature boy tried to crawl through the ropes to get away.

"He's going for the ropes immediately!" my lady friend shrilled, and as the wretch made gestures toward his throat, to convey the idea that O'Connor had used a strangle hold, she shrieked, "You're not choking, you're faking!"

The fellow grabbed O'Connor and got him down for a second, but Yukon Eric roguishly climbed through the ropes, came around the ring, and put O'Connor on top again. The crowd condoned this infraction of the rules, because it was done by an honest man. In another instant, O'Connor had pinned either Neilson's or Lisowski's shoulders to the canvas, and the score was deuce.

The rubber fall was the most thrilling of the three, but unhappily the curfew rang while all four men were trading punches in the center of the ring, and the hapless, helpless referee wrung his hands in despair. The nature boys held each other's hands up as if they'd won, but the eleven thousand old men and women just booed. So did I. It had stepped up all our metabolisms, softened our arteries, strengthened our faith in the invincibility of right, and built up a hell of a return match. The disqualification man's complexion had visibly improved, from light olive to canary yellow, and I will lay you ten to one he survives until Yukon Eric faces the wolf pack again.

As for Mrs. Immaculate, she got her husband out of there winging, and I heard her say, as she hustled him out to the aisle, "We can just get back to Staten Island in time for the wrestling on television."

In my mind, I had named the husband William the Silent, and he made good for me; he didn't say anything.

꾸 꾸

I have always believed in the therapeutic value of attending horse races. It fills the lungs and empties the mind.

A New Yorker's Derby

꾸 꾸

MAY 29, 1955

THE WAYS of Epsom on Derby Day take a good deal of knowing, and since I get there only at seven-year intervals, I don't suppose I shall ever know them well.

This is all the more likely because I began in 1948, when I was already a fair age. I have learned, however, that it is always wise, on entering Tattersalls, to rent binoculars at the booth behind the big stand. They guarantee no prospect more interesting than the backs of gray top hats, which come into your line of vision whenever you level up a horse. But the five-pound deposit you are required to leave on the binoculars assures the means of dignified retreat if your calculations go amiss. It is the best of savers. It is of course essential not to retrieve the deposit before the last race. In 1948 I hauled myself back to London by my binocular-straps.

I have learned also that a French horse always wins when I am present, and the Volterra stable owns at least part of the horse. The late M. Volterra had one-and-a-half of the first two past the post in 1948—a half share in My Love, the winner, and all of Royal Drake, the runner-up. Mme Volterra owned only one of the first two horses Wednesday, but it was the right one. It would therefore be madness not to back a French horse, particularly when a Volterra owns even a cutlet. I am not mad.

A third Epsom commonplace is that the English are a deeply kind nation, and that Derby favorites are often a creation of sentiment. Last Wednesday morning, for example, I read pages by experts who really know quite a lot about racing, evoking the probability of a Derby in which Acropolis, an untried colt, would prove himself one of the great racehorses of all time. Their reason for believing he would win a stiff race at a mile and a half was that he had run a fast time trial at a mile and a quarter. The emotional basis of it all, I am sure, was that Acropolis was owned by a noblewoman, ninety-three years old, who had selected him as a yearling. The poetic fitness of a win for such a combination had proved first attractive, then irresistible, to the hardened professionals. In 1948, as I remember it, the favorite's chief qualification was that the Maharajah of something or other had named him after his infant son.

Another factor which improves the odds is the British tendency to underrate invaders. I am sure that Harold the Saxon had information from Chantilly that William the Conqueror was very ordinary and couldn't act uphill. As a result a French horse is always likely to be what we transatlantics call an overlay. I failed to convert the night porter at my hotel to this doctrine. He said, "I don't trust them."

The most important Derby Day truth for me is that I have more fun there than at any other race I know. On one side of the course there are the decorative people, consciously and happily picturesque, exercising the English talent for being dressed up and enjoying it. It is a very great talent, whose effects I had no chance of appreciating during the khaki-and-Utility war, when I lived here longest.

On the other side of the track there is the endless Crazy Gang routine of the touts: "I said the 'orse wouldn't stay, but 'e *did* stay, 'e stayed in one place." "You couldn't find a better soldier in the British Army than I was—when you could find me." This is the Self-deprecating Tout, who wins his public's confidence by the establishment of his own human frailty.

"I didn't get this motorcar from Godfrey Davis, the 'ire-car man, to impress you for the day. I've *always* 'ad a car. I'm a responsible businessman. In the tel-e-phone book. You can look me up. I don't go racing so often nowadays, but when I *do* go, I 'ave a *reason* for it." This is the

Successful Tout, who sells by dynamism. I suppose he would call it the American method.

In the last seven years, I think, there has been a falling-off in the Grotesque Tout. Prince Monolulu, older and mellower, did not shout when he saw me this year, "I've got a 'orse!" He said deferentially, "Could you use a 'orse?" The Rocket Man was similarly subdued. He had discarded his Mae West for a coachman's hat like the doorman at Hatchett's in Piccadilly. The American method seems to get the half-crowns.

With a press badge you can slip back and forth between the two forms of entertainment, regulating the dosage, as if you were producing your own revue. Ten minutes of comedy and then down to the paddock for a touch of "Florodora" flash with the crinoline girls and the Moss Brothers' men's chorus.

One of the things I haven't learned about Epsom—shall I pick it up in 1962 or 1969?—is how to get fed properly. On the grandstand side of the course I found, when I had my first intimations of malnutrition in 1948, that the only visible antidote consisted of wide white expanses of flaccid bread agglomerated around panes of what I took to be cellophane. The *vendeuse* explained it was "Ham, love. We have rationing, love."

I attributed the ignominy, like all others, to Mr. Attlee. Last Wednesday I perceived that three years of free enterprise had not thickened the ham in buffet sandwiches by an eighth of a millimeter, and the elegantly draped elbows one receives in the ribs on the way to the buffet are as hard as they used to be in utility garments.

In quest of something more in keeping with the costumes, a *mayonnaise de langouste* and a pheasant, perhaps, with a magnum of *sirop de cacao,* I climbed two winding flights of stairs into a kind of belfry marked "Luncheons." Here, with a glow of nostalgic pleasure, I found again my old love, the wartime queue. The racegoers stood in Indian file in a passageway leading, as I supposed, to the luncheon, although from their faces it may well have been the guillotine.

If I had tagged on at the end, I would have been lucky to emerge in time for the St. Leger, so I dashed back to the common folk and lunched on a bison—"a bison of eels," was the full title the *garde-manger* at the barrow gave the dish, and I followed it by a red-hot bag of cold fish-and-chips, a mystery of the British cuisine comparable, but not in many ways, to a baked Alaska.

When I had finished, I understood why fish-and-chips is not served in the enclosures. Had I been wearing appropriate headgear, I should not have been able to doff it without greasing the brim. (My early suspicion that the toppers contained vacuum jugs or chafing dishes had been dispelled by observation of the luncheon queue. It was obvious the *incroyables* were as faminous as I.)

I was therefore on the *qui vive,* as the invaders say, for the tip which I eavesdropped from the lips of Mme Volterra herself on the way over from the walking ring to the paddock before the Derby. (It merely confirmed my resolution to do Phil Drake, but without such ante-post support resolutions have been known to waver.) I was not with, but near, Mme Volterra, and, quite naturally, looking at her, when I heard her say to one of her *chevaliers du chapeau gris,* "*Une chose qui est certaine, c'est que mon cheval a bien mangé.*" (Another Epsom axiom is that it is well to understand the raiders' language.) Mme Volterra looked like a woman who doesn't joke about food.

And if, as she said, her horse had eaten well, I knew he was the only living being on Epsom Downs who had done so. I dashed off to put a fiver on his lovely dark nose, and when he turned loose that run in the stretch—from seventeeth place to first—I knew where he got the stamina. It was a triumph for French cooking as well as for French cunning.

Jump: 1960

COMPETITIVE running outdoors has always struck us, and most other New Yorkers, as mildly bizarre, perhaps because outdoors is where a man is supposed to have his clothes on. *Indoor* track meets, though, have always been phrenetically popular here; the overheated lake of carbon dioxide thinly laced with oxygen that fills Madison Square Garden on such occasions offers justification for the athletes who race about in shirts and shorts. The whole *ambiance* is at once intimate and insane, with a good healthy metropolitan reek of hot dogs and beer to cut the cigarette smoke, and the sixteen-pound shots narrowly missing unwary high jumpers.

The track itself is a narrow wooden ellipse of 160 yards—eleven laps to the mile—with only two places on it where a man can run straight and at top speed for a couple of seconds. A runner attaining high speed on the inside of the curves, where he naturally wants to be, often falls, or is pushed, off the track altogether. When there's a large field in action, the center of the Garden sometimes looks like the subway shuttle station at Times Square. Because indoor meets draw so well, foreign running stars are imported, at great expense, to "compete," although a scramble over the boards has as much relation to an Olympic run as a fence climb has to a bobsled race. (A famous British runner named Mike Rawson came off the track at the National Amateur Athletic Union indoor championships last week with a thin smile, like a polite man who has given up trying to get into a revolving door.)

While the runners bat each other about on the track, encouraged by the strains of a band, the field athletes—jumpers, vaulters, and weight throwers—perform within the ellipse, and N.A.A.U. officials put up giant placards advertising the heights the agile chaps are about to negotiate. It's a constant competition for audience attention, like the circus. The band, it seems to us, tries systematically to play a little faster than the runners want to run, as if to cheat them into new records. Since there are few big indoor meets a year, indoor-running records are broken with satisfying regularity; the athlete is matching his performance against perhaps two dozen indoor winners in the same year, while the outdoor runner is up against thousands. We have never heard of a large indoor meet where somebody didn't break some kind of world's (indoor) record. The jumpers and vaulters, however, compete under precisely the same conditions in the Garden as outdoors, and the records they sometimes beat *are* world's records.

The people who attend the big indoor meets are like opera buffs; you seldom see them anywhere else, and they buy up all the tickets weeks in advance. As nobody else thinks of a track meet very long before it happens, the enthusiasts are the only ones who get there, and one of their chief prides is saying, afterward, that they saw some chap or other break a record. It's as if they had once heard Tetrazzini sing *Rigoletto*. Another of their joys is to wave to one another, with either a program or a hot dog in hand, across the terraced sea of white shirts and congested faces, like opera fans at Sherry's between the acts.

At last week's meet, it was apparent from the heights the jumpers and vaulters were attempting when we came in that it was going to be a good night for records. A tall, slim, cinnamon-colored freshman from Boston University named John Thomas, who, we knew from the newspapers, had already jumped 7 feet this season, was clearing with ease, one after another, heights that only a few years ago would have been incredible—6 feet 7, 6 feet 9, 6 feet 10, 6 feet 11, and then 7 feet. At 7 feet 1¼, a new world's record, he hesitated. He failed on his first two tries (he had a right to three), and then—several times, it seemed to us —he took a couple of little, springy steps, ran up to the bar, which was only a shade above the top of his head, and at the last instant swerved aside, just measuring.

While this was going on, one of the track buffs beside us turned his back on the arena and spotted a friend he hadn't seen since the last indoor championships sitting about eighteen rows behind and above him. Waving a hot dog *and* a program, he shouted, "Hey, Sid!" We turned, too, creature of weak concentration. Sid waved back, looking straight at the fellow beside us, and while we weren't watching, Thomas, with what we still think a censurable lack of consideration, ran forward in earnest and jumped higher than anybody else in the world had ever jumped.

"Most graceful thing we ever saw," we were saying by the time we got to the exit.

Fun-Lover

A FEW DAYS AGO, I took a ride up to a resort hotel called the Pines, at South Fallsburg, in the Catskills, to have my first look at Charles L. Liston, the challenger for the world heavyweight championship, who is training there. Early in the spring, Liston and Floyd Patterson, the champion, were sure that the New York State Athletic Commission would let them fight for the title here in late June, so Liston engaged training quarters. Then the Commission barred the match, and it had to be postponed while the promoter, Championship Sports, Inc., picked a site in another state. (It is now set for September 25 at the White Sox ball park in Chicago.) But Liston had meanwhile started to train, and he decided to continue, as if for two fights; he planned to reach peak form in July and then knock off for a couple of weeks and "slop in," as the fancy phrases it, after which he would go back to training, with not so much ground to regain as if he had spent all the interim loafing. Mr. Liston had been described to me by a colored fight trainer I know as "a big, hard, heavy-handed man," and one who loafs as intensely as he works.

My interest in the contemplated contest is cultural, and has nothing to do with the Commission's reasons for exiling it, which have a political look. There is a gubernatorial election in the fall, and the prize ring has had a bad press lately. Besides, Liston has been called a hard case, although his mother, down in Forrest City, Arkansas, recently told a reporter that he was always a good boy. I was never one to low-grade a mother, so when Mr. Hal Conrad, a press agent for C. S., Inc., invited me to the Pines, I was glad to go. I had heard disparate evaluations of the challenger; one qualified observer had told me he was the best big man since Joe Louis, and another had said he was too slow to compete with the champion, who is less big but gets around faster. All I can say after seeing Liston is that he is as strong as an ox but considerably more agile, and that his stern exterior conceals surprises.

The Pines is a resort of only moderate size compared to the really big hotels in the Catskills; a place called the Concord, which I saw from the expressway going up, looked like the Castle of Chapultepec. I found Liston's training quarters in a split-level pavilion there called the 19th Hole, because of its proximity to a putting course. The lower floor of the 19th Hole is given over to bedrooms, and the upper to a long lounge, with kitchen and lunch counter, which is operated as a canteen in the full summer season. Three members of Liston's faction were on the putting green, trying to talk one another out of putts. They adjourned their game at Conrad's hail, and told us that Liston had gone cycling—a rough test for a bike, since at this stage of his training he weighs nearly an eighth of a ton. Conrad introduced the largest of the three putterers as Willie Reddish, the challenger's head trainer, and I tried to pump him about his principal's disputed talents. Reddish is a big, light-colored, good-natured man who was a pretty good heavyweight himself in the thirties, though never of the top grade. It is often possible to gauge a winning fighter's temperament by his trainer's, which will be just the opposite—a process like mirror-reading. A moody fighter or a worrier does best under an easygoing type, who can make him laugh at himself; the good-tempered fighter needs a martinet to remind him that life is serious.

One reason it has been hard to learn much about Liston is that all but one of his fights since his novice days have been extremely short. Ten of the last eleven have gone an average of three and a fraction rounds, or about ten minutes, apiece, and two of the victims were pretty good fighters. In the one exception, a highly cautious fellow named Eddie Machen lasted twelve rounds by continuous evasive action, but he left Liston as much of a mystery as before. The ten knockouts showed what kind of puncher Liston was, Reddish told me—"a couple could have gotten tough, but he made them easy by knocking them out."

The fight that went the distance was even more conclusive, Reddish said, because it proved that Liston wouldn't tire: "He went twelve rounds at high speed, chasing a man running away from him, and he finished the twelfth as fresh as he started the first. When a man come to stay, if he got experience, he is hard to take out."

I asked him what Liston did best in the ring, and he said, "Everything —short punches, long punches, either hand."

The assistant trainer, Joe Polano, a grizzled type in a visored cap, who is an expert at repairing cuts between rounds, said he had never had to perform his specialty for Liston's benefit, because Liston never cut. (In ring language, the verb "to cut" is often passive in sense.) "Still," Mr. Polano said, "you never know when they're going to start."

The third putter, a slim young colored man named Ray Munson, said he was the challenger's personal secretary and had no technical information to impart. Liston's faction also includes a sparring partner, Jim McCarter; a camp secretary, Archie Parolli; and a factotum, Ted King. Reddish, Munson, McCarter, and King all sport down-turned pencil mustaches that follow the curve of the upper lip, and when I saw Liston I was not surprised to note that the camp mustaches were discreet copies of his. (This is a practice that began, I believe, when all of Archie Moore's sparring partners sported imperials like his, and all of Ray Robinson's grew long sideburns.)

Conrad and I walked over to the main building, half the distance of the Belmont Stakes, for a dairy lunch, and when we returned, at half past two, Reddish and Polano were laying out the gear for a workout in a gymnasium, with a raised regulation ring, that had been set up under a new small-circus tent. Since it was a weekday and the full resort season had not yet begun, there were only a few spectators—nonpaying, like me. The others included the hotel proprietors and a couple of small, fat boys. Reddish had said that Liston wouldn't do much, because it was only his second day of sparring and he had only one partner. The partner, McCarter, now quietly bandaging his own hands, told me that he had played fullback for the University of Washington and had been an alternate on the Olympic boxing team that went to Melbourne in 1956. He had turned professional only lately, and had had eleven fights, winning eight, all on the Pacific Coast. Liston then entered, a big, hard man if ever I saw one—six feet one, with wide shoulders, long arms, big hands, a torso like a tree, and calves stuffed with muscle. He was wearing green tights and heavy sweatclothes, which made him look even bulkier, and he was scowling as if he enjoyed it. If he wins the title, he will be the first scowling champion since John L. Sullivan. He, too, began to bandage his hands, with a care that indicated the amount of power he puts behind them; he used endless yards of gauze bandage, wrapping a small sponge between two layers over the knuckles of each hand.

The two men warmed up with two no-contact rounds without gloves —feinting and motioning punches, which they checked in the air. All I could see was that Liston was a well-schooled conventional boxer, standing even straighter than Louis and using a long left that resembled a thick-bodied snake with a darting head. The man looked ponderous but the hands were fast. There was hardly more to see when the men put on gloves and sparred three rounds, conventionally but carefully. Liston gave an impression of power, but he was not trying to hurt, and McCarter was content to keep the big man moving. Often, after a straight left, Liston would drop his body and throw a left hook to the ribs. It was evident, though, that, unlike Johansson, he was a two-handed fighter.

Liston followed the sparring with a long, earnest attack on the heavy bag—nothing fancy, but at times vindictive. The light bag was less in his line. Hundreds of sit-ups followed, then rope-skipping for two sides of a long-playing record. The second selection was "Night Train," and he pounded out the sound of the wheels running through the night, his feet coming up just high enough to let the rope pass under them, as if he were treading a body into the floor. During the rope-jumping, he flared up in mock anger at King, the camp clown, who had been snapping pictures of him. "You fired!" he shouted. "You working for me or for the publicity department? Let them pay you!" King pantomimed despair but seemed not much concerned. He gets fired often, but is always rehired. Liston went on to do more hundreds of sit-ups, with his legs strapped to a board slanting steeply upward, then let Reddish carom medicine balls off his iron torso, and wound up with a specialty—standing on his head and hands, swaying like a bifurcated pendulum, and taking all the weight on the top of his head and the muscles of his neck. Physically, it was a tremendous workout, and he was not breathing hard at the end of it.

When it was over, he put on a heavy robe and motioned to me to approach and ask him questions. He reacted to them as if they were medicine balls thrown at his middle; he let them bounce.

I asked him when he first knew that he could knock out a man with a short punch—the great test of a hitter.

"When I hit Williams," he said. (Cleveland Williams, on March 21, 1960.)

Thinking that he might confess a boyhood doubt, I asked him whether he had ever worried before a fight.

He said "No."

I asked him whether he had ever worried *during* a fight, and his answer was the same.

"It's enough if one man worry," he elaborated.

I asked him if he had a model, and he said "Joe Louis." The conversation languished.

Everybody moved over to the 19th Hole lounge, where Liston led me to a seat on a banquette against one wall, and we had tea while he sweated. Members of his faction were on stools strung along the lunch counter, and I heard Munson say to Polano, "Did you give Sonny the two dollars I gave you for him?" ("Sonny" is Liston's *diminutif*.) Polano said "Yeah." At that, there was a roar of animal wrath, and a huge shadow whizzed by my shoulder as Liston rushed toward the cut man. "You lie, you hound!" he shouted. "Gimme my two bucks!" A vast fist shot out, and I heard a tremendous smack as Polano went down, amid a shower of teeth. Pulling a pistol from a pocket of his dressing gown, the challenger, reverting to the alleged errors of his youth, blazed away twice. Groaning, Polano struggled along the floor toward me, imploring protection. Liston aimed again, then, changing his mind, pointed the pistol at me and fired a third time. I threw up my hands and, in doing so, spilled my tea. Everybody shouted happily.

"The man from the Baltimore *Sun,* he run into the fireplace when we done that," Polano said proudly from the floor. "The teeth is white beans. I catch the punch on the palm of my hand, see? That makes the smack."

Liston was jumping up and down as if skipping rope. "It's blanks, see?" he said, showing me the pistol, which was, in repose, a pretty obvious toy.

I told them that they were the best show off Broadway, and Liston, who had stopped scowling long since, said, "You come see us again, hear? You come back!" He had on a broad, unpublicized grin.

Willie Reddish said, "We got to make a little fun so the time pass. That fight seem far away, but it'll be here."

Toros: 1958

❧❧ ❧❧

A MAN we know went out to the other end of Long Island recently to sell a place he has there, and came back without selling it. When we saw him, he said he had gone to the house to have a last look around before he clinched the deal, and, on opening the gate, had been greeted by two bull calves, which the dairy farmer across the road had turned onto his lawn to graze and to keep the land in heart—an exchange of services that had been going on for quite a time.

"The two calves were at a stage I had never before noticed in the male cow," our friend, a city fellow, said. "I always thought of calves as awkward, and bulls as big and mean. These were only about a foot higher than a Great Dane, but quite a lot heavier, and spotted black and white, and they were nimble. They circled me at a distance wherever I walked, bounding in arcs like porpoises going around a ship.

"I walked back to the rail fence that divides my front lawn from my pasture. My neighbor ordinarily uses that for his cattle, too, but he had no cows in it the other day—growing a winter crop of some kind of grass, I suppose. I leaned on the fence looking across the land, which is pretty but has never really been of any use to me—too far from town, and I'm not a farmer, anyway. One of the calves came up behind me and gave me a nudge, just to show what he could do if he wanted to. I whipped around, and he was out of hitting range but ready to counter if I wanted to make anything out of it. Balanced on his feet, head down but one eye rolling up to keep me in view. No pawing the ground blindly. When he saw I wasn't mad, he ran away laughing.

"It made me think. These brave bulls that are killed in the ring are bred to be suckers, from full brothers of bulls that have died bravely. 'Brave' means to charge where there is motion. The calves are encouraged to do the same thing. It's like breeding from boxers who can't keep a left out of their puss, and then teaching the kids to drop their shoulder. [Our man's vocabulary contains a variety of incongruous pigments, which sometimes run together.] I decided to hang onto the place, and develop a strain of bulls to lick bullfighters. What the sport lacks now is competition. Can you imagine a baseball league where the team in the cellar didn't win one in three?"

We shook our head, and he went right on. "Conditioning is important. First, I'll hire a guy to teach the calves to stay away from the moving cape. It should be simple. All he will need is a boxing glove loaded with tea foil under the cape. He waves the cape, the calf charges, and, boom, he hits the calf in the nose. A calf of the intelligence of even the class of fighters on television will learn to work toward his sparring partner's left, away from the cape. He will gallop around in circles until the guy is dizzy, and then get him, the way the calf got me. It seems to be instinctive with a bull calf of normal I.Q. The matadors I've seen pictures of—their legs are gone. I don't think they jump enough rope. They could never meet that kind of attack.

"I wouldn't try to do it in one generation—maybe not even in two. I'd breed from the bulls that wouldn't follow a feint and that had the best footwork—the cuties. About the third generation, I'd start matching my bulls with a six-round class of bullfighter, who would maybe get a feature *corrida* only in the Spanish equivalent of West Hartford. After my bulls ran up a record, I would parlay one of them against the three greatest bullfighters in the world—I don't remember the names, but say, for argument, El Gazpacho, El Aficionado, and Tome Coca-Cola. The first two names I made up, but I happen to know that the third is genuine; I saw it painted all over the outside of a bullring in Mexico. My bulls would kill every bullfighter in the world."

"What have you got against bullfighters?" we asked.

"Nothing," he said, "but it would stop an awful lot of bad writing."

Ahab and Nemesis

BACK IN 1922, the late Heywood Broun, who is not remembered primarily as a boxing writer, wrote a durable account of a combat between the late Benny Leonard and the late Rocky Kansas for the lightweight championship of the world. Leonard was the greatest practitioner of the

era, Kansas just a rough, optimistic fellow. In the early rounds Kansas
messed Leonard about, and Broun was profoundly disturbed. A radical
in politics, he was a conservative in the arts, and Kansas made him think
of Gertrude Stein, *Les Six,* and nonrepresentational painting, all novel-
ties that irritated him.

"With the opening gong, Rocky Kansas tore into Leonard," he wrote.
"He was gauche and inaccurate, but terribly persistent." The classic
verities prevailed, however. After a few rounds, during which Broun
continued to yearn for a return to a culture with fixed values, he was
enabled to record, "The young child of nature who was challenging for
the championship dropped his guard, and Leonard hooked a powerful
and entirely orthodox blow to the conventional point of the jaw. Down
went Rocky Kansas. His past life flashed before him during the nine
seconds in which he remained on the floor, and he wished that he had
been more faithful as a child in heeding the advice of his boxing teacher.
After all, the old masters did know something. There is still a kick in
style, and tradition carries a nasty wallop."

I have often thought of Broun's words in the years since Rocky Marciano, the reigning heavyweight champion, scaled the fistic summits, as
they say in *Journal-Americanese,* by beating Jersey Joe Walcott. The
current Rocky is gauche and inaccurate, but besides being persistent he
is a dreadfully severe hitter with either hand. The predominative nature
of this asset has been well stated by Pierce Egan, the Edward Gibbon
and Sir Thomas Malory of the old London prize ring, who was less preoccupied than Broun with ultimate implications. Writing in 1821 of a
milling cove named Bill Neat, the Bristol Butcher, Egan said, "He pos-
sesses a requisite above all the art that *teaching* can achieve for any
boxer; namely, *one hit* from his right hand, given in proper distance, can
gain a victory; but three of them are positively enough to dispose of a
giant." This is true not only of Marciano's right hand but of his left
hand, too—provided he doesn't miss the giant entirely. Egan doubted
the advisability of changing Neat's style, and he would have approved
of Marciano's. The champion has an apparently unlimited absorptive
capacity for percussion (Egan would have called him an "insatiable glut-
ton") and inexhaustible energy ("a prime bottom fighter"). "Shifting,"
or moving to the side, and "milling in retreat," or moving back, are in-
novations of the late eighteenth century that Rocky's advisers have carefully kept from his knowledge, lest they spoil his natural prehistoric
style. Egan excused these tactics only in boxers of feeble constitution.

Archie Moore, the light-heavyweight champion of the world, who
hibernates in San Diego, California, and estivates in Toledo, Ohio, is a

Brounian rather than an Eganite in his thinking about style, but he naturally has to do more than think about it. Since the rise of Marciano, Moore, a cerebral and hyper-experienced light-colored pugilist who has been active since 1936, has suffered the pangs of a supreme exponent of *bel canto* who sees himself crowded out of the opera house by a guy who can only shout. As a sequel to a favorable review I wrote of one of his infrequent New York appearances, when his fee was restricted to a measly five figures, I received a sad little note signed "The most unappreciated fighter in the world, Archie Moore." A fellow who has as much style as Moore tends to overestimate the intellect—he develops the kind of Faustian mind that will throw itself against the problem of perpetual motion, or of how to pick horses first, second, third, *and* fourth in every race. Archie's note made it plain to me that he was honing his harpoon for the White Whale.

When I read newspaper items about Moore's decisioning a large, playful porpoise of a Cuban heavyweight named Nino Valdes and scoop-netting a minnow like Bobo Olson, the middleweight champion, for practice, I thought of him as a lonely Ahab, rehearsing to buck Herman Melville, Pierce Egan, and the betting odds. I did not think that he could bring it off, but I wanted to be there when he tried. What would *Moby Dick* be if Ahab had succeeded? Just another fish story. The thing that is eternally diverting is the struggle of man against history—or what Albert Camus, who used to be an amateur middleweight, has called the Myth of Sisyphus. (Camus would have been a great man to cover the fight, but none of the syndicates thought of it.) When I heard that the boys had been made for September 20, 1955, at the Yankee Stadium, I shortened my stay abroad in order not to miss the Encounter of the Two Heroes, as Egan would have styled the rendezvous.

In London on the night of September 13, a week before the date set for the Encounter, I tried to get my eye in for fight-watching by attending a bout at the White City greyhound track between Valdes, who had been imported for the occasion, and the British Empire heavyweight champion, Don Cockell, a fat man whose gift for public suffering has enlisted the sympathy of a sentimental people. Since Valdes had gone fifteen rounds with Moore in Las Vegas the previous May, and Cockell had excruciated for nine rounds before being knocked out by Marciano in San Francisco in the same month, the bout offered a dim opportunity for establishing what racing people call a "line" between Moore and Marciano. I didn't get much of an optical workout, because Valdes disposed of Cockell in three rounds. It was evident that Moore and Marciano had not been fighting the same class of people this season.

This was the only fight I ever attended in a steady rainstorm. It had begun in the middle of the afternoon, and, while there was a canopy over the ring, the spectators were as wet as speckled trout. "The weather, it is well known, has no terrors to the admirers of Pugilism of Life," Egan once wrote, and on his old stamping ground this still holds true. As I took my seat in a rock pool that had collected in the hollow of my chair, a South African giant named Ewart Potgieter, whose weight had been announced as 22 stone 10, was ignoring the doctrine of apartheid by leaning on a Jamaican colored man who weighed a mere 16 stone, and by the time I had transposed these statistics to 318 pounds and 224 pounds, respectively, the exhausted Jamaican had acquiesced in resegregation and retired. The giant had not struck a blow, properly speaking, but had shoved downward a number of times, like a man trying to close an overfilled trunk.

The main bout proved an even less grueling contest. Valdes, eager to get out of the chill, struck Cockell more vindictively than is his wont, and after a few gestures invocative of commiseration, the fat man settled in one corner of the ring as heavily as suet pudding upon the unaccustomed gastric system. He had received what Egan would have called a "ribber" and a "nobber," and when he arose it was seen that the latter had raised a cut on his forehead. At the end of the third round, his manager withdrew him from competition. It was not an inspiring occasion, but after the armistice eight or nine shivering Cubans appeared in the runway behind the press section and jumped up and down to register emotion and restore circulation. *"Ahora Marciano!"* they yelled. "Now for Marciano!" Instead of being grateful for the distraction, the other spectators took a poor view of it. "Sit down, you chaps!" one of them cried. "We want to see the next do!" They were still parked out there in the rain when I tottered into the Shepherd's Bush underground station and collapsed, sneezing, on a train that eventually disgorged me at Oxford Circus, with just enough time left to buy a revivifying draught before eleven o'clock, when the pubs closed. How the mugs I left behind cured themselves I never knew. They had to do it on Bovril.

Because I had engagements that kept me in England until a few days before the Encounter, I had no opportunity to visit the training camps of the rival American Heroes. I knew all the members of both factions, however, and I could imagine what they were thinking. In the plane on the way home, I tried to envision the rival patterns of ratiocination. I could be sure that Marciano, a kind, quiet, imperturbable fellow, would plan to go after Moore and make him fight continuously until he tired

enough to become an accessible target. After that he would expect con-
cussion to accentuate exhaustion and exhaustion to facilitate concus-
sion, until Moore came away from his consciousness, like everybody else
Rocky had ever fought. He would try to remember to minimize damage
to himself in the beginning, while there was still snap in Moore's arms,
because Moore is a sharp puncher. (Like Bill Neat of old, Marciano hits
at his opponent's arms when he cannot hit past them. "In one instance,
the arm of Oliver [a Neat adversary] received so paralyzing a shock in
stopping the blow that it appeared almost useless," Egan once wrote.)
Charlie Goldman would have instructed Marciano in some rudimentary
maneuver to throw Moore's first shots off, I felt sure, but after a few
minutes Rocky would forget it, or Archie would figure it out. But there
would always be Freddie Brown, the "cut man," in the champion's corner to repair superficial damage. One reason Goldman is a great teacher
is that he doesn't try to teach a boxer more than he can learn. What he
had taught Rocky in the four years since I had first seen him fight was
to shorten the arc of most of his blows without losing power thereby,
and always to follow one hard blow with another—"for insurance"—
delivered with the other hand, instead of recoiling to watch the victim
fall. The champion had also gained confidence and presence of mind;
he has a good fighting head, which is not the same thing as being a
good mechanical practitioner.

"A *boxer* requires a *nob* as well as a *statesman* does a HEAD, coolness
and calculation being essential to *second* his efforts," Egan wrote, and
the old historiographer was never more correct. Rocky was thirty-one,
not in the first flush of youth for a boxer, but Moore was only a few
days short of thirty-nine, so age promised to be in the champion's favor
if he kept pressing.

Moore's strategic problem, I reflected on the plane, offered more
choices and, as a corollary, infinitely more chances for error. It was possible, but not probable, that jabbing and defensive skill would carry him
through fifteen rounds, even on those old legs, but I knew that the mere
notion of such a *gambade* would revolt Moore. He is not what Egan
would have called a shy fighter. Besides, would Ahab have been content
merely to go the distance with the White Whale? I felt sure that Archie
planned to knock the champion out, so that he could sign his next
batch of letters "The most appreciated and deeply opulent fighter in the
world." I surmised that this project would prove a mistake, like Mr.
Churchill's attempt to take Gallipoli in 1915, but it would be the kind
of mistake that would look good in his memoirs.

The basis of what I rightly anticipated would prove a miscalculation went back to Archie's academic background. As a young fighter of conventional tutelage, he must have heard his preceptors say hundreds of times, "They will all go if you hit them right." If a fighter did not believe that, he would be in the position of a Euclidian without faith in the 180-degree triangle. Moore's strategy, therefore, would be based on working Marciano into a position where he could hit him right. He would not go in and slug with him, because that would be wasteful, distasteful, and injudicious, but he might try to cut him up, in an effort to slow him down so he could hit him right, or else try to hit him right and then cut him up. The puzzle he reserved for me—and Marciano—was the tactic by which he would attempt to attain his strategic objective. In the formation of his views, I believed, Moore would be handicapped, rather than aided, by his active, skeptical mind. One of the odd things about Marciano is that he isn't terribly big. It is hard for a man like Moore, just under six feet tall and weighing about 180 pounds, to imagine that a man approximately the same size can be immeasurably stronger than he is. This is particularly true when, like the light-heavyweight champion, he has spent his whole professional life contending with boxers—some of them considerably bigger—whose strength has proved so near his own that he could move their arms and bodies by cunning pressures. The old classicist would consequently refuse to believe what he was up against.

The light-heavyweight limit is 175 pounds, and Moore can get down to that when he must, in order to defend his title, but in a heavyweight match each Hero is allowed to weigh whatever he pleases. I was back in time to attend the weighing-in ceremonies, held in the lobby of Madison Square Garden at noon on the day set for the Encounter, and learned that Moore weighed 188 and Marciano 188¼—a lack of disparity that figured to encourage the rationalist's illusions. I also learned that, in contrast to Jack Solomons—the London promoter who held the Valdes-Cockell match in the rain—the I.B.C., which was promoting the Encounter, had decided to postpone it for twenty-four hours, although the weather was clear. The decision was based on apprehension of Hurricane Ione, which, although apparently veering away from New York, might come around again like a lazy left hook and drop in on the point of the Stadium's jaw late in the evening. Nothing like that happened, but the postponement brought the town's theaters and bars another evening of good business from the out-of-town fight trade, such as they always get on the eve of a memorable Encounter. ("Not a bed could be had at any of the villages at an early hour on the preceding evening; and Uxbridge was crowded beyond all former precedent," Egan wrote of the night before Neat beat Oliver.) There was no doubt that the fight had caught the public imagination, ever sensitive to a meeting between Hubris and Nemesis, as the boys on the quarterlies would say, and the bookies were laying eighteen to five on Nemesis, according to the boys on the dailies, who always seem to hear. (A friend of mine up from Maryland with a whim and a five-dollar bill couldn't get ten against it in ordinary barroom money anywhere, although he wanted Ahab.)

The enormous—by recent precedent—advance sale of tickets had so elated the I.B.C. that it had decided to replace the usual card of bad preliminary fights with some not worth watching at all, so there was less distraction than usual as we awaited the appearance of the Heroes on the fateful evening. The press seats had been so closely juxtaposed that I could fit in only sidewise between two colleagues—the extra compression having been caused by the injection of a prewar number of movie stars and politicos.

The tight quarters were an advantage, in a way, since they facilitated my conversation with Peter Wilson, an English prize-ring correspondent, who happened to be in the row behind me. I had last seen Mr. Wilson at White City the week before, at a time when the water level had already reached his shredded-Latakia mustache. I had feared that he had drowned at ringside, but when I saw him at the Stadium, he assured me that by buttoning the collar of his mackintosh tightly over his nostrils, he had been able to make the garment serve as a diving lung, and so survive. Like all British fight writers when they are relieved of the duty of watching British fighters, he was in a holiday mood, and we chatted happily.

There is something about the approach of a good fight that renders the spirit insensitive to annoyance; it is only when the amateur of the Sweet Science has some doubts as to how good the main bout will turn out to be that he is avid for the satisfaction to be had from the preliminaries. This is because after the evening is over, he may have only a good supporting fight to remember. There were no such doubts—even in the minds of the mugs who had paid for their seats—on the evening of September 21.

At about ten-thirty the champion and his faction entered the ring. It is not customary for the champion to come in first, but Marciano has never been a stickler for protocol. He is a humble, kindly fellow, who even now will approach an acquaintance on the street and say bashfully, "Remember me? I'm Rocky Marciano." The champion doesn't mind waiting five or ten minutes to give anybody a punch in the nose. In any case, once launched from his dressing room under the grandstand, he could not have arrested his progress to the ring, because he had about forty policemen pushing behind him, and three more clearing a path in front of him. Marciano, tucked in behind the third cop like a football ball-carrier behind his interference, had to run or be trampled to death. Wrapped in a heavy blue bathrobe and with a blue monk's cowl pulled over his head, he climbed the steps to the ring with the cumbrous agility of a medieval executioner ascending the scaffold. Under the hood he seemed to be trying to look serious. He has an intellectual appreciation of the anxieties of a champion, but he has a hard time forgetting how strong he is; while he remembers that, he can't worry as much as he knows a champion should. His attendants—quick, battered little Goldman; Al Weill, the stout, excitable manager, always stricken just before the bell with the suspicion that he may have made a bad match; Al Columbo—are all as familiar to the crowd as he is.

Ahab's party arrived in the ring a minute or so later, and Charlie Johnston, his manager—a calm sparrow hawk of a man, as old and wise in the game as Weill—went over to watch Goldman put on the champion's gloves. Freddie Brown went to Moore's corner to watch *his* gloves being put on. Moore wore a splendid black silk robe with a gold lamé collar and belt. He sports a full mustache above an imperial, and his hair, sleeked down under pomade when he opens operations, invariably rises during the contest, as it gets water sloshed on it between rounds and the lacquer washes off, until it is standing up like the top of a shaving brush. Seated in his corner in the shadow of his personal trainer, a brown man called Cheerful Norman, who weighs 235 pounds, Moore looked like an old Japanese print I have of a "Shogun Engaged in Strategic Contemplation in the Midst of War." The third member of his group was Bertie Briscoe, a rough, chipper little trainer, whose more usual charge is Sandy Saddler, the featherweight champion—also a Johnston fighter. Mr. Moore's features in repose rather resemble those of Orson Welles, and he was reposing with intensity.

The procession of other fighters and former fighters to be introduced was longer than usual. The full galaxy was on hand, including Jack Dempsey, Gene Tunney, and Joe Louis, the *têtes de cuvée* of former-champion society; ordinary former heavyweight champions, like Max Baer and Jim Braddock, slipped through the ropes practically unnoticed. After all the celebrities had been in and out of the ring, an odd dwarf, advertising something or other—possibly himself—was lifted into the ring by an accomplice and ran across it before he could be shooed out. The referee, a large, craggy, oldish man named Harry Kessler, who, unlike some of his better-known colleagues, is not an ex-fighter, called the men to the center of the ring.

This was his moment; he had the microphone. "Now, Archie and Rocky, I want a nice, clean fight," he said, and I heard a peal of silvery laughter behind me from Mr. Wilson, who had seen both of them fight before. "Protect yourself at all times," Mr. Kessler cautioned them unnecessarily. When the principals shook hands, I could see Mr. Moore's eyebrows rising like storm clouds over the Sea of Azov. His whiskers bristled and his eyes glowed like dark coals as he scrunched his eyebrows down again and enveloped the Whale with the Look, which was intended to dominate his willpower. Mr. Wilson and I were sitting behind Marciano's corner, and as he came back to it, I observed his expression, to determine what effect the Look had had upon him. More than ever, he resembled a Great Dane who has heard the word "bone."

A moment later the bell rang, and the Heroes came out for the first round. Marciano, training in the sun for weeks, had tanned to a slightly deeper tint than Moore's old ivory, and Moore, at 188, looked, if anything, bigger and more muscular than Marciano; much of the champion's weight is in his legs, and his shoulders slope. Marciano advanced, but Moore didn't go far away. As usual, he stood up nicely, his arms close to his body and his feet not too far apart, ready to go anywhere but not without a reason—the picture of a powerful, decisive intellect unfettered by preconceptions. Marciano, pulling his left arm back from the shoulder, flung a left hook. He missed, but not by enough to discourage him, and then walked in and hooked again. All through the round he threw those hooks, and some of them grazed Moore's whiskers; one even hit him on the side of the head. Moore didn't try much offensively; he held a couple of times when Marciano worked in close.

Marciano came back to his corner as he always does, unimpassioned. He hadn't expected to catch Moore with those left hooks anyway, I imagine; all he had wanted was to move him around. Moore went to his corner inscrutable. They came out for the second, and Marciano went after him in brisker fashion. In the first round he had been throwing the left hook, missing with it, and then throwing a right and missing with that, too. In the second he tried a variation—throwing a right and then pulling a shoulder back to throw the left. It appeared for a moment to have Moore confused, as a matador might be confused by a bull who walked in on his hind legs. Marciano landed a couple of those awkward hooks, but not squarely. He backed Moore over toward the side of the ring farthest from me, and then Moore knocked him down.

Some of the reporters, describing the blow in the morning papers, called it a "sneak punch," which is journalese for one the reporter didn't see but technically means a lead thrown before the other man has warmed up or while he is musing about the gate receipts. This had been no lead, and although I certainly hadn't seen Moore throw the punch, I knew that it had landed inside the arc of Marciano's left hook. ("Marciano missed with the right, trun the left, and Moore stepped inside it," my private eye, Whitey Bimstein, said next day, confirming my diagnosis, and the film of the fight bore both of us out.) So Ahab had his harpoon in the Whale. He had hit him right if ever I saw a boxer hit right, with a classic brevity and conciseness. Marciano stayed down for two seconds. I do not know what took place in Mr. Moore's breast when he saw him get up. He may have felt, for the moment, like Don Giovanni when the Commendatore's statue grabbed at him—startled because he thought he had killed the guy already—or like Ahab when he saw the Whale take down Fedallah, harpoons and all. Anyway, he hesitated a couple of seconds, and that was reasonable. A man who took nine to come up after a punch like that would be doing well, and the correct tactic would be to go straight in and finish him. But a fellow who came up on two was so strong he would bear investigation.

After that, Moore did go in, but not in a crazy way. He hit Marciano some good, hard, classic shots, and inevitably Marciano, a trader, hit him a few devastating swipes, which slowed him. When the round ended, the edge of Moore's speed was gone, and he knew that he would have to set a new and completely different trap, with diminished resources. After being knocked down, Marciano had stopped throwing that patterned right-and-left combination; he has a good nob. "He never trun it again in the fight," Whitey said next day, but I differ. He threw it in the fifth, and again Moore hit him a peach of a right inside it, but the steam was gone; this time Ahab couldn't even stagger him. Anyway, there was Moore at the end of the second, dragging his shattered faith in the unities and humanities back to his corner. He had hit a guy right, and the guy hadn't gone. But there is no geezer in Moore, any more than there was in the master of the Pequod.

Both came out for the third very gay, as Egan would have said. Marciano had been hit and cut, so he felt acclimated, and Moore was so mad at himself for not having knocked Marciano out that he almost displayed animosity toward him. He may have thought that perhaps he had not hit Marciano *just* right; the true artist is always prone to self-reproach. He would try again. A minute's attention from his squires had raised his spirits and slaked down his hair. At this point, Marciano set about him. He waddled in, hurling his fists with a sublime disregard of probabilities, content to hit an elbow, a biceps, a shoulder, the top of a head—the last supposed to be the least profitable target in the business, since, as every beginner learns, "the head is the hardest part of the human body," and a boxer will only break his hands on it. Many boxers make the systematic presentation of the cranium part of their defensive scheme. The crowd, basically anti-intellectual, screamed encouragement. There was Moore, riding punches, picking them off, slipping them, rolling with them, ducking them, coming gracefully out of his defensive efforts with sharp, patterned blows—and just about holding this parody even on points. His face, emerging at instants from under the storm of arms—his own and Rocky's—looked like that of a swimming walrus. When the round ended, I could see that he was thinking deeply. Marciano came back to his corner at a kind of suppressed dogtrot. He didn't have a worry in the world.

It was in the fourth, though, that I think Sisyphus began to get the idea he couldn't roll back the Rock. Marciano pushed him against the ropes and swung at him for what seemed a full minute without ever landing a punch that a boxer with Moore's background would consider a credit to his workmanship. He kept them coming so fast, though, that Moore tired just getting out of their way. One newspaper account I saw said that at this point Moore "swayed uncertainly," but his motions were about as uncertain as Margot Fonteyn's, or Artur Rubinstein's. He is the most premeditated and best-synchronized swayer in his profession. After the bell rang for the end of the round, the champion hit him a right for good measure—he usually manages to have something on the way all the time—and then pulled back to disclaim any uncouth intention. Moore, no man to be conned, hit him a corker of a punch in return, when he wasn't expecting it. It was a gesture of moral reprobation and also a punch that would give any normal man something to think about between rounds. It was a good thing Moore couldn't see Marciano's face as he came back to his corner, though, because the champion was laughing.

The fifth was a successful round for Moore, and I had him ahead on points that far in the fight. But it took no expert to know where the strength lay. There was even a moment in the round when Moore set himself against the ropes and encouraged Marciano to swing at him, in the hope the champion would swing himself tired. It was a confession that he himself was too tired to do much hitting.

In the sixth Marciano knocked Moore down twice—once, early in the round, for four seconds, and once, late in the round, for eight seconds, with Moore getting up just before the bell rang. In the seventh, after that near approach to obliteration, the embattled intellect put up its finest stand. Marciano piled out of his corner to finish Moore, and the stylist made him miss so often that it looked, for a fleeting moment, as if the champion were indeed punching himself arm-weary. In fact, Moore began to beat him to the punch. It was Moore's round, certainly, but an old-timer I talked to later averred that one of the body blows Marciano landed in that round was the hardest of the fight.

It was the eighth that ended the competitive phase of the fight. They fought all the way, and in the last third of the round the champion simply overflowed Archie. He knocked him down with a right six seconds before the bell, and I don't think Moore could have got up by ten if the round had lasted that long. The fight by then reminded me of something that Sam Langford, one of the most profound thinkers—and, according to all accounts, one of the greatest doers—of the prize ring, once said to me: "Whatever that other man wants to do, don't let him do it." Merely by moving in all the time and punching continually, Marciano achieves the same strategic effect that Langford gained by finesse. It is impossible to think, or to impose your thought, if you have to keep on avoiding punches.

Moore's "game," as old Egan would have called his courage, was beyond reproach. He came out proudly for the ninth, and stood and fought back with all he had, but Marciano slugged him down, and he was counted out with his left arm hooked over the middle rope as he tried to rise. It was a crushing defeat for the higher faculties and a lesson in intellectual humility, but he had made a hell of a fight.

The fight was no sooner over than hundreds of unsavory young yokels with New England accents began a kind of mountain-goat immigration from the bleachers to ringside. They leaped from chair to chair and, after they reached the press section, from typewriter shelf to typewriter shelf and, I hope, from movie star to movie star. "Rocky!" they yelled. "Brockton!" Two of them, as dismal a pair of civic ambassadors as I have seen since I worked on the Providence *Journal & Evening Bulletin*, stood on Wilson's typewriter and yelled "Providence!" After the fighters and the hick delinquents had gone away, I made my way out to Jerome Avenue, where the crowd milled, impenetrable, under the el structure.

If you are not in a great hurry to get home (and why should you be at eleven-thirty or twelve on a fight night?), the best plan is to walk up to the station north of the Stadium and have a beer in a saloon, or a cup of tea in the 167th Street Cafeteria, and wait until the whole mess clears away. By that time you may even get a taxi. After this particular fight

I chose the cafeteria, being in a contemplative rather than a convivial mood. The place is of a genre you would expect to find nearer Carnegie Hall, with blond woodwork and modern functional furniture imported from Italy—an appropriate background for the evaluation of an aesthetic experience. I got my tea and a smoked-salmon sandwich on a soft onion roll at the counter and made my way to a table, where I found myself between two young policemen who were talking about why Walt Disney has never attempted a screen version of Kafka's *Metamorphosis*. As I did not feel qualified to join in that one, I got out my copy of the official program of the fights and began to read the high-class feature articles as I munched my sandwich.

One reminded me that I had seen the first boxing show ever held in Yankee Stadium—on May 12, 1923. I had forgotten that it *was* the first show, and even that 1923 was the year the Stadium opened. In my true youth the Yankees used to share the Polo Grounds with the Giants, and I had forgotten that, too, because I never cared much about baseball, although, come to think of it, I used to see the Yankees play occasionally in the nineteen-'teens, and should have remembered. I remembered the boxing show itself very well, though. It happened during the spring of my second suspension from college, and I paid five dollars for a high-grandstand seat. The program merely said that it had been "an all-star heavyweight bill promoted by Tex Rickard for the Hearst Milk Fund," but I found that I could still remember every man and every bout on the card.

One of the main events was between old Jess Willard, the former heavyweight champion of the world, who had lost the title to Jack Dempsey in 1919, and a young heavyweight named Floyd Johnson. Willard had been coaxed from retirement to make a comeback because there was such a dearth of heavyweight material that Rickard thought he could still get by, but as I remember the old fellow, he couldn't fight a lick. He had a fair left jab and a right uppercut that a fellow had to walk into to get hurt by, and he was big and soft. Johnson was a mauler worse than Rex Layne, and the old man knocked him out. The other main event, *ex aequo*, had Luis Angel Firpo opposing a fellow named Jack McAuliffe II, from Detroit, who had had only fifteen fights and had never beaten anybody, and had a glass jaw. The two winners, of whose identity there was infinitesimal preliminary doubt, were to fight each other for the right to meet the great Jack Dempsey. Firpo was so crude that Marciano would be a Fancy Dan in comparison. He could hit with only one hand—his right—he hadn't the faintest idea of what to do in close, and he never cared much for the business anyway. He knocked

McAuliffe out, of course, and then, in a later "elimination" bout, stopped poor old Willard. He subsequently became a legend by going one and a half sensational rounds with Dempsey, in a time that is now represented to us as the golden age of American pugilism.

I reflected with satisfaction that old Ahab Moore could have whipped all four principals on that card within fifteen rounds, and that while Dempsey may have been a great champion, he had less to beat than Marciano. I felt the satisfaction because it proved that the world isn't going backward, if you can just stay young enough to remember what it was really like when you were really young.

La Bonne Vie

Light Lunch

ONE WINTER I lunched at the Hôtel du Commerce in Vendôme with a friend who was an instructor in a school for Armenian orphans in a château that a New York rug merchant had bought from the Duc de Dodon Rochefoucauld. The rug man had not thought fit to hire the Duc's chef for the orphans, and my *convive* brought a hearty appetite to the meal, which was served at the head of a long table, with a half-dozen *commis-voyageurs* ranged around the other end of the board.

Paniguian, my friend, was twenty-four and I was twenty-three. We were both confirmed gluttons. We ate the precise menu that the *commis-voyageur* at Vire had described, with some amendment in the wine department. We had a bottle of the landlord's best local wine to begin with and then a Corton-Clos du Roi with the pheasant. The gentlemen of commerce were patronizing when we sat down and placed our napkins in our laps. They tied theirs around their necks, so that they could forget caution in grappling with their grub. But when we cleaned the serving platters of *rillettes*, of *pâté de lièvre*, of *jambon cru du pays*, of *andouilles* (inferior to those of Vire, but acceptable), and even of salt herring and scraps of *gigot* left over from yesterday's Sunday dinner and freshened with onion, they were admirative. They still felt superior, though. One was sportsman enough to warn us, "Attention, there's more to come!"

It was presumption on his part to think we didn't know.

After we devastated the *tripes à la mode de Caen*, a look of speculation broke water in their faces, as in a pool shark's when his intended victim runs 15 from the break.

Our performance on the beefsteaks and soufflé potatoes was so apocalyptic that I saw one of them pause, his fork halfway to his mouth, to watch us—a pause so unusual, for a Frenchman eating, that I thought for a moment he had a stroke. When we had eaten five or six beefsteaks apiece while each of them was despatching a humdrum three, the waitress cleared the table, and all of us regarded one another with satisfaction, like men who have rowed a creditable race in the same boat. The drummers' fear that we would eat all the beefsteaks was assuaged. They were full and could afford to be complimentary.

"Here you truly ring the bell!" one drummer said, and another corroborated, "What one sends oneself, it's something!"

The waitress placed a cheese tray and a couple of baskets of Saint-Jeans, which we call seckel pears, before the drummers, and went away.

One called down to us, "Why aren't you having any cheese? Are you full already?"

Then his paternal bonhomie changed to an expression of compound hate, a mixture of xenophobia (the franc was falling) and the Spirit of the Barricades. He saw the waitress bringing in the pheasant, just for us.

It was a remarkable pheasant, served on a skinned and lightly toasted loaf of bread, in which a trough had been made and filled with a salmi of the bird's insides. I have never since believed the legend that all game must be hung, because I had seen the gunner bring in the pheasant early that morning. It remains the best bird in my memory.

Long before we had eaten all and crushed each bone in our teeth, the drummers had disappeared. They could not bear watching us and had elected to take their coffee and *eau de vie* in a café down the street. After we had done full justice to the goat cheese in ashes, the seckel pears, and the puckered baked apples with cores of jelly, we called for the *patron* and congratulated him on an unforgettable meal. We offered him a glass of his own best Armagnac, taking a gamble that, since we were not in Normandy, he might respond by buying us the next round.

The *patron* said modestly that it was the regular Monday lunch, all except that little bird that he had been fortunate enough to come by that morning, and it was too bad we hadn't come later in the week, when he made an effort.

"You know how it is on Monday," he said. "After the substantial repasts of Sunday, nobody has any appetite."

This has developed from a merely culinary into a geographical digression, but I can never approach the memory of that meal without wanting to go into it. It has the same attraction for me as Costello's saloon. I seldom encounter a pheasant nearly so good nowadays, and when I do, an *hors d'oeuvre* and possibly the tripe is all I can manage at one meal besides the bird. (I am writing this on a lunch exclusively of turtle soup, as I am trying to take off weight.)

Dietetics

⁕⁕ ⁕⁕

Mens sana in corpore sano is a contradiction in terms, the fantasy of a Mr. Have-your-cake-and-eat-it. No sane man can afford to dispense with debilitating pleasures; no ascetic can be considered reliably sane. Hitler was the archetype of the abstemious man. When the other krauts saw him drink water in the Beer Hall, they should have known he was not to be trusted.

⁕⁕ ⁕⁕

Khrushchev, too, looks like the kind of man his physicians must continually try to diet, and historians will someday correlate these sporadic deprivations, to which he submits "for his own good," with his public tantrums. If there is to be a world cataclysm, it will probably be set off by skim milk, Melba toast, and mineral oil on the salad.

⁕⁕ ⁕⁕

A man who is rich in his adolescence is almost doomed to be a dilettante at table. This is not because all millionaires are stupid, but because they are not impelled to experiment. In learning to eat, as in psychoanalysis, the customer, in order to profit, must be sensible of the cost.

⁕⁕ ⁕⁕

In general, the Bretons practice only one method of preparing their lobsters, true or spiny—boiling them in seawater, which is fine if what you want to taste is lobster. In lobster *à l'américaine*, on the other hand, the sauce, which cannot be produced without the lobster, is the justification of the indignity inflicted on him. If the strength of this dish, then, lies in the sauce (as I deem indisputable), its weakness, from a non-French point of view, lies in the necessity of mopping up the sauce with at least three linear meters of bread. Bread is a good medium for carrying gravy as far as the face, but it is a diluent, not an added magnificence; it stands to the sauce of lobster *à l'américaine* in the same relationship as soda to Scotch.

But a good pilaf—each grain of rice developed separately in broth to the size of a pistachio kernel—is a fine thing in its own right. Heaped on the plate and receiving the sauce *à l'américaine* as the waitress serves the lobster, the grains drink it up as avidly as nymphs quenching their thirst. The grains do not lose form or identity, although they take on a bit of *rondeur*. Mere rice cooked any old way won't do the trick; it turns to wallpaperer's paste. The French in general are almost as bad with rice as the Chinese, who are the very worst. The Armenians, Greeks, and Turks are the best with it. The conjunction of my Greek cook's *langouste* and his pilaf was a cultural milestone, like the wedding of the oyster and the lemon.

❧ ❧

Personally, I like tastes that know their own minds. The reason that people who detest fish often tolerate sole is that sole doesn't taste very much like fish, and even this degree of resemblance disappears when it is submerged in the kind of sauce that patrons of Piedmontese restaurants in London and New York think characteristically French. People with the same apathy toward decided flavor relish "South African lobster" tails—frozen as long as the Siberian mammoth—because they don't taste lobstery. ("South African lobsters" are a kind of sea crayfish, or *langouste*, but that would be nothing against them if they were fresh.) They prefer processed cheese because it isn't cheesy, and synthetic vanilla extract because it isn't vanillary. They have made a triumph of the Delicious apple because it doesn't taste like an apple, and of the Golden Delicious because it doesn't taste like anything.

In a related field, "dry" (non-beery) beer and "light" (non-Scotch-like) Scotch are more of the same. The standard of perfection for vodka (no color, no taste, no smell) was expounded to me long ago by the then Estonian Counsul General in New York, and it accounts perfectly for the drink's rising popularity with those who like their alcohol in conjunction with the reassuring tastes of infancy—tomato juice, orange juice, chicken broth. It is the ideal intoxicant for the drinker who wants no reminder of how hurt Mother would be if she knew what he was doing.

❦ ❦

I am still of the opinion that Lower Normandy has the best seafood, the best mutton (from the salt meadows of the Avranches region), the best beef, the best butter, the best cream, and the best cheese in Europe, and that the ideal light lunch is a dozen *huîtres de Courseulles,* an *araignée de mer* (spider crab) with a half pint of mayonnaise on the side, a dish of *tripes à la mode de Caen,* a partridge Olivier Basselin, poached in cream and cider and singed in old Calvados, a *gigot de pré-salé,* a couple of *biftecks,* and a good Pont l'Evêque. I can no longer stand up to it in one sitting, as the Irishmen say in the story books, but that is not the fault of the menu. It is my metabolism that has collapsed.

❦ ❦

To insure the regional character of my meal, I ordered an *araignée,* to be followed by *raie au beurre noir.* The *araignée,* a beast of loathly aspect in a state of nature, is a warty, long-legged creature with a carapace resembling a slightly flattened baseball. It looks more like a land crab than a water crab. It is of a despicable khaki color, which gives it protective coloration on mud bottoms, and it has acquired a trick of tangling seaweed around its legs, possibly to make itself appear innocuous or inedible. Whatever its object, it has created the latter impression so successfully on the New England and Long Island coasts that I have never known anybody there to eat one. It is a great bait grabber, and when Americans fishing for blackfish or flounder haul one of these crabs aboard, they consider it a calamity instead of a stroke of luck and dash the crab to death, or stamp on it, before they throw it back into the sea—the men in the party swearing and the women, if there are any aboard, shuddering. What doesn't occur to those fishermen is that the *araignée,* placed in hot water, will turn red like any other crustacean, and so lose its repulsive color. It turns a peculiarly beautiful red, in fact—the color of those old-fashioned rambler roses that smell like raspberries. On the other hand, the *tourteau,* so popular in Britain, where "crab" means only *tourteau,* will blush no deeper than a yellowy pink, attractively set off by black claw tips, while our own blue crab assumes in hot water the angry color of a newborn baby.

Set down on the plate right side up, the cooked *araignée* has the appearance of an ambulant rosy-red apple. The Norman cook has already made a discreet incision around the periphery of the carapace, permitting the spider eater, after he has sufficiently admired his specimen, to lift the top like a lid and attack the white interior from above. There is a good deal to eat in an *araignée;* while there are none of the large chunks of meat you find in a lobster or *langouste,* every part of it except the lid may be profitably scrunched between molars. The long legs, passed between the incisors, yield their sweet juice to a gentle pressure. Just as the nectarine combines peach and plum, the taste of the *araignée* suggests both lobster and crab, with the tantalizing added suggestion of *oursin,* or sea urchin.

Skate is a less peculiarly regional dish, but in support of my choice of this relative of the shark, I appropriate a statement by a woman I once knew about Long Island fluke. "Once plucked from the water, they lose their flavor as quickly as corn on the cob," she said, and the observation is equally pertinent to the skate. The *raie au beurre noir* of West 48th Street or Soho is to the *raie au beurre noir* of Port-en-Bessin what the Joe Louis of 1951 was to the Joe Louis of 1938. The inland chef's sole recourse in preparing skate is to stoke the *beurre noir* with capers until the *raie* taste no worse than deep-frozen Pacific swordfish bought in cellophaned slabs from a supermarket.

***

The wine was a thin *rosé* in an *art nouveau* bottle, with a label that was a triumph of lithography; it had spires and monks and troubadours and blondes in wimples on it, and the name of the *cru* was spelled out in letters with Gothic curlicues and pennons. The name was something like *Château Guillaume d'Aquitaine, grand vin.*

"What a madly gay little wine, my dear!" M. Cliquot said, repressing, but not soon enough, a grimace of pain.

"One would say a Tavel of a good year," I cried, "if one were not a complete bloody fool." I did not say the second clause out loud.

My old friend looked at me with a new respect. He was discovering in me a capacity for hypocrisy that he had never credited me with before.

***

We ordered a couple of dozen *escargots en pots de chambre* to begin with. These are snails baked and served, for the client's convenience, in individual earthenware crocks, instead of being forced back into shells. The snail, of course, has to be taken out of his shell to be prepared for cooking. The shell he is forced back into may not be his own. There is thus not even a sentimental justification for his reincarceration. The frankness of the service *en pot* does not improve the preparation of the snail, nor does it detract from it, but it does facilitate and accelerate his consumption. (The notion that the shell proves the snail's authenticity, like the head left on a woodcock, is invalid, as even a suburban house-wife knows nowadays; you can buy a tin of snail shells in a supermarket and fill them with a mixture of nutted cream cheese and chopped olives.)

Monsieur Mirande

M. Mirande had an equally rich life between meals. He had pleasure of women. Currently pleasure and women are held matters incompatible, antithetical, and mutually exclusive, like quinine water and Scotch. Mirande also gave women pleasure; many women had pleasure of him. This is no longer considered a fair or honorable exchange. Women resent being thought of as enjoyables; they consider such an attitude an evidence of male chauvinism. They want to be taken seriously, like fallout.

The function of the sexes, if I read the authors of the age aright, is mutual boredom.

It has become customary to write freely of the sexual connection, but always with solemnity. One may respectably write of his sexual initiation, provided it was a disaster. Holden Caulfield never got to the post. Henry Miller may write about revelers self-woven into a human hooked rug, because his ecstasy is solemn. (Arriving in Paris at thirty-nine, he wrote about *la noce* like a child making a belated discovery of the banana split.) *Lady Chatterley's Lover* is acceptable because it is "a *serious* work of art." It is impossible, for the best of reasons, to prove it is a work of art, but it is easy to show that it is serious, the legalizing word. The jocund work of art is still beyond the pale. This is no damn joke.

The wretched how-to-do-it books about copulation are serious in intention, solemn in tone; the do-it-yourselfs will soon be with us.

The one thing about the glorious diversion that is no longer written, or if still written never published, is that it remains the most amusing as well as the most instructive of human activities, and one of the most nearly harmless.

Observations

❧ ❧

❧ ❧

A SQUIRMER is a stripteaser who, having exhausted the possibilities of the vertical, exercises her art horizontally, recumbent on a chaise longue above the back bar with its array of spuriously labeled liquor bottles. Supine, she produces alternate clockwise and counterclockwise ventral vibrations, synchronized with opposed mammary rotations and what she conceives to be a facial expression of extreme passion. With her legs, meanwhile, she performs a calisthenic of easily penetrable symbolism.

❧ ❧

I have always found the New England accent endearing in women. There is a suggestion of primness about it that is as aphrodisiac as a starched gingham dress.

❧ ❧

Mother . . . had bloomed in an age when all blond little girls with blue eyes wanted to grow up to be Lillian Russells. Miss Russell was a butterscotch sundae of a woman, as beautiful as a tulip of beer with a high white collar, or a two-dollar valentine, or a brace of borzois in white leather body harness. If a Western millionaire—one of the Hearst or Mackay kind—could have given an architect carte blanche to design him a woman, she would have looked like Lillian.

❧ ❧

The profession of ingenue exists no longer. There was a girl in *Little Mary Sunshine* who had the gist of it, but she will have no chance to develop. In her next job she may have to play an agoraphobic Lesbian in love with her claustrophobic brother. The tragic siblings will be compelled to tryst in a revolving door. It is the kind of play people like to write now, because it can be done in one set, in this case the door.

※ ※

At the Crédit, I would be received with scornful solemnity, like a suitor for the hand of a miser's daughter. I was made to sit on a bare wooden bench with other wretches come to claim money from the bank, all feeling more like culprits by the minute. A French bank, by the somber intensity of its addiction to money, establishes an emotional claim on funds in transit. The client feels in the moral position of a wayward mother who has left her babe on a doorstep and later comes back to claim it from the foster parents, who now consider it their own. I would be given a metal check with a number on it, and just as I had begun to doze off from the effects of a good lunch, the *côte rôtie*, the brisk walk, and the poor ventilation, a *huissier* who had played Harpagon in repertoire at Angers would shake me by the shoulder. I would advance toward a grille behind which another Harpagon, in an alpaca coat, held the draft, confident that he could riddle my pretensions to the identity I professed. Sometimes, by the ferocity of his distrust, he made me doubt who I was. I would stand fumbling in the wrong pocket for my *carte d'identité*, which had a knack of passing from one part of my apparel to another, like a prestidigitator's coin, and then for my passport, which on such occasions was equally elusive. The sneer on Harpagon's cuttlefish bone of a face would grow triumphant, and I expected him to push a button behind his grille that would summon a squad of detectives. At last, I would find my fugitive credentials and present them, and he would hand over the draft. Then he would send me back to the bench, a *huissier* would present me with another number, and it all had to be done over again—this time with my Kafka impersonation enacted before Harpagon, at another grille, who would hand out the substantive money. Finally, with two hundred times twenty-six francs, minus a few deductions for official stamps, I would step out onto the Boulevard des Italiens —a once-a-month Monte Cristo. "Taxi!" I would cry.

※ ※

The fellows I met at the Center were Americans, most of whom were living in Montparnasse and were writing or trying to learn how to paint.

None of them was trying to learn how to write, because in the 1920s that was supposed to come naturally, like falling off a bar stool.

❧ ✿

I liked to box, and I had an illusion that if I boxed a lot, I could eat and drink a great deal and even stay up late with the girls. The exercise would burn all that out. I was too young to know that if you do those three things often, you will feel with increasing infrequency like boxing, and boxing is no fun unless you feel like it. This is because boxing makes you want to eat, but eating does not make you want to box. I had not yet heard the great Sam Langford say, "You can sweat out beer and you can sweat out whiskey, but you can't sweat out women." Sam had never had to contend with my toughest opponent of all, sheer gluttony.

German Women

❧ ✿

WHEN I WAS a small child, I had had a succession of German governesses all indistinguishably known to me as *Fräulein*. They had been servile to my parents and domineering to me, stupid, whining, loud, and forever trying to frighten me with stories of children who had been burned to a crisp or eaten by an ogre because they had disobeyed other *Fräuleins*. The fairy tales of anthropophagic stepmothers and princes turned into white mice gave me nightmares. Once when I was very small I was escorted by the current *Fräulein* through the torture tower in Nuremberg and made to look down a deep well into which, she told me, it was customary to throw bad little boys. It was really the place where the jolly Meistersingers had been accustomed to drop the mangled corpses of people who disagreed with them, like a slot for used razor blades. She had bought me a little miniature of the Iron Maiden as a souvenir of our promenade, complete in detail, she liked to point out. Only Germans could be so thorough, she said with pride—there were miniature spikes inside the hollow maiden's hollow eyes, just like the spikes in the big one, that pierced the victim's brain. I suppose German-lovers would have called it *gemütlich*. Banse and Goebbels and their war by fear are in the main line of German culture, not twentieth-century deviations. Only people with hollow hearts can so count on the fears of others. The *Fräuleins* had shared a national habit of digging their fingernails into the flesh of my arm. When I was five years old I would rather have died with my milk teeth in a governess' ankle than tie the kind of bow in my shoelaces that she had wanted to make me tie. Anybody who had had a German governess could understand Poland.

My wars against the *Fräuleins* left me with a blurred recollection of injustice and struggle, like the collective memory of the Irish, for whom I have an anomalous sympathy even when they are at their most difficult. The *Fräulein*, I have often thought since, was a remarkably effective device for siphoning off from the parents the hostility that analysts assure us is the parents' due. Careful bootleggers in Harlem during prohibition used to pass suspected alcohol through an old felt hat, on the theory that the denaturing agent would remain there. The *Fräulein*, in the segment of a segment of society that I was young in, fulfilled the function of the felt hat. As full of discharged hostility as the hat of fusel oil, she shifted to another job when the child outgrew her, leaving it to its parents as harmless as a baby rattlesnake milked of venom. I credit to this system the patience that a number of elderly Germanistic friends of mine still manifest with regard to their mothers. To the child who began conscious life under the rule of a *Fräulein*, even the least bearable mother will always appear an angel. The device seems to me, looking back, more sensible than that of the kind nanny, described in middle-class English novels. The nannies siphon off not the hostility but the affection, leaving the heroes of the novels incapable of liking anybody else for the rest of their lives.

Rule Needed

NOTHING is more useful in the conduct of human affairs than the time limit—the count of ten in the prize ring, the five years of the statute of limitations on felonies, and the five years of a husband's absence after which his wife is allowed to presume him dead. Arbitrary such periods must be, but fixed with some regard to the reasonable. If a fighter can't get up at ten, for example, the chances are that he can't at eleven, or shouldn't; if a husband hasn't come home in x years, the chances are that he won't in x plus 1, and anyhow he should have the good taste to stay away. Without devices like these, there would be no steadiness in life; no citizen would know where he was. We are in favor of a reasonable rule of closure in the United States Senate—if a speaker can't convince his colleagues in x hours, it is almost certain he won't in x plus 27 or in $27x$—and in favor of a fixed date for compliance with laws and Supreme Court decisions. (There are fixed dates for meeting taxes and mortgages, and although we hate to think of them, we suppose they are necessary.)

What we are getting at, by a long enough route, we hope, to avoid the charge of subversion of State Department foreign policy—and the consequent risk of being denied a passport by a Pennsylvania congressman—is that the world lacks a Count of Ten on Fallen Statesmen. How long after a ruler is chucked out on his *de-facto* ear by an ungrateful country does he remain *de-jure* chief of government, and how far does he have to be chucked to be out of bounds?

If the United Nations, following a big, rousing debate, set a maximum interval between the time a regime loses effective control of its country and the time it ceases to be the legal government, international relations would be simplified. No matter what the UN decided—six months, ten years, twenty years—it would be all to the good. (As a parallel, there is no immutable reason territorial waters should extend three miles from the shore, as they do, or twelve, as the United States claimed during prohibition, but there must be an international definition of territorial waters or we'd all be shooting one another.) In the name of decency, we are for a fixed minimum interval, too—of at least until the palace charwomen finish wringing the blood from their mops. There could be adjustments later.

No government anywhere today has an unflawed original title: England's government is based on conquest (1066) and revolution (1688), France's on a whole pinwheel of revolutions, ours on a revolution, a forced solder job in 1865, and the Tilden-Hayes election of 1876. Yet each of the three would find it intolerable if an outside power indefinitely withheld recognition and treated with the Anglo-Saxon Nationalist government or the House of Valois or the Sons of the Confederacy. In brief, we're advocating some kind of order. There would be nothing at all, of course, to prevent the de-legalized crowd from starting a revolution in order to get back. After the third out, they go into the field. A revolution is an internal affair, though, and until it succeeds, outsiders should recognize the regime the revolution is against. One government, like one husband, at a time. Let the UN pass an Enoch Arden law.

Bobance, Man of Taste

OFTEN, in the last twenty years, I have thought of Assistant Lieutenant Bobance, retired, under whom I served in Burgundy in 1927 in a successful campaign that has never been confided to military history. Usually these thoughts occurred while I sat at a restaurant table with a glass in my hand. The wine in my glass was often good, but even when it was excellent I was aware that Assistant Lieutenant Bobance would not have approved of my method of wine tasting. I was paying for my drinks, and that was a violation of the Bobance strategic doctrine.

The only blood for which my old commander thirsted was the blood of the grape, and he seldom thirsted long. He was a master of concealment and surprise, and since the publishing mode continues to be for military biographies, I have felt impelled to set down this tribute to a great soldier.

The fact is that Assistant Lieutenant Bobance and I used to drink Vosne-Romanée, Romanée Conti, Chambolle-Musigny, and the veritable Richebourg without paying a sou. Together we reeled in the white dust of the Burgundian roads, sweating through every pore vintages that I shall never again be able to afford.

One evening, when he fell on his face only fifty feet from his own door, Mme Bobance helped me drag him into the café of which he was the proprietor and cried that she was an unhappy woman. "What a life!" she wailed. "What a life he leads me! Instead of encouraging the clients to drink in his own house, he gets black with them outside. Our competitors profit from my misfortunes."

Actually, I spent very little money outside of the Bobances' inn, where I was stopping, but Bobance had never seen fit to enlighten madame; he did not wish to reveal our procedure.

Assistant Lieutenant Bobance, retired, was a portly man with a round head and a face like a mustachioed tomato. He was not of the countryside in which he kept his inn, l'Auberge de l'Écu d'Or. The Assistant Lieutenant was a Lorrainer, a native of Nancy, and the Burgundians considered him neither a good weather prophet nor a good judge of wines. For the rest, they admitted that Assistant Lieutenant Bobance was a cultivated man who had been in Indo-China and who, to hear him tell about it, had been a great hero in the war. There was only one war to talk about then, that of 1914. But they did not invite him into their cellars and ask him for his opinion, because he could not tell you whether the wine of a new *cru* would gain finish in five years or perish ignominiously. Oenologically speaking, he had lacked early advantages. So the Assistant Lieutenant could only dream of all the good wine stored in the cellars of the vicinity while he drank his own sour *vin ordinaire*. He could also, of course, drink *les apéros* from behind the bar, but his wife was always watching and ready to make a scandal, because *apéritifs* are dear. And, after all, they aren't the same thing.

I think that when I entered the inn of the Écu d'Or, Assistant Lieutenant Bobance recognized me not as the funnel through which the best wines of the Côte d'Or were to trickle gratuitously down his throat but merely as a fat American in knee pants, demanding board and lodging. Instantly he told me that the tariff of the house was twenty-five francs —amounting to a dollar—a day for a room and three meals. When I appeared astonished, he thought I had sensed the swindle. He had, in truth, quoted a rate two-thirds higher than his normal one. "Wine included," he said hastily. "All the wine you can drink with meals. The good wine of the district." This was a lie, because it was the very worst wine of the district. I accepted his terms and became a guest of the Écu d'Or.

My bedroom was over the cow barn. The chamber next to mine was tenanted by a Polish couple. The husband went to work on the railroad at five o'clock in the morning, and since they used their limited time intensively, I got my best sleep late. When I rose, at eight or nine, I would have my cup of chocolate and a piece of bread in the café of the inn and then walk out among the vineyards. It was September and the roads were warm and dusty; the grape leaves looked yellow on the hills. On the roads around the Écu d'Or, the signposts are like wine cards: pointing to the south, they say Vougeot, Chambolle, Vosne-Romanée, Nuits-Saint-Georges, Beaune. The inn was within the communal limits of Gevrey-Chambertin. I had no practical reason for being in that region. In Paris, the Côte d'Or had seemed an interesting place to be, and it was on the direct line between the capital and Marseille, where I was to board a liner in a couple of weeks. But since the French believe that there must be a logical reason for everything, word got about that I was an American wine buyer. The *vignerons* were too tactful to ask direct questions. It is my impression, however, that Assistant Lieutenant Bobance told them plenty.

After dinner on my second evening, he cajoled me into playing a game rather like parcheesi, with nuances in the rules that I never quite understood. Because of the nuances, which he explained to me very carefully as the situations calling for them arose, he won five consecutive games. At the end of each, I bought him and myself a drink. Three or four farmers from the district watched us from another table. Each had one drink, which he made outlast our five. As I started out to cross the courtyard to my room, carrying my candlestick, I could see that Bobance had joined the farmers at their table.

The following day, the Assistant Lieutenant proposed that we take an afternoon walk together. He said he supposed I was interested in wines. I said, naturally, that I was. Bobance informed me that some of the local proprietors had a cooperative winery. One of them, a M. Rameau, had been in the café on the previous evening and had suggested that the Assistant Lieutenant bring me to the winery for a visit. I said that I would be charmed. When Bobance went into the kitchen to announce that he was taking the afternoon off, I could hear madame's whining voice raised in some objection. Then the rich parade-ground voice of the Assistant Lieutenant: "I will pass you a few slaps!" And Mme Bobance, shrilly: "What a life! What a life!" Bobance emerged, breathing hard, and we set out.

The narrow white side road that we took ran through fields of sourish grapes, not fully ripe. We nibbled them as we walked. After about a third of a mile we came to an *estaminet*. The sweat rolled down the lobes of Bobance's ears and he looked as if he might collapse. "It's worse than Morocco," he said. "And besides, I really ought to see how my competitors' affairs march." So we went into the *estaminet* and I bought a drink. This happened a couple of times before we arrived at the Caves Syndicales des Viticulteurs Réunis du Vicinage, a low concrete structure, the rear of which was built into the side of a hill. I recognized M. Rameau when he came to greet us as one of the men who had been at the Écu d'Or.

"It was extremely nice of you to come on such a hot afternoon," he said ceremoniously. "Come into the interior, where it is cool."

In there, for a moment, I couldn't see at all, but I could feel Bobance nudge my ribs with his elbow. "Not too much enthusiasm for the first wine," he mumbled in my ear. "The afternoon is long."

M. Rameau, who had disappeared into the shadows, returned with three large metal drinking cups and led the way to the first barrel he proposed tasting. Using a syphon, he drew off three drinks. I was the putative buyer, but it would have been discourteous to omit Bobance from the round. Moreover, my landlord obviously had influence over me. I drank.

"There is no room for discussion about that," I said. "It's a good wine. Honest. A taste of the earth. But still, all the same, a bit young, eh?"

M. Rameau was not displeased. "Over here," he said, "we have another *cru*, les Violettes. You are going to see."

The three of us drank deep. I witheld my comment momentarily, but smacked my lips.

"Another shot?" M. Rameau asked gaily. He had Bobance's empty cup in his hand before he finished his question.

We all drank, and I said, "It has finesse, agreed, but it lacks a little body."

M. Rameau led us on. We had forgotten the heat outside, and I sensed that M. Rameau, after his third drink, found us sympathetic. Like Bobance, he was willing that our quest for perfection should lead to many casks. To ensure this result, I relied upon an alternation of comments: "It has bouquet, it has velvet, but it lacks, all the same, of vigor" and "It has strength, all right, it is a mouthful, it warms you the heart, but concede, my dear Rameau, that it is, all the same, rough." Almost any wine must fall in one or the other category. How many hours we remained submerged in the darkness of the cave I could not estimate. My voice sounded mechanical in my ears, like a phonograph record of a French lesson. From somewhere in the dark, Rameau continued to hand out full cups; I pushed them back into the shadows empty. Since we of-

ten lingered over one cask, it sometimes happened that I made contradic-
tory comments on the same *cru*. Rameau politely ignored such anomalies.
Bobance, invisible, was only a continuous gurgle in the obscurity.

"These are honest wines," Rameau said. "They are bottled in the commune of origin, not like the wines in the big warehouses in Beaune and
Nuits-Saint-Georges. They haven't been worked, mixed with stuff from
other vineyards." He was drawing wine of a sort he called le Clos St.
Jacques. I drank some, and to save my soul I could not say anything
against it. I knew Bobance would be angry, but I had to end the game.
From being so long in the cave, I was beginning to feel like a stalagmite.

"This wine," I said, "is perfect. It is the most remarkable wine of
France."

The effect upon Rameau was incredibly felicitous. "You are exactly
of my advice!" he shouted. "This wine is grown upon my own three
acres! Of all the wines in the cellar, you pick precisely the wine of Rameau. We must celebrate this with marc!" So we began drinking the
marc, the old Burgundian brandy, distilled from Rameau's wine.

Days later, it seemed, we staggered out into the light. Green-and-
orange jellyfish, rising before my eyes like Roman candles, obscured my
vision at first, but after a while they cleared away and I could see that
it was still daylight, with the sun low in all four quarters of the sky and
a little rabbit hopping along the road and Assistant Lieutenant Bobance
running after it shouting, *"Faisons la carrousse!"*

On succeeding afternoons, Bobance and I visited other cellars. The
entire countryside soon knew about me. Rameau had spread the word
that I was a Daniel among wine tasters. As yet I had not mentioned
buying even one case of wine. None of the proprietors wished to offend
me by introducing the subject. When we ran out of strictly local cellars,
I hired the village taximan to drive Bobance and me to Nuits-Saint-
Georges, eight miles away. My legend had preceded us. We were wel-
comed to the cellars of the largest wholesale firm. Bobance was a little
frightened. After all, he would have to continue to live in the district
when I was gone. But after the first six free drinks, he was all right.

I asked the *chef de cave*, "Is this wine of homogeneous origin or has
it been worked, *hein?*"

"Of course it has been worked," he said. "By blending good wines,
you get a better wine."

I said that I preferred straight wines.

He admitted that he had some vintage Burgundies and led us on to
untampered-with *crus* of Romanée and Vosne-Romanée.

"You know," I said kindly, after drinking about three pints, "you do yourself a great disservice. If you had château bottling, as they have in Bordeaux, people would have more faith in the authenticity of your wines."

The *chef de cave,* a hairy, grizzled man with rheumy eyes and a face like Vercingetorix, rose in the air like a gamecock. "Bordeaux!" he howled. "Bordeaux! *La mise en bouteille au château!* What a filthy deception. Ah, monsieur, if you only knew what they do to the wine *in* the château!" He laughed bitterly. "They mix glucose in their wine!" he shouted. "They mix Algerian vinegar in their wine! Besides, it is known that only a girl with the greensickness can find any taste in the very best of clarets. Come with me! I will show you wine."

He dragged us off to a cask of Richebourg that was just about to be bottled. We filled ourselves with Richebourg as a mosquito sucks blood. And the *chef de cave* stood over us, enormous, ominous, with a wooden mallet in his hand, as if forcing us to drink hemlock. "Ah, ah!" he repeated. "Tell me, is there wine in Bordeaux like that? *Their* châteaux! *Their* châteaux! Ah, oh, euh, ah!"

That was the night Assistant Lieutenant Bobance fell on his face. And later, as I lay on my bed over the cow barn, I could hear Mme Bobance screaming, "What a life! What a life!" And Assistant Lieutenant Bobance: "Peace, woman! Peace! It was only a tour of *dégustation.* We went to taste a little wine."

On a return trip, which I made to the Côte d'Or not very long ago, I failed to find my old chief. I had lunch at the inn he formerly conducted, but the new proprietor said M. Bobance, from whom he had bought the place, had moved to Dijon and drunk himself to death. "After the death of madame, he was inconsolable," he said.

French Without Scars

A FINE WAY to acquire facility in the use of French idioms is to be beaten up by a couple of Frenchmen. I made this discovery in peacetime, in 1926, in an alley off the Rue Nationale in Tours, at about 2:45 A.M. The École Berlitz is welcome to this tip on payment of a small royalty.

I had spent most of the previous afternoon in the vineyards across the Loire from the city, walking about with a knowing air and occasionally picking a small, sour grape and eating it. The year was destined to be remembered in the valley of the Loire for the conspicuous worthlessness of its wines, but I had no way of knowing that. Somebody had presented me with a book called *The Wines of France,* and I was completing a tour of the great vineyard regions, an enterprise that, at the time, I thought strikingly original.

In my travels, I did not like to associate with compatriots. If you were just going to talk to other Americans, what was the benefit of being in France? The trouble was I did not feel at home with the French themselves, because I always missed my second shot when I talked to them. I could usually compose an adequate opening sentence, for example, "It will be good this year, the vintage, *hein?"* But when the person I spoke to replied, "On the contrary, it is not scarcely the pain to pick the raisins," or made some other equally pessimistic answer, I invariably wished I hadn't begun. "Goodbye," I would say, "I will see you soon." As the psychiatrists would put it, I was becoming withdrawn.

It must have been eight o'clock when I returned to my hotel, the Métropole, at Tours. I changed from knickers into long trousers and then decided not to eat in the hotel dining room, where they had international cuisine and a Levantine headwaiter, but to look up a place called Le Colibri, which a girl in Angers had recommended to me. It was truly chic, she had said, a place such as you wouldn't expect to find in the provinces.

Le Colibri didn't look like much when I found it, more than a kilometer from the hotel. There were a few tables, a bar, and a fellow singing a comic song about Mussolini, who was more unpopular than usual in France that summer. I sat down at a table and ordered something to eat. It appeared that Le Calibri did not serve serious food—a sandwich was the best I could hope for. By that time I was so hungry that I said a sandwich would be all right—a sandwich and some red wine. I had expected local wine in a plain bottle, but the waiter brought me a bottle of Nuits-Saint-Georges 1915, with one of those deadly French sandwiches consisting of a loaf of bread sliced longitudinally and a paper-thin slice of ham hidden between the halves. There I sat with my excellent bottle of wine and my deplorable sandwich, and before I had finished the Nuits-Saint-Georges I began to feel sorry for myself, in a pleasant way. I was a lone exile and I felt that I could not tell any of the people in the bar about it because they would ask me why I didn't go home. Then I would have to tell them that I didn't go home because I enjoyed thinking of myself as a lone exile. So I had a bottle of champagne—Irroy, I think—and drank it all, rather slowly, continuing to pity myself. When I ordered a second bottle of champagne, a girl named Roberte came and sat at my table, and I gave her a couple of glasses of wine. I felt that I couldn't finish the bottle anyway. Roberte had a wide face and her neck seemed to be made of lard. Sometimes it is difficult to be a Francophile.

I stayed in Le Colibri for a long time, drinking slowly, and finally the place began to close. Waiters were moving tables around and the boss came over and said he was very sorry. I paid the check, which wasn't bad, because francs were about thirty-five to the dollar, and the *patron* and I were both satisfied. He thought he had cheated me, but I knew how much it would have cost me to get feeling that way in New York. Then I found myself walking in the street with Roberte. It was all right; I knew what I was doing. I had told her I didn't like her, but she said that the *patron* wanted her to walk part way home with me so I wouldn't get lost. It was raining and she had an umbrella and there were no taxis in Tours at that hour of the morning.

We got on the Rue Nationale, which is long and straight, and then I knew where I was, but Roberte walked me about halfway to the hotel. She told me she was going to Rennes the next day and that that was a nice town, too, if you knew your way around. She said there was a shortcut to the *pension* where she was stopping, through an alley by the burlesque theater. I offered to see her home and we walked a little way into the alley together. Then she insisted that I had come far enough, and said good night.

When I turned back toward the street, I saw that two fellows had walked into the alley after me. They wore black, wide-brimmed hats and they looked more like students than toughs.

One of them put his right hand on my left arm and said, "Where are you descended?" The idiom was unfamiliar to me until he said, "At what hotel?"

"At the Métropole," I told him.

I guess he was just making conversation, because he hit me in the eye. I threw my right, but he didn't stagger. That puzzled me, because he was a small man. It is quite possible that I hadn't even touched him. The other one pitched in and they hit me a good many times. I kept swinging, but my knuckles were unscuffed when I got to my room later. We must have made a lot of noise in that echoing alley, scuffling over the cobblestones and swearing. Eventually, I landed on the back of my neck. I could hear two men running, their feet pounding on the cobbles, and when I got up I couldn't see anybody. I took two reluctant steps after them for honor's sake. I knew there was no danger of my catching them.

My glasses had been broken and I had a lot of small cuts on my face from the glass, but otherwise I was all right. I walked on down the Rue Nationale to the Métropole, feeling very stupid. There were six hundred francs in my wallet, untouched—a circumstance which seemed at that time of no particular significance. There wasn't a policeman in sight.

The glass door of the hotel was locked. I knocked loudly, and as I waited for the porter, I remembered the new phrase and that this was the hotel where I was "descended." The night porter took a look at me and burst into a smile of ineffable jollity—nothing so enlivens a Frenchman as the contemplation of spectacular catastrophe. "Ah, old man," he said, "you're well arranged, eh?" I carried his colloquialism and my wounds to bed with me.

Early the following afternoon, I dressed and went looking for a barber, thinking he could clean my face up a bit with hot towels. When I appeared in the door of the Métropole barbershop, the *maître-coiffeur* whistled. He seemed as pleasantly aroused as the porter had been.

"I am well arranged, eh?" I snapped as I sat down in the first chair. Naturally, I had to tell the barber all about my misadventure, and since I couldn't talk French very fast, he filled in the gaps. He was an imaginative man. I began by relating that I had drunk two or three bottles of wine.

He smothered me with a hot towel and said, "You were in train to tap the bell, *hein?*" When he took the towel off my face, I asked him what that meant. He said it meant to eat or drink well.

I got along to the part of the story where I took a punch at the little man, and the barber said, "You tapped on top!" I knew I hadn't tagged the fellow at all, but by that time I was beginning to color the story slightly, so I said "Of course." "Ah!" said the barber. When I got to where they knocked me down and went home, he was in raptures. "They saved themselves!" he exclaimed "Monsieur, you are a brave."

I could have clasped him in my arms. With that short phrase *"Ils se sont sauvés!"* he had rescued my self-esteem. Instead of being beaten up by two insignificant youths in an alley, I had won a great victory. As I thought over the incident, I could see that they had been lucky to escape with their lives. It was evident, as the barber said, that they were professional characters of small interest who had followed me with the object of de-pocketbooking me, but I had resisted. "Did they get your money?" he asked. I told him they hadn't. I couldn't remember their asking for the money, and, reconsidered in the light of the barber's question, my resistance had certainly been successful. When I left the barber chair, I had the skeleton of a story. It took on flesh and color with repetition.

At Blois (Hôtel du Château), where I told the story next, the number of my assailants had increased to three types of small interest. They had followed me with the object of de-pocketbooking me (a verb I had already begun to find useful). They didn't render themselves account. I had tapped on top! And rudely! In the end, they had saved themselves, fortunately for them. At Vendôme (Hôtel du Commerce), four dirty mugs figured in my narration. I had taken them two by two and knocked their heads together. It seemed a natural development.

Continuing, at a hamlet called La Ville-aux-Clercs (Hôtel de l'Écu d'Or), I told a postman and an egg buyer that five *apaches,* but real ones of real ones—trust me, I knew the type well—had attacked me with knives and brass knuckles, but that by a few quick strokes of *la boxe américaine,* which they had doubtless observed in moving pictures, I had disengaged myself. The *apaches* had done well to save themselves! "But I was well arranged, old man!" I remembered to concede here. The postman said he had once seen an American movie actor, Reginald Denny, dispose of a considerable number of gangsters in the same fashion. For weeks, wherever I went, people who saw my face wanted to know what had happened to me. I told each new acquaintance my latest revised and expanded version. It established a rapport that had hitherto been lacking. By adopting comments from my listeners, I got fresh phrases to incorporate in my narrative—"They passed me through the tobacco" and "I was advised to carry plaint to the police station, but the cops, what? Bah!" This last embellishment always pleased taxi drivers. At each rendition, I increased the number of fellows who had saved themselves.

I can acknowledge now, when I am being frank with myself, that my assailants were just two men who hadn't liked my looks and who succeeded to a considerable extent in altering them. There was a good deal of antiforeign feeling in France that summer because of the slump in the franc. But this theory never formed part of my recitation. By the time I got back to Paris, the scars had faded, but Mme Anna, behind the desk of the small hotel where I stopped on the Avenue Montaigne, sensed at once that I was a changed man.

"Monsieur talks currently now," she said. "Before, he appeared to have fear to talk French. He has lost his timidity."

"*Eh, bien!*" I said. "Once you've licked nine uninteresting types simultaneously in an alley at Tours, you render yourself account!" And when I heard myself say it in French, I believed it.

Far West

The Mustang Buzzers: 1953

THE PRESENT high demand for dog and cat food has made mustanging, or the rounding up of wild horses, a gainful employment out in the West, for the horses are marketable at four cents a pound on the hoof, which is half as much as cattlemen are getting for old cows these days.

Early this winter, when my wife and I were staying at a guest ranch on the western rim of Pyramid Lake, north of Reno, we were told that excellent mustanging country was close at hand, in the mountains and draws west and north of the lake. Our informants were two mustangers, Mr. Hugh Marchbank and Mr. Bill Garaventa, who operate from a camp some forty miles up the long, lonely road that skirts the western edge of the lake and ends fifty miles farther along in Gerlach, an oasis of five bars and a general store.

Mr. Marchbank, a bachelor, refers to himself as a jack-Mormon, which means that although he was born into the Church of the Latter-Day Saints, he no longer pays tithes or holds with the tenet of total abstinence. The only part of Mr. Marchbank's L.-D.S. heritage that creeps up on him now and then is one long abjured by the working Saints: he can sometimes see good in more than one woman at a time. Mr. Marchbank owns so freely to this atavistic foible that when he failed to show up one day for a business engagement with his partner, Mr. Garaventa jumped to the conclusion that he had either got shot by an unnamed widow or run off with her.

Mr. Garaventa cannot round up wild horses alone, because he would be like a pitcher without a catcher. He operates from an airplane, buzzing the mustangs and urging them along with an occasional shotgun blast at their tails, and if he had no collaborator, he would have to drive them into a corral, land on a flat, and run back in time to shut the gate behind them. It is Marchbank's job to take charge after Garaventa brings the wild horses down from the canyons where they live to within sight of the padres—the disingenuous tame horses who act as decoys in the mouth of the corral trap. Padres are named for the priests who walk ahead of condemned men. Garaventa was considerably disappointed by Mr. Marchbank's defection, for the day was clear and windless—the kind of day he needs for his thread-the-needle flying in the canyons. But he announced that all was off until Hugh reappeared.

About a week later, a rancher from up north, stopping in at the bar of our ranch on his way down to Reno, said that Bill had had word from Hugh that he would be back in a couple of days. The bar is the only one in the 120 miles between Gerlach and Sparks, a suburb of Reno, and if you spend enough time there, you are sure to hear about everything that happens along the road.

"Seems Hugh had an uncle up to Winnemucca who got killed in a mine accident, and he had to go up and bury him," this rancher said.

"I saw Hugh at the Round Up Bar in Reno a couple of nights ago," Harry Drackert, boss of the ranch, said after the rancher had left, "and he didn't look like he come from a funeral, unless they embalmed the wrong fellow. He said those bar stools was a lot softer than a stock saddle."

Along toward closing time the same night, Hugh himself stopped by the bar, bound in the other direction—toward that hard stock saddle and Bill Garaventa. He must have been mourning especially hard in town, because his cheeks were sunken and his eyes were a dull Wedgwood blue instead of their customary bright cobalt. But his brow was unfurrowed and he appeared to be bearing up. Hugh looked slightly flummoxed when my wife said she was sorry to hear about his uncle, but then he rallied, and said a man that age had had no right to be swimming a horse across the Snake River in such cold weather.

"The horse's tail froze and come away in his hand, and he got carried down the stream," he said.

My wife said she had heard that his uncle got killed in a mine.

Hugh said it was hard lines on a fellow to have two uncles pass out on him in one week. "I was feeling low even before I heard the bad news," he went on, "because I'd been romancing a woman that had a bag of loot in each hand, and her parents took her away to Honolulu. I went down to San Francisco to see her off, and I would have sailed with her, but they wouldn't let me on board with my Oklahoma Gladstones—you know, paper boxes tied up with string. I come back to Reno to rest up, and while I was drinking a green mint high, I heard about my poor old uncles. It broke me up."

It was the kind of story, I knew, that would be sure to win Bill's sympathy. Bill had told me about the aftermath of a weekend he himself had spent in Reno. He had taken his plane down to the Sparks airport for repairs, and on Sunday he was flying her back into the Smoke Creek country, so he could run horses early Monday. He flew over the Paiute reservation at a height of about fifty feet, looking down now and then for horses, and he had a terrible head. Outsiders may not hunt horses on the reservation, but you never can tell when a band will stray out into the public domain, so it pays to know where they are. Suddenly, Bill saw the most outrageous horse he had ever gazed upon; in fact, it appeared to be a camel. He went back and buzzed the strange beast, and it was unmistakenly a camel. Then he saw Martin Green, a Paiute he knew, galloping along on a normal horse but wearing a fur coat. Bill could only figure that the Paiutes had gone on the warpath for the first time in seventy-five years and plundered a traveling circus and a department store. But that didn't seem plausible, so he went on the wagon. It wasn't until a month later, when he drove down to Reno with some mustangs, that he learned that a moving-picture company had been on the reservation making a film about the Gobi Desert, which in spots the reservation resembles, and that the apparition had been a real Hollywood camel. Martin had been a fierce Mongol horseman.

Hugh is a lean man with a long, honest face and a modest smile. His partner, Bill, is a bald-headed, barrel-chested, bowlegged man, who wears a flying jacket with his jeans and cowboy boots. They both feel ambivalent toward their work—proud because it calls for a lot of skill but defensive because there is a special human sentimentality about horses, and, as horsemen, they aren't immune to it.

"I like *good* horses," I once heard Hugh rationalize over a can of beer, sounding like Brother David, the Episcopal missionary on the Paiute reservation, when he is distinguishing between devout and backsliding Indians. "But those wild ones are no good to nobody, suffering out in the cold and so poor they ain't none of them worth breaking." And then, as if seeking moral support from the horse's mouth, he added, "Gentle horses hate them mustangs. They can't stand the smell of them." He has an equivocal feeling about eating horsemeat, too. "I've ate it when there wasn't anything else," he told me, "and it's just as good as range beef. But it's a lot like eating your brother." Bill, a great epicure, won't eat horsemeat at all, possibly because he's afraid he would like it.

Hugh looked a bit worn by all his romance and sorrow, but he said they'd be running next morning if they had good weather. The sky was full of stars. He pushed on at midnight, and shortly after dawn three of us began to get ready to follow him. We were my wife, myself, and a fellow waiting for a divorce, named Bob. We used a Plymouth I had hired from a rent-a-car place in Reno. Harry was unable to accompany us; he had to go to Carson City to get a yearling that a fellow named Cliff had been breaking for him down there. This fellow was in the Nevada State Penitentiary doing a life term for murder, so he had plenty of time to give to his work. In the Nevada Penitentiary, the convicts get a chance to work at their regular trades and earn a little outside money; it keeps them contented. Cliff had been made foreman of the horse barn. "He's conscientious," Harry said. "Nice little fellow, too." One of the things about racetracks that irk Harry is the number of obstreperous horses you see. "No reason a thoroughbred shouldn't be broke as well as any other kind of horse," he says. "Makes them better racing tools." Harry was at one time the champion bronc rider of the world, but he doesn't have the time to break all his horses himself, so he has to farm some out. "The fellow Cliff killed wasn't no good anyway," he said, "and if Cliff had just left well enough alone, they would have acquitted him, but he made a couple of mistakes, like cutting hisself with a knife and saying the other fellow done it, and the D.A. crossed him up on fingerprints and cast a reflection on his honesty." Another mistake Cliff had made, in Harry's opinion, was to put on a clean shirt and a pressed suit every day of his trial at Las Vegas, where he had killed this worthless man. "It set the jury against him," Harry said.

The route to the mustang corral was noteworthy. The lake, at our right, was Prussian blue against the naked, snow-tipped *djebels* on the other shore, and the tufa islets stood up like castles and churches. Pyramid Lake was the Paiutes' Mediterranean, the center of their Stone Age world, which continued into the nineteenth century, and it is still theirs, inside the reservation's barbed-wire fence. The boundary of the reservation follows the shoreline anywhere from a mile to ten miles inland. North of the lake, the reservation runs up into the desolate mountains for ten miles. The road to Gerlach lies within the boundary. After it leaves the lake behind, there is nothing to look at except sagebrush flats and the kind of mountain they have in North Africa—bare, and brown or gray, dotted with juniper around the crotches. At some places on the road, through a gap between minor ranges to the west, which nobody calls by name, you can see clear over to the main line of the Sierra Nevada. The bleak ground pullulates with jack rabbits, who support a handsome population of hawks and coyotes, all very beautiful and in the same color key as the mountains—gray, sandy, and tawny. There is great speed in all these animal forms. In the summer, the little lizards

travel with the velocity of hummingbirds. From the road, you can now
and then see bands of white-faced cattle, and you can tell their owners
by the different ways the beasts have been harmlessly mutilated. A strip
of skin cut back and allowed to dangle from the throat is a bell wattle,
Art Heller's mark. A similar strip hanging from the breast is a brisket
dewlap, Bill Ceresola's. Both men are local ranchers whose cattle have
a way of getting over into Indian territory, and these so-called neckties
can be seen farther away than ear nicks or brands. Most of the bushes
are silvery gray the greater part of the year. The coloration of the land-
scape, except for the lake, is no more vivid than that of a Siamese cat,
but the shadows can do great things with the hills toward sunset. Beyond
the mountains on the other side of Pyramid, there is Winnemucca, another lake, perhaps half as large, that has dried to salt and lies shimmer-
ing like an African chott. North of the reservation, there is the Smoke
Creek Desert, which is smaller than the Sahara, but no joke.

Several miles north of the lake, we hit Bonham's ranch, a group of
four neat buildings by the road. It is about a third of the way between
Harry's and Gerlach. You can buy gas but not liquor at Bonham's and
liquor but not gas at Harry's. I do not know whether this reflects differ-
ing principles or a trade agreement, but it is essential information for
the pilgrim to Gerlach. A wind sock on a pole proclaimed a meadow
alongside the road to be Bill Garaventa's airport. His plane was missing
when we got there, but we hadn't pushed far beyond when we saw it,
maybe fifty feet in the air and five miles away. It was going the same
way we were, and not much faster; Bill's top speed is only about eighty,
and he generally loafs anyway. It was late for him to be just starting for
the mountains, and I couldn't make out what he was about. Then I saw
the long line of the mustang corral on the sloping side of a hill to our
left, about a mile back from the road. It was a narrow V, perhaps a
quarter of a mile long, with the open end facing north, toward the
mountains from which Bill brought the mustangs. Its sides were camou-
flaged with brush that had stayed summer-dark so it made a black line
against the gray. Beyond it, the hill rose more steeply, to a great red rock.
A horse taking the natural way down around that rock would head
straight into the mustangers' trap.

There were no horses in sight as our car drew even with the dark
stockade, but just as I concluded that we either had missed the chase
or would have to wait hours for it, an escaping horse burst out from the
wide end of the corral, running north like a well-meant long shot. It
ran flattened out, as if it had a premonition of its fate, and I had hardly
had time to look at it before another horse, with a rider on it, broke into

view about ten lengths behind. The rider was Hugh—I could tell him
by the fifty-dollar white hat he always shelters under—and he was sailing along as if he had never heard of ratholes. I had stupidly forgotten
to bring field glasses, but I had the advantage of a grandstand that kept
up with the racers. They ran almost parallel to the road, their course
and ours only very gradually converging. The horses were running across
a decided slope and over ground that was peppered with rocks and
pocked with animal warrens, but they moved as smoothly as more effete
racers move on a level turf course. I knew Hugh would have something
under him that could run, but the wild horse ran like a good one, too.
It is true he had nothing to carry, while Hugh, with rope and saddle,
must have weighed nearly two hundred pounds. I have frequently seen
outriders at the track catch riderless runaways, and even police horses
on bridle paths can usually spot the weight. The difference here seemed
to be that the wild horse was running with a purpose. A gentle horse
that runs away doesn't know what to do with its liberty; it runs with an
intention of being caught.

I could see that Hugh was coming up on the fugitive. He rode bend-
ing forward only slightly, his long legs straight down, his hands low;
no longer gangling, he looked better in a saddle than on a bar stool, no
matter which he said he liked. The airplane, hovering over the chase,
had turned in front of it and now swooped. Hugh got on the near side
of the wild horse and rode him off to the right, turning him away from
the straight line to his distant home country. That took the heart out
of him. The chase was obviously going to cross the road ahead of us,
and with the amateur's fear of getting too closely involved in the action,
we stopped. We thought that if we followed on, we might get between
Hugh and the mustang.

The race passed out of view, and then we could see the plane, a yellow
Cub, coming in our direction. When Bill got over us, he yelled and
waved down the road in the direction we had come from. We understood
that he wanted us down there, so we turned and went back. Bill flew
lower and yelled to my wife, who was driving, to pull off the road, because he wanted to land. We did and he did. He had plenty of room.
"Help me pull the airaplane off the road!" he yelled as he climbed out.
This was a light chore—it wheeled as easily as a baby carriage—and
when it was stowed in the sagebrush, Bill asked us to take him up the
road to where Hugh was waiting with the wild horse, which he had
caught and roped shortly after he had gone out of our sight; Bill had
seen the catch from the air. "I can give him a hand hobbling that old

stud," he said, switching from his flying to his buckarooing personality. He was carrying a coiled rope, which he kept by him in the cockpit.

He said he had brought six horses down from the mountains—not a very good hunt, but the herd he found up there had split into small bands and all he could do was pick out one. He had found them on Twin Peak, between Smoke Creek and Buffalo Creek—more than twenty miles north of where we were—and had chivied them across the intervening country in barely two hours, keeping them at a lope all the way. When they saw the tame padres, all six had followed them into the wide mouth of the corral, but an old stud and two yearlings had taken alarm and doubled back. Hugh had had to close the gate behind the three that were all the way in and then take out after the old fellow, which explained the mustang's long lead when he burst into our view. The yearlings had gone off down a draw to the west.

"He's a big son of a gun for a mustang," Bill said of the old horse. "Must weigh nearly a thousand."

"He would have got away if you hadn't run him twenty miles before the race," my wife said unexpectedly. "If that had happened at Jamaica, the stewards would have ordered him scratched." She is always for the underprivileged. "You ought to let him go," she said.

This proposal did not appeal to Mr. Garaventa to any perceptible degree, but he didn't know quite what to answer. Finally, to induce sympathy he said, "Supposing I got killed in that old airaplane?"

"It would serve you exactly right," my wife said. She is a great protector of animals, especially cats (for which she often buys horsemeat), and she took a highly partisan stand.

I was relieved when we pulled up alongside Hugh and his captive, and Bill got out. Hugh and the wild horse were about a hundred yards east of the road, waiting there and looking at each other. Hugh had put a loop around the old stud's neck, and the other end of the rope was secured to the horn of the saddle on Hugh's well-lathered mount, a dark bay mare with white stockings. The mare maintained her pull on the rope, preventing the old horse from bolting, and Bill, deft as a deckhand on a tug, ran in with his extra rope and slipped a noose under one of the captive's hind feet. With Hugh and the mare pulling one way and Bill the other, they threw the old horse, and then Bill, operating unexcitedly among the thrashing hoofs, tied the two forelegs together and secured them to the hind foot he had already noosed. When this was done, he released Hugh's rope from the stud's neck. Hugh dismounted, and the two partners hauled and kicked the hobbled old rover to his feet. The rope left him just sufficient play to walk a little. He lurched forward, as if he was unable to understand why he couldn't walk as usual, and then dropped his neck and began to graze.

This old stud was a bright bay; the wet red fur on his chest reminded me of a robin's breast. He had the tremendous neck and forequarters that stallions develop with age and that make Derby winners look so ungainly in pictures of them taken ten years after they have quit racing. His neck and chest were scarred from battles; he had probably killed more competitors than a Restoration beau. Wattles of balled fur stood out on his neck where strips of skin had been torn back by other studs and hadn't grown smooth. He was blind in his left eye, and most of his right ear had been chewed away. He was a square sort of horse, half-legged and heavy, and fully fifteen hands, which is tall for a mustang, and his general makeup supported a story Hugh had told me—that the mustangs in the Smoke Creek country are descended in part from draft stock abandoned by unsuccessful dry farmers. He had a proud head— wide between the eyes, Roman-nosed, and authoritative.

"He must be eighteen years old," Hugh said.

"Look at that head!" my wife cried. "Pure Arabian!"

It wasn't, but I knew what she meant—wild and noble. I felt a bit blue myself, but I can't explain why. There was nothing friendly about the old stud.

Meanwhile, Hugh had taken the saddle off his mare and was leading her back and forth by the side of the road to cool her out. Her official name was Gold Lee, but she answered to the name of Witchy. She was one of Harry Drackert's mares, Hugh told me, by the quarter horse Goldfield out of Anna Lee, and he was giving her a trial to see if he wanted to buy her.

"She can go pretty good, but she's green to rope from," he said. "We caught that horse about two miles back, but instead of giving me a chance to lass' him, she went right on past and made me miss. She's been raced, and passing is all she knows. I didn't have no second rope, and by the time I got my rope back, that old stud had gone ahead. We went about three miles." A quarter horse, as the phrase implies, is not bred to hold top speed for more than a quarter of a mile, and what Hugh had done was move Witchy in a series of short bursts, "favoring" her in between, he said. "This is good country to run horses in, because it's level," he went on. (Everything is relative, of course.) "If that old fellow could have got onto a hill, he would've lost us. Ain't no gentle horse can follow them among the rocks." What Hugh calls a hill is pretty nearly a precipice.

The sun was high now, and Hugh was as wet as the mare. He emptied a can of beer from a supply we had brought along, and then saddled up again for the ride to the corral, leaving the old stud behind to graze. The rest of us got into the Plymouth and started back for the corral, too. As we left, we saw him jog off through the sagebrush, having ridden a ten-thousand-dollar race for a total reward of twenty dollars —his half of the price of a forty-dollar mustang. Passing the airplane, we dropped Bill, who took off to look for the yearlings that had got away. A little farther along, a trail of wheel marks left the road, leading up to the southern end of the corral. Hugh and Bill had made this path by driving pickup trucks over it.

Three-quarters of the way down the corral toward the V point, there was a gate, which was left open during a hunt until the horses got past and was then closed behind them, and fifty yards farther down was another gate, which closed off the bottom of the V.

When we got to the corral, there were five horses in the upper compartment—two padres, wearing bridles, and the three prisoners, who looked like stubby bumpkins compared to the cowboys' horses. The padres, a chestnut named Billy and a bay named Slim, were eating hay from a feed rack and ostentatiously snubbing the mustangs. The wild horses, apprehensive and lonesome, tried to shoulder up to the decoys for company. (Wild horses will not eat hay, Bill had told me, because they are not used to cut fodder.) But the padres, as if fearing recrimination, sent them off with hearty kicks; so the shill turns on the fleeced sucker. "Never saw the guy before," I fancied Slim saying to Billy. Embarrassed, the wild horses stood shifting from feet to feet. They were a brown stallion with a white face and three white stockings, a bay mare, and a bay yearling. The yearling was surely the mare's son, because two homelier but more resemblant animals never lived. The stallion, which I guessed to be about nine years old, was smaller than the old fellow up the road, but just as battle-scarred. He may or may not have been the mare's mate, but her gaze seemed to me to reproach him for the fix the three found themselves in. I imagined he avoided her eye.

Now Hugh arrived and, dismounting, led Witchy through the gate. The uncurried stallion nuzzled the neat runner, but Witchy, towering above the old reprobate, turned and kicked him in the belly. Then she shrugged her shoulders and joined the two padres at the feed rack. The wild horses scrounged back in the most distant corner of the pen, the mare snuggling against the stallion forgivingly, the old scoundrel professing to ignore her.

Hugh, having fastened the first gate behind him, opened the second, and drove the three captives through it, thus shutting them off from the gentle horses. He drove them by throwing a few handfuls of earth and yelling. They appeared cowed. When they were in the point of the V, he shut the second gate behind them and fastened it with a rope. But now the captives seemed seriously disturbed. Although the elegant strangers had rejected them, their nearness had been reassuring. The three mustangs began trotting about their pen.

The gate, strung to a pole by two ropes instead of hinges, was made of two vertical and three horizontal planks, with two more planks nailed X-wise over them for reinforcement. It was about six feet high. The old planks were powder-dry, and the nails were loose. The stallion went back on his haunches, awkwardly threw himself forward and up, and smashed through the top bar of the gate with his knees. He got his forelegs over the second bar and knocked the whole business askew with his hindquarters as he came down on the other side, with cuts on the insides of all his legs. The mare and the yearling simply trampled through after him. Having achieved this feat, they stood shivering while the gentle horses pretended not to notice them. When you think how spooky wild horses are—they are terrified by the mere aspect of anything like a gate or a feed rack or a watering trough—you can understand what a big decision the old stallion had had to make. But the outer gate was stronger and higher, and anyway he didn't try it. A gate, he must have figured after his lacerating experience, is something that cuts your legs.

"It was about time we put another gate together anyhow," Hugh remarked after the old stallion's leap. "There's a million horses been through this corral since we slung that one. Cheer up, old boy," he added to the stallion consolingly. "You won't mind them cuts when you get your rind off." And to all three horses he recited a little rhyme:

> Far from water, and far from wood,
> You're going to leave this place for good.

My wife, who was cooing at the stallion and urging him to jump a section of the fence that she thought was low enough, did not hear Hugh, which was as well for both of them. Bill returned, not having found the yearlings, and he and Hugh saddled Billy and Slim to go down and get the ancient stud in the field and bring him back to join the unhappy family.

"After that, we'll go over to a old dry ranch and pull enough planks off the barn to make a new gate," Hugh said. "If you come up tomorrow, we'll be running horses again."

But Bob said he thought one day of mustanging was probably pretty much like another, and I said I thought I had the general idea. So we lit out for the guest ranch, and made it. On our way down, we saw three coyotes running beautifully across a flat, and a bit farther on we passed a dead one, poisoned. Everybody has trouble, even in Nevada.

Two days later, Hugh and Bill stopped in at the bar on their way down to Reno. They had two trucks—they each own a pickup—and fourteen horses in them. They had had a good hunt the day after we were there, they said, and had added ten horses to the four we saw taken. The horses stood crosswise in the trucks, alternate horses facing in the same direction, and the wind from the lake blew through their tails and manes.

"That makes our catch for this season two hundred," Bill said, "and we been averaging thirty-two dollars a horse. Pretty soon we'll go along up to Idaho. Snow ought to be driving them northern horses out of the mountains."

"Pickings getting pretty slim around here," Hugh said. "Better leave a few for seed."

"And what will happen when the horses are *all* gone?" my wife asked the partners. She thinks Hugh and Bill are darlings, but she wishes they would find a nicer way of making a living, like being outriders at a race-track.

"Then them cats of yours will have to get used to these ten-cent cows, ma'am," Hugh answered, in his most courtly fashion. "But I sort of think the wild horses will last me out."

Note— They did.

Book Review,

Editorial

❦ ❦

A Talkative Jerk

THE TRADITIONAL Englishman of Gallic fiction is a naïve chap who speaks bad French, eats tasteless food, and is only accidentally and episodically heterosexual. The sole tolerable qualities ever allowed him are to be earnest, in an obtuse way, and physically brave, through lack of imagination.

When I began reading *The Quiet American,* in its British edition, on a plane between London and New York last December (Viking has just now brought it out in this country), I discovered that Mr. Graham Greene, who is British, had contrived to make his Quiet American, Pyle, a perfect specimen of a French author's idea of an Englishman. I had bought *The Quiet American* at the waiting-room newsstand, on the assurance of the young lady attendant that it was good light reading.

Pyle is as naïve as he can be and speaks French atrociously. He dotes on bland horrors in food: "A new sandwich mixture called Vit-Health. My mother sent it from the States." (In American, I think, a thing like that is called a sandwich *spread.*) Pyle's choice of idiom convinced me that he is a thinly disguised Englishman. But I was impressed by the *toupet* of Mr. Greene, sneering down at Pyle from the gastronomic eminence of a soggy crumpet. A British author snooting American food is like the blind twitting the one-eyed. Finally, Pyle says he has never had a woman, even though he is thirty-two. He is earnest, though, in an obtuse way, and physically brave, through lack of imagination.

This exercise in national projection made me realize that Mr. Greene, the celebrated whodunist, trapped on the moving staircase of history, was registering a classical reaction to a situation familiar to me and Spengler. When England, a French cultural colony, outstripped the homeland after Waterloo and the Industrial Revolution, all that remained for the French to say was "Nevertheless, you remain nasty, overgrown children." The Italians of the Renaissance said it to the French, and I suppose the Greeks said it to the Romans. It is part of the ritual of handing over.

When Greene undertook the composition of Pyle's sparring partner, he had more difficulty. He had already presented one basically English type as a Quiet American. Now he had to have somebody to contrast him with unfavorably—an Articulate Englishman. Such a person is a contradiction in popular-fiction terms, like a scrutable Oriental. To produce one, Greene had to defenestrate all the traits by which a whodunit reader identifies an Englishman—the tight upper lip, the understatement, the cheerful mask of unintelligence skillfully exploited to confuse the enemy. I needed a full thirty seconds in the company of the result —Fowler, the correspondent in Saigon of a London newspaper published in a grim Victorian building near Blackfriars station—to see that Greene had run out at the turn.

Fowler is a sophisticated MacTavish. He knows French writing from Pascal to Paul de Kock and speaks the language like a native, although not necessarily of France. He has brought with him from Bloomsbury, of all places, the gustatory savvy of a Prosper Montagné: "I sat hungerless over my apology for a chapon duc Charles." (He has, in fact, an edge on Montagné, who includes no such *plat* in his *Grand Livre de la Cuisine.*) He is as active sexuallly as a North African jack and has a taste in women unaffected by the flicks, which glorify convex Marilyns and Ginas. Fowler prefers flat women with bones like birds, and he likes them to twitter on his pillow while he smokes opium. He associates informally with foreign-language-speaking people. None of these, especially the last, is a traditional British characteristic. Yet Fowler, from the moment I laid eyes on him, which was at about the time the takeoff sign flashed FASTEN SAFETY BELTS—NO SMOKING, had a familiar air, like a stranger who resembles somebody whose name you can't remember.

Suddenly I made him. He was a mockup of a Hemingway hero— *donc* an American, *donc* One of Us. Fowler is not a Hemingway hero by Hemingway, of course. He is nearer the grade of Hemingway hero that occurs in unsolicited manuscripts. "What distant ancestors had given me this stupid conscience? Surely they were free of it when they raped and killed in their paleolithic world" is a fair example of Fowler in his jungle gym of prose. But he can also bring the beat down, quiet and sad, for contrast. Like "Ordinary life goes on—that has saved many a man's reason." Original but not gaudy. I hyphenated him Bogart-Fowler *sur le chung* (a bit of Indo-French I soaked up from Greene).

There are aspects of Bogart-Fowler that lead me to think he may be an American by birth, although probably a naturalized British subject. His familiarity with the minutiae of American life that irritate him hint at a boyhood spent in a town like Barrington, Rhode Island. When he thinks that Phuong, his bird-boned baby doll, is about to marry Pyle, Fowler wonders, for example, "Would she like those bright, clean little New England grocery stores where even the celery was wrapped in cellophane?" Perhaps, when he was a child, he tried to eat the cellophane.

Maybe Fowler's father, a vicar, left Rhode Island because of a broken home, taking young Bogart with him, although he knew the boy was not his own son—a situation always rich in potential traumata. Back in Bloomsbury, he imparted to the little changeling an implacable hatred of milk shakes, deodorants, and everything else American. There—but this is again a hypothesis—Bogart-Fowler may have got a job writing readers' letters to a newspaper published in a grim Victorian building near Blackfriars station, and then fourth leaders about the wiles of chaffinches, which have bones like birds.

"Good chap, that," the old Press Lord had said, with a wintry smile, as he spread Marmite on his fried beans *maison du coin lyonnaise* and read the fourth leader. "Make a jolly good foreign correspondent." I had often wondered how some of my British newspaper friends got abroad.

I stopped there, though, because I have never been a man to let a hypothesis run away with me, and considered another possibility—that Fowler, born British, had merely been the Washington correspondent of the newspaper near Blackfriars long enough to take on a glaze of loquacity. If so, when had he got out of the Press Club bar in time to shop for celery for his wife? He had a wife; it says so in the book.

I found, as I read at Mr. Greene, that Fowler's pre-Saigon past interested me a lot more than what happened to him after he got there. Where, for instance, had he learned his distaste for reporters who asked questions at army briefings? Had he perhaps been not a reporter at all but a press-relations officer with Montgomery? In Saigon, he gets his information from a sick Eurasian assistant who comes around to his digs every evening to share a pipe. Greene leaves the newspaper part of Fowler's past a mystery, such as where he had learned what was a proper *chapon duc Charles* and what was an apology for one. Had Fowler, during this obscure period, discovered that "good little French restaurant in Soho" that is as hard to verify as the Loch Ness monster? And where is it? Yes, Fowler's past is a blank, except in one department. He tells Pyle that before coming to Saigon he had forty-odd plus four women, of whom only the four were important to him, especially one in a red kimono. On Topic A he is a Talkative Englishman, native or natural- ized.

At that point, I fell into one of those short, deep airplane sleeps, ten minutes long, that you hope have been longer, and, waking, found my hand where I had left it, around half a glass of Scotch-and-soda.

The book was open at the same place: Fowler telling the Quiet Ameri- can about sex.

"One starts promiscuous and ends like one's grandfather," he says. (Dead, I thought, anticipating the next word, but it wasn't.) "One starts promiscuous and ends like one's grandfather, faithful to one woman" was the complete sentence. Fowler has *had* his fun; now he is a moralist. "We are fools," he concedes, "when we love." Still, he never leaves the Quiet American in any doubt about who of the two of them is the bigger fool. Poor old Q. A. Pyle, cold-decked by Mr. Greene, never suspects that Fowler is an American, too. Greene has fixed it so Pyle doesn't read fiction, except Thomas Wolfe, and Fowler is not in Wolfe. Pyle takes Fowler for a Legit Brit., the soul of honor. That is why he trusts him.

I wandered downstairs to the lounge bar, dragging *The Quiet Ameri- can* with me. It was slow, but it was all I had, because I was making the trip on short notice and the other books on the stand had looked even less promising. I had a copy of the *British Racehorse*, but I had read through that early and lent it to one of the hostesses, who said she thought the Aly Khan was cute. Between drinks and dozes, I gnawed away at the novel, as though it were a gristly piece of apology for a *chapon duc Charles,* until at an unremembered point I began to won- der when Greene himself had realized that a possible second American had infiltrated his Eastern Western, and if that was the sort of thing that made him mad at us. Reading a bad book is like watching a poor fight. Instead of being caught up in it, you try to figure out what is the matter.

I signaled to the Aly Khan's fan for a fourth drink. The book was written in imitation American, too—brutal, brusque sentences tinkling with irony, not at all like fourth leaders about chaffinches. Does Greene ever get homesick for Lewis Carroll?

"They pulled him out like a tray of ice cubes, and I looked at him." . . . "Death takes away vanity—even the vanity of the cuckold who mustn't show his pain." . . . "I was a correspondent; I thought in head- lines." . . . "She was the hiss of steam, the clink of a cup, she was a certain hour of the night and the promise of rest." The last quote is a switch to the poetic, but it is an *American* style of poetry—simple, dynamic, full of homely, monosyllabic comparisons. It reminded me of a lyric I used to sing:

> *You're the cream in my coffee, you're the salt in my stew,*
> *You're the hiss of my and the bliss of my*
> *Steamy dreamy of you.*

Poor old Greene was in the position of the Javanese politician who told a correspondent he hated the Dutch so specially hard because he could think only in Dutch.

Mr. Greene's irritation at being a minor American author does not justify the main incident of the book, which is a messy explosion in downtown Saigon, during the shopping hour, put on by the earnest but unimaginative Pyle in collaboration with a bandit "general" in the hope of blowing up some French officers. (The French postpone their parade, and the explosion merely tears up women and children.) When I reached that point, most of the way through, I had had breakfast and was trying to kill the two last deadly hours before Idlewild. I thought I might as well finish the book so that I could give it to the hostess, a brunette from Rye, New York.

I should perhaps explain here that the book begins with Pyle in the morgue. That is the big gag: A Quiet American. It then goes on to the events that led up to his arrival there. The trouble that starts immediately and keeps on happening is known technically as Who Cares? Near the three-eighths pole, it appears that Pyle, who is a cloak-and-dagger boy attached to the Economic side of the American Legation, is helping the bandit get plastic, which can be used in the manufacture of bombs as well as many other things. I figured the bandit was fooling naïve young Pyle. Not at all. Pyle knew all about the bombs and the contemplated explosion. So did the whole American Legation. The Minister must have O.K.'d it. The way Mr. Greene, through Fowler, tips the reader to this is Fowler is in a café and two young American Legation girls are there eating ice cream—"neat and clean in the heat," a pejorative description for Fowler, who is a great sweat-and-smell man:

> *They finished their ices, and one looked at her watch. "We'd better be going," she said, "to be on the safe side." I wondered idly what appointment they had.*
> *"Warren said we mustn't stay later than eleven-twenty-five."*

The two girls go out, and a couple of minutes later the big bomb goes off.

All the Legation personnel had been warned.

At this point, I, as startled as Fowler, remembered something—a miching little introductory note in the front of the book, about how all the characters are fictitious. I turned back to it, not bothering to follow Fowler out of the café and into the horrors of the square, to which I knew he would do stark justice—brusque, brutal, ironic.

"Even the historical events have been rearranged," the part of the note I wanted to see again said. "For example, the big bomb near the Continental preceded and did not follow the bicycle bombs."

Greene was, then, writing about a real explosion, a historical event, which had produced real casualties. And he was attributing the real explosion to a fictitious organization known as the State Department. If the State Department had promoted the historical explosion, I thought, it was a terrific news story and a damned shame. We needed a new State Department.

But whether it had or hadn't, anybody who read the book would wonder whether the State Department was engaged in the business of murdering French colonels and, in their default, friendly civilians. In France, which is traversing a period of suspicion, rapidly approaching hatred, of all foreign governments, the effect would be particularly poisonous when the book was translated. I knew that Mr. Greene, like James Hadley Chase and Mickey Spillane, is a great favorite of French readers of whodunits. ("Not for a long time have Anglophobia and anti-Americanism been so much at work in Paris," Stephen Coulter of the Sunday *Times* wrote lately. "It is a rooted French political axiom: 'When in trouble blame the foreigners.'")

Then I remembered something else. In Paris, where I had been until the day before I began my plane passage, I had noticed, without much interest, that *L'Express,* a bright new newspaper, had already begun the publication of a new serial: *Un Américain Bien Tranquille,* by Graham Greene. The serials in Paris newspapers are generally translations of fairly stale books, and they are frequently retitled to appeal to French taste. I therefore had assumed the *feuilleton* in the *Express* was a book Greene wrote years ago (but of which I had read only a review) about an American who has an affair with an Englishwoman and is punished for the sacrilege. The *Express,* a tabloid, was crowded for news space even at sixteen pages, a format it had struggled for two months to attain. It is a universal belief among French editors, however, that a newspaper must have a *feuilleton.* The readers demand it, and read it more faithfully than anything else in the paper. I could imagine the *Express's* hundred thousand readers getting to the two-neat-girls installment and then asking their friends at lunch, *"Tu l'as vu dans l'Express? C'est les Amer-loques qui ont fait sauter deux mille français sur des mines atomiques en Indochine."* People everywhere confuse what they read in newspapers with news.

L'Express is only a weekly now. *Un Américain Bien Tranquille* was an irresponsible choice for the editors, but they needed circulation desperately. They didn't get it. *L'Express* went 245 numbers before it gave up its struggle to survive as a daily, and it still annoys me to think that a sixteenth of each of at least a hundred was devoted to Mr. Greene's nasty little plastic bomb.

There is a difference, after all, between calling your oversuccessful offshoot a silly ass and accusing him of murder.

R. I. P. —*John Lardner*

JOHN LARDNER once wrote, "You may have noticed that these playwrights who are not afraid of emotion tend to write things for the stage that explain all too clearly why other writers *are* afraid of emotion." He was one of the other writers. His style reminded a reader of a jockey riding a race with something in hand; he never scrubbed or whipped. Yet it is hard to write with any restraint at all about his death at forty-seven.

The style accorded with the man. As a man and as a writer, Lardner was reserved. His humor was direct without being blunt, his use of understatement graceful without being soft. He was as easy to like as he was hard to know. We had the pleasure of his benevolent acquaintance from the time he was a boy. His first piece for *The New Yorker* appeared on December 26, 1931, when he was nineteen. The last that he read the proofs on ran on March 19 this year, a week before he died. Oddly, both were about broadcasting—the first, a slight bit of straight-faced humor about a radio storyteller; the last, one of the numerous television departments he wrote during the past two and a half years.

In the time between, Lardner wandered far and wrote about most things under the sun. A younger brother, David, was a *New Yorker* war correspondent when he was killed at Aachen in 1944. In the following year, John wrote for us accounts of the fighting on Iwo Jima and Okinawa that were as good as J. W. De Forest's reporting of combat in the Civil War, which in our opinion is almost perfect. David's death may have brought emotion closer to the surface, but without troubling the medium or dulling the eye. John was naturally brave; when he saw blinding bomb flashes by night, he used to walk *toward* them to see better. After the war, Lardner substituted for the late Wolcott Gibbs as drama critic of *The New Yorker,* during Gibbs's long absences, and did so with a felicity of which the quotation at the beginning of this notice is sufficient evidence. Then he chose to devote himself to writing about television.

John grew up in the shadow of a father who was a great writer. This is a handicap shared by only an infinitesimal portion of any given generation, but it did not intimidate him. He made his own way. As a humorist, reporter, sportswriter, and critic, he found his style—a mixture, unlike any other, of dignity and gaiety, precision and surprise. He was a funny writer, and, though he would never have admitted it, an artist. In one of his last pieces, he wrote that his father "struggled constantly to make his stuff as good and as true as it could be." He might have been writing about himself.

Through all the years we knew him, John remained outwardly the same: handsome, grave, and equable, only the corners of his mouth, and of the eyes behind the thick lenses, betraying occasionally his private amusement with what he thought about. If he was sad—and there was much in his life that might have made him so—he never talked about it. He was often for long hours a tall, vertical silence in front of a bar with a cigar in his hand, dominating by his dignity a saloonful of noisy newspapermen, yet there was nobody idiot enough to resent this withdrawal. He did not mind jokers who suggested that he must be an Indian. At long intervals, he would look down at the floor and, after another long interval, up at the ceiling and blow a smoke ring. He had not worked for the *Herald Tribune,* his first employer, since 1933, but to the last he maintained a sentimental affiliation with the saloon next door. We think we will never enter it without turning our head to the right, by reflex, to look in his favorite corner, or know a night that we won't be sad not finding him.

Harold Ross—The Impresario

❧ ❧

IT IS HARD for a writer to call an editor great, because it is natural for him to think of the editor as a writer *manqué*. It is like asking a thief to approve a fence, or a fighter to speak highly of a manager. "Fighters are sincere," a fellow with the old pug's syndrome said to me at a bar once as his head wobbled and the hand that held his shot glass shook. "Managers are pimps, they sell our blood." In the newspaper trade, confirmed reporters think confirmed editors are mediocrities who took the easy way out. These attitudes mark an excess of vanity coupled with a lack of imagination; it never occurs to a writer that anybody could have wanted to be anything else.

I say, despite occupational bias, Ross, the first editor of *The New Yorker*, was as great as anybody I ever knew, in his way. He was as great as Sam Langford, who could make any opponent lead and then belt him out, or Beatrice Lillie, who can always make me laugh, or Raymond Weeks, who taught romance philology at Columbia and lured me into the Middle Ages, or Max Fischel, who covered New York Police Headquarters for the *Evening World,* and was the best head-and-legman I ever saw. The head helps the legs when it knows its way around.

Given the address of a tenement homicide, Max would go over the roofs and down while the younger men raced down to the street and then around the block and up. They would arrive to find him listening sympathetically to the widow if the police had not already locked her up, or to a neighbor if they had. People in jams liked to talk to him because he never talked at them.

Ross was as great as Max, or as a man named Flageollet, who kept a hotel with eight rooms at Feriana in Tunisia and was one of the best cooks I have known, or another named Bouillon, who had a small restaurant on the Rue Sainte-Anne in Paris. (It is odd that I should have known two great cooks with comestible names.) He was as great as Eddie Arcaro, the rider, or Gen. George Patton or Bobby Clark and Paul McCullough, or a number of women I have known who had other talents. Ross would not have resented any of these comparisons, and the ones with Max and Patton would have flattered him particularly, because he was a newspaper and army buff. One thing that made him a great editor was his interest in the variety of forms greatness assumes. He saw it in the entertainers he hired, as cheaply as possible so that they would work harder, to appear in his Litterographic Congress of Strange (Great) People of the World. The Greatest One-Gag Cartoonist, the Greatest Two-Gag Cartoonist, the Greatest Cartoonists Waiting for a Gag; the Greatest One-Note Male Short-Story Writer, the Greatest Half-Note In-Between Short-Story Writer, the Greatest Demi-Semi-Quaver Lady Short-Story Writer Ending in a Muted Gulp; The Greatest Woman Who Ever Married an Egyptian, the Greatest Woman Who Ever Married a Patagonian, the Greatest Woman Who Ever Married a Dravidian Pterodactyl. These latters' stories always began: "My mother-in-law could never get used to my wearing shoes," and still do, although sales territory is becoming rapidly exhausted; the only franchises still available to marry into are the Andaman Islands and Washington Heights. Ross cherished half-bad Great talents too; he knew there will never be enough good ones to go around.

E. B. White once said to me that the relation between Ross and him was like that of two railroad cars—they met only at one point. White was with Ross from the beginning of the magazine in 1925, but he admits he knew only one Ross personally and a couple of dozen others by intuition, hearsay, brag, or reputation. Ross had some raffish friends I envied him and some stuffed-shirt friends I wouldn't be seen dead with. He was equally proud and I think equally fond of all of them. He liked anybody who had a lot of money or a good story to tell, and since these are minerals seldom found in conjunction, he prospected around. *The New Yorker* he made reflected this idiosyncrasy, but not what the kids now call dichotomy. There was no conflict; he just had more interests than most people. I think that a number of men who knew Ross underrated him because, coming up on him always from one direction, they found him sometimes preoccupied with what was going on in another ring.

It was as if a wire-walker expected a ringmaster to be as exclusively interested in high-wire acts as he was. Of course Ross couldn't write as well as Thurber or Joe Mitchell, or draw as well as Steinberg. He didn't know as much as Edmund Wilson is supposed to, and there were at any given period of *The New Yorker's* existence eighty-four people around who knew more about France or the East Side or where to buy a baby bottle with an aquamarine nipple for Christmas. But he had his own greatness—he put the show together. Why he wanted to I don't know. What made Arcaro a jockey?

Early in December, 1951, when Ross had been ill since the previous April, I said to Bill Shawn, who was doing his work and has since succeeded him, "If I knew he was going to die, I'd put my arm around his shoulder and say I'd always liked him. But if he recovered, he'd never forgive me."

That was at a time when the doctors had not admitted his condition was critical, but when the length of the illness had made us all suspicious. He died about a week later, but I think he knew that I liked him, in a way, and I know he liked me, in a way, and that's about as close as I ever got to him in an acquaintance of eighteen years, sixteen of them on *The New Yorker*.

The only letter of his I have chanced to preserve is one I got in Reno, Nevada, in the summer of 1949. He felt there was a great story in Reno, but did not know just what it was. He wrote, "But of course you are a better reporter than I am. (The hell you are!)" He couldn't give a compliment without taking it back in the next sentence—afraid you'd get a swelled head, I suppose. I disappointed him with a slight report on Reno I wrote then, but I took east the seed of a much better story, which germinated until I went out to Nevada again in the fall of 1953 and reported and wrote it. He never saw it, of course.

He was a great hunch man, which is part of being a great editor. Many aspects of life entranced him imprecisely, and he knew that where there was entrancement there was a story, if he could just bring the right kind of man into its vicinity. Like a marriage broker, he could bring together a couple, writer and subject, who ought to hit it off. But sometimes not even Ross could make them go to bed together.

He was also good at sensing a mismatch. Immediately after the end of the war I told him that I would like to travel in the unknown—to me—interior of this country and write about the Midwest as I would of any other strange land.

"You wouldn't like it, Liebling," he said. "You wouldn't like it."

I spent the winter of 1949-50 in Chicago, and he was dead right.

Later in my Nevada summer he came to Reno with some of his Hollywood pals—Chasen and Capra and Nunnally Johnson—on a holiday. He was very happy, happier than I have seen him in any other setting. He liked the West (as distinguished from Mid-) and pretending to be a Westerner. (He had left the West when a kid, and by the time I knew him was an indefinitely urban type, though never a New Yorker.) He got me to sit in with him at the open poker game in the Bank Club, together with the old sheepherders and railroad pensioners. There are always at least three one-armed men in that game—brakemen who fell under trains. I played a half hour, lost twenty dollars and got out. He stayed an hour and said he won sixty. Later he went back, played until five in the morning, and returning to the Riverside Hotel, cashed a check for five hundred. I heard about it at breakfast from the night manager of the game room, who was just going off duty. At lunch Ross told me he had cleaned up, but I knew better.

When he was young, vaudeville was the chief national entertainment industry, and I often thought he would have made a first-class booker for variety shows. This is no faint compliment, for I adored vaudeville, which lasted well on into my own youth. So must Ross have done; he had a great affection for old comics like Joe Cook and Chasen. He put on a weekly variety bill of the printed word and the graphic gag—always well balanced and sufficiently entertaining to bring the audience back next week. He booked the best acts he could, but he knew that you couldn't get the best specialists in every spot every week. When he had no headline comic, he built the show around a dancer or even a juggler. One week he might have a cartoon that people would remember with pleasure for years. The next it might be a good profile, and the week after that the Fratellini of prose, Sullivan and Perelman, or a tear-jerking fiction turn by Dorothy Parker or O'Hara. Vaudeville, too, had its sacred moments; next to a good laugh there is nothing so nice as a sniffle.

Ross tried to polish old acts or develop new ones, but he never let his notion of what he wanted get in the way of his clear apprehension of what was to be had. In the late 1930s, when all his new writers came from newspaper staffs where they had sweated through the depression, he said to me, "Liebling, I wish I could find some young conservative writers who could write, but there aren't any."

He was by inclination a kind of H. L. Mencken conservative himself, but he wouldn't book a dancer who couldn't dance just because he liked the shape of her *derrière*. This is a higher integrity than either right-wing or left-wing editors possessed in those days. The writing in the *New Masses* was as bad, in a different way, as the writing in *Time*. (The transition, as Whittaker Chambers found out, was easy.) Ross's loyalty was to his readers. He treasured Alva Johnston, an earlier convert from the newspaper fold than we were, who wrote excellent profiles and at the same time held that stupid Presidents were best, because they let big businessmen run the country, and businessmen had brains.

Alva's only objection to Herbert Hoover was that he was too bright. He was a hard man to satisfy; it is a pity he did not live to see Eisenhower. Ross relished Johnston's concurrent political opinions as *lagniappe*; he wouldn't have given a hoot about them if he hadn't esteemed

Alva's technique of defining character by a series of anecdotes on an ascending scale of extravagance, so that the reader of the sixth installment wolfed yarns that he would have rejected in the first.

Nor did Ross insist on playing types of acts that had lost their vogue. During the late twenties and very early thirties *The New Yorker* frequently ran a type of profile of rich and successful men that was only superficially distinguishable from the Success Stories in the late *American Magazine*. (The difference was that the *New Yorker* writer might attribute to the protagonist some supposedly charming foible like wearing crimson ties although he had attended Princeton.) The hallmark of this kind of profile was a sentence on the order of "Although Jeremy P. Goldrush is as rich as rich, you would never think from his plain old two-hundred-dollar suits that he was more than an ordinary weekend polo player."

After a couple of these heroes had landed in state prisons, Ross became receptive to portraits in a less reverent style. Although Ross loved the smell of success, he was emotionally irreverent and always enjoyed learning that a fellow he had accepted as a monument to society was in fact a sepulchre with a runny coat of whitewash.

He made the same good adjustment to World War II as to the depression. He would have preferred not to have it, but he didn't deny it was on. That got me a break. He sent me to France in October, 1939. I attracted the assignment by telling McKelway how well I could talk French. McKelway could not judge. Besides, I was a reasonable age for the job: thirty-five.

Ross was forty-seven then, and in the newspaper world where we came out in different decades, twelve years is a great gap. When we talked I called him "Mr. Ross." I was never an intimate of his—just an act he booked and learned to appreciate, though never highly enough in my opinion. I think that all the reporters of my *New Yorker* generation—Mitchell and Jack Alexander and Dick Boyer and Meyer Berger and I —had the same classical ambivalent son-to-father feeling about him. We were eager to please him and cherished his praise, but we publicly and profanely discounted his criticism. Especially we resented his familiarity with the old-timers—the Companions of the Prophet—and his indulgence for them. Our admiration for their work was not unqualified or universal. (I still think *The New Yorker's* reporting before we got on it was pretty shoddy.)

I find it hard to admit how jealous I was one day in 1946 when Wolcott Gibbs, who was very ill, called up while Ross and I were working over proofs. Ross told him to take care of himself and said, "Don't worry

about money." That was white of him, I thought, but he had never said
that to me. It was a true sibling emotion. In fact, Ross thought that a
healthy writer wouldn't write unless he had had to emit at least two
rubber checks and was going to be evicted after the weekend. It was an
unselfish conviction, a carry-over from his newspaper days. He reminded
me of a showman I knew named Clifford G. Fischer—the impresarial
analogy pops up constantly when I think of Ross. Fischer spoke to actors
only in a loud scream, and when I asked him why, replied, in a low
conversational voice he used on non-actors, "Because they are abnormal
people. To abnormal people you got to talk in an abnormal voice."

Ross liked writers, but he would no more have thought of offering a
writer money than of offering a horse an ice-cream soda. "Bad for them,
Liebling," he would have said. But you could promote a small advance
if you were in a bad jam. What continually amazed me about Ross, and
convinced me of his greatness, was that he took the whole show seriously
—from the fiction, which I seldom can read, to the fashion notes that I
never try to. He knew no more of horse racing than a hog of heaven,
but he knew how to find and keep Audax Minor, G. F. T. Ryall, whose
tone is precisely right for *The New Yorker*. Here again he had the in-
stinct of a showman, who wants the whole bill to be good, while I have
that of an educated seal, who thinks that when he plays "Oh, say can
you see" on the automobile horn, it is the high spot of the evening. After
that the crowd can go home.

A lot has been written about Ross as an editor of manuscript, as distinguished from Ross the editor-impresario. There should be different
words for the two functions in English as there are in French—*directeur*
for the boss and *rédacteur* for the fellow who works on the copy. Ross
did both, but he impressed me less as *rédacteur* than as *directeur*. His
great demand was clarity. This is a fine and necessary quality, but you
can go just so far with it. You cannot make subtlety or complexity clear
to an extraordinarily dull reader, but Ross in editing would make himself
advocatus asinorum. He would ask scores of marginal questions, including many to which he full well knew the answers, on the off chance
that unless all were pre-explained in the text some particularly stupid
woman might pick up a *New Yorker* in a dentist's waiting room and
be puzzled. Out of the swarm of questions there were always a few that
improved the piece—on an average, I should say, about 2¾ per cent,
and none that did any harm, because you could ignore the silliest and
leave Shawn to talk him out of the rest.

I never thought this quest for clarity naïve. It was part of a method
he had thought out for putting his "book" across in the early days. If the

silliest *New Yorker* readers could go through a piece on a "sophisticated" subject and understand every word, they would think themselves extremely intelligent and renew their subscriptions. But there are subjects not susceptible of such reduction; the only way of making clear pea soup is by omitting the peas. Ross continued his queries compulsively long after the time when *The New Yorker* had to recruit readers. A point had been reached when the silly ones would pretend to understand even if they didn't. This vestigial reminder of the "book's" early hard times was exasperating, but not serious. The writer got his way in the end. Just because he was a great editor, Ross knew when to back down.

I have heard that he made a fetish of Fowler's *Modern English Usage,* a book I have never looked into. (It would be like Escoffier consulting Mrs. Beeton.) He never suggested the book to me, nor told me how to write that mythical thing, the *"New Yorker* style." What is affected as a *"New Yorker* style" by undergraduate and British contributors is, to judge from specimens I have seen, a mixture of White's style, Gibbs's and S. J. Perelman's, but as none of these three is like either of the others, the result is like a "Romance language" made up by jumbling French, Portuguese and Romanian. It is not a satisfactory medium of communication. I don't know anybody who has written a good story for *The New Yorker* in *"New Yorker* style."

Personally, I had a tough first year on *The New Yorker,* from the summer of 1935 to the summer of 1936, because I brought to it a successful newspaper short-feature method that was not directly transferable to a magazine, especially in long pieces. It would have been like running a mile in a series of hundred-yard dashes. I rescued myself by my reporting on a profile of Father Divine. I found out more of the inner inwardness and outward outerness of that old god in a machine than anybody else had. The machine was a hundred-and-fifty dollar Rolls-Royce acquired during the depression when nobody else wanted a car that burned that much gas. The old newspaperman in Ross came to the top; he stopped my salary of sixty-five dollars a week and gave me a drawing account of ninety. I have never been out of debt to *The New Yorker* since.

And still, that isn't the whole story. It is hard to be entirely kind to Ross, and he found it hard to be entirely kind to others, as I recalled earlier on. But through five years of war I liked to know that he was behind me, unashamedly interested in what I was doing and seeing, like a kid watching a high-wire act, and that my copy would run as I wrote it. He never usurped the right to tell me what I saw, or to turn my report into a reflection of an editorial conference in Rockefeller Plaza strained through a recollection of Plattsburg in the First World War. That used to happen constantly to the collective journalists who worked for Henry R. Luce. Ross appreciated a good story, too. He seldom gave unqualified praise to a person—and who deserves it?—but he once cheered me with a note about the "unbelievably high quality" of a piece. He was a ham and understood them.

I wish I had told him once how much I liked him.